PRAISE FOR Wealth & Wisdom

"As a professional trader for the last 20 years, many of the quotes found in this book are truly words to trade by. You could read ten thousand pages of books on market psychology, and not get anywhere near the money-making (and saving) knowledge you can find inside *Wealth & Wisdom*."

– *Dave Lutz,* macro trader

"There has not been a concise, effective and well thought out book on investing and building wealth in quite some time. *Wealth & Wisdom* is that book. In a well-managed and unique structure, the reader not only receives a complete history of the time-tested, emotional platforms the market demands for success on the topic but at the same time, a process to de-mystify the art and science of investing. Having been blessed to work with the author and his other seasoned colleagues at Tocqueville for years, I can attest firsthand that the reader will find George McAuliffe's insights in *Wealth & Wisdom* to be extremely valuable over the years ahead as you move toward your successful wealth management goals."

– *Michael W. Williams,* Genesis Asset Management

"As someone who has spent one a day a week for the past 15 years looking for the best quotes I can find for my clients, I know a good quote book when I find one. I have them all. *Wealth & Wisdom* is a very welcome and much needed addition to my library. It is full of timeless wisdom and that is a priceless gift to the reader."

– *Kiril Sokoloff,* founder and Chairman of 13D Research and publisher of *What I Learned This Week*

Wealth & Wisdom

Wealth
&
Wisdom

*Timeless Quotations
and Comments About
Money and Investing*

George B. McAuliffe, III

Milico Press

Wealth & Wisdom – Timeless Quotations and Comments About Money and Investing
George B. McAuliffe, III

Copyright © 2014 by George B. McAuliffe, III
All Rights Reserved

Editing and Copyediting: Heidi W. Moore and Marianne Wallace
Design and Layout: Amy Manzo Toth
Cover art: Fabrice Frere
Author photo: Tamara Zouboff

Published in the United States by Milico Press
www.milicopress.com

ISBN 978-0-9915274-0-3

Print Version 1.0

To my children Camilla, Julian, and Nicholas

May the advice herein serve you well.

It is a good thing for an uneducated man to read books of quotations. Bartlett's
Familiar Quotations *is an admirable work, and I studied it intently.*
The quotations, when engraved upon the memory, give you good thoughts.
They also make you anxious to read the authors and look for more.

– *Winston Churchill,* Roving Commission: My Early Life.

Contents

Foreword

Long before Twitter capped the maximum length of a tweet at 140 characters, wise people with pens and styluses were jotting down adages. "Buy low, sell high," one of their number said. The unnamed author of this aphorism did more than proffer the best and simplest item of investment advice ever recorded. He or she also wrote an 18-character guide for living.

Between these covers is collected some of the best and wittiest of the world's short-form financial wisdom. The ancients and the moderns take turns advising us when to buy, when to sell (if at all) and how to think. From the likes of Harry S. Truman, Sophie Tucker, Thomas Edison, Mark Twain, Fred Schwed, Jr., Samuel Johnson, Babe Ruth, Abraham Lincoln, Benjamin Franklin, Bernard M. Baruch, Socrates, Lao Tzu, Finley Peter Dunne and—especially, for my money—the late Robert G. Kirby, we learn more in a few words than most fat tomes can teach.

"We are normally put in the category called `value investors,'" Kirby, chairman emeritus of the Capital Guardian Trust Co., is quoted as saying. "This has always surprised me a bit, because it seems to imply [the existence] of another category called `non-value investors.'" Of course, such a class exists and its numbers are legion. You can tell them by the manic gleam in their eye. "In a buying frenzy, there is, through the effect of contagion, a universal urge to participate in the whirlwind of speculation," quoth Marc Faber.

I am gratified to see that the editor of this aphoristic assortment, George McAuliffe, lines up with the angels on the matter of financial counsel. Don't begrudge the author of, just for instance, a fortnightly financial newsletter, his or her subscription price, he strongly and sensibly implies. Thus, "Free advice is worth the price."–Robert Half. And, "What you get free costs too much."–Jean Anouilh. Still, McAuliffe, who makes his living in money management, does not deny the anti-Wall Street opposition its voice: "A stockbroker is someone who invests other people's money until it is all gone."–Woody Allen.

Perhaps the film maker should heed Jean Paul Getty, who urged, "Buy when everyone else is selling," or Baron Rothschild, the author of the immortal line, "Buy when there is blood in the streets," timely counsel, indeed, for these tense times. If Allen is listening, I would urge him to go out and read, in its entirety, Fred Schwed's *Where Are the Customers' Yachts?* excerpts from which adorn these pages. "Investment and speculation are said to be two different things," wrote Schwed, for instance, "and the prudent man is advised to engage in the one and avoid the other. This is something like explaining to the troubled adolescent that

Love and Passion are two different things. He perceives that they are different, but they don't seem quite different enough to clear up his problems."

As for selling, the sages quoted herein hold differing views. "Nobody ever lost money taking a profit," said Bernard Baruch. "Never buy at the bottom and always sell too soon," said Jesse Livermore. "Our favorite holding period is forever," said Warren Buffett. Maybe Buffett has the best idea. The famously tax-averse, pro-tax advocate didn't get super-rich by making a partner of Uncle Sam.

No book, even one so easily and pleasurably perused as this one, reads itself. The advice and wisdom it contains is sometimes Delphic, and the quoted wise men frequently disagree. It falls to you, dear reader, to distinguish true value from ersatz. Which will it be, for instance, the contention that there is nothing new under the sun, or—to borrow from, among others, Henry Ford and Michelangelo—that to live is to learn? Harry Truman seemed to side with the first-named camp: "The only thing new in the world is the history you don't know," he said.

Disagreement—a civil and constructive kind of disagreement—extends to the institution of the market itself. "To know values is to know the meaning of the market," Charles Dow, father of the Dow Jones indices, is recorded here as saying. He seems to have a point, but what about old Baruch, to whom is attributed, "The stock market is people," a phrase that, while not directly addressing the question of meaning, suggests the market may mean a great many things to a great many different participants. Maybe Benjamin Graham has the clarifying perception: "The market is always making mountains out of molehills and exaggerating ordinary vicissitudes into major setbacks."

But let Bernard-Paul Heroux have the final, comforting word: "There is no trouble so great or grave that cannot be much diminished by a nice cup of tea."

James Grant, editor of *Grant's Interest Rate Observer*.

Preface

This is a book for sensible people interested in wealth and appreciative of good quotations. There are no graphs, formulas, higher mathematics, or shortcuts; just common sense, for that is all you really need to wisely invest.

Regarding good quotations, I have always collected them—from turning down pages and underlining in my first copy of *Bartlett's*, to manually typing them into my first computer, to the search, cut-and-paste ease that we know today. A really good quotation has a timeless nature. It matters little whether it was uttered by an ancient or a modern—the wisdom captured, or the foible of human nature exposed, remains as relevant today (and certainly tomorrow) as the day when first written.

Investing is the same. Watch the market go up and down once or twice during a decade, and one eventually realizes that there are no really new investing opportunities or new questions to ask concerning them. The opportunities are always new in very predictable ways, and the questions are drawn from the same list that an investor in London or Antwerp in the 1600s could have used. It is just a matter of always trying to apply basic common sense and good judgment.

Similarly, discussions with clients concerning their money and wealth have evolved little. The concerns are always the same: how to make it, how to keep it, and how to prevent the next generation from losing it. And again, the answers are not convoluted; they already exist in the words of wise people: simplicity, common sense, and good judgment.

Which brings us back to my ever-growing collection of quotations, by now largely focused on investing and wealth. While continuing to clip wise bon mots, it became apparent that any modest realizations I had made on these topics had all long ago been discovered and expressed much more cleverly and concisely than I ever could. And yet, I still felt I had something to say on these topics. The opportunity for this book, I finally saw, lay in organizing and curating these already-existing nuggets of wisdom.

Such memorable and wise quotations abound out in the wild but are most often stumbled upon randomly, and most often not presented in proper context or with sufficient explanation. Similarly, others more talented than I have written wonderful investment books (see the "Further Readings" section), but these are often more serious, solid and substantial books not always suited for the amateur looking for that first nudge in the right direction. To organize and recapitulate investing and wealth common sense wisdom, to set the amateur on the right path, to entertain my fellow practitioners, and to give everyone an appetite to read more from those quoted, all this is what I hope to have achieved here.

George B. McAuliffe, III

Introduction

Why write an investing and financial wisdom book composed mostly of the clever words of others? Very simply, because when it comes to money, there are no new ideas (or they are exceedingly rare), and all the existing wisdom has already been written about endlessly (and much more cleverly than I possibly can). However, what I do not see out there is a compendium, for the layman, of all the good bits of wisdom that have already been immortalized in prose. This, therefore, is my attempt to assemble, curate, and comment on everything already said that I view as wise and insightful, correct, concise, and useful.

> *Everything has been said before, but since nobody listens we have to keep going back and beginning all over again. – André Gide.*

Truly New Financial Ideas Are Highly Unlikely

Finance, commerce, and investing have existed for millennia. It is inconceivable that new ways to make money might suddenly arise.

> *It is not once nor twice but times without number that the same ideas make their appearance in the world. – Aristotle.*

> *History is a gallery of pictures in which there are few originals and many copies. – Alexis de Tocqueville.*

Since there are no new ways to make money, you need only rediscover all the old ways.

> *All intelligent thoughts have already been thought; what is necessary is only to try to think them again. – Johann Wolfgang von Goethe.*

> *You don't have to rediscover lessons that have been well made by others before you. – Thomas Russo.*

> *There are certain old truths which will be true as long as this world endures. – Theodore Roosevelt.*

> This book is an attempt to compile all those intelligent thoughts that pertain to investing in one place, curate them as to topic, and add sufficient context and explanation so that their enduring truth and wisdom will be clearly understood by all.

Everything we see touted as "new" today is really some retread or amalgam of existing knowledge.

Past events shed light on the future. For the world has always been the same, and everything that is and will be, once was; and the same things recur, but with different names and colors. – Francesco Guicciardini.

There are no new ways to make money. There are no new ways to lose money. It is all just variations on a theme. History repeats itself. So please, read this book and assimilate a few of the principles herein.

When one encounters something labeled as "new," especially in the domain of money, one should therefore be highly suspicious.

Fresh ideas are not always the best ideas. – fortune cookie, author unknown.

There are only two areas where new ideas are terribly dangerous —economics and sex. – Felix Rohatyn.

ALL INVESTING WISDOM HAS ALREADY BEEN WRITTEN

Just as there are no truly new investing ideas, these ideas have all been written about before.

A library may be regarded as the solemn chamber in which a man may take counsel with all who have been wise and great and good, and glorious among the men that have gone before them. – George Dawson.

Truly good books are more than mines to those who can understand them. They are breathings of the great souls of past times. Genius is not embalmed in them, but lives in them perpetually.
– William Ellery Channing.

A classic is a book that has never finished saying what it has to say.
– Italo Calvino.

Like old ideas only needing to be rediscovered, so too should the classic investment books be rediscovered.

Better than a thousand days of diligent study is one day with a great teacher. – Japanese proverb.

The ancients tell us what is best. – Benjamin Franklin.

Focus on books that have stood the test of time. The current hot bestseller that advises on how to invest in the current hot and popular asset class may be entertaining and may provide a useful window into current market sentiment, but it is unlikely to provide any enduring edification. Read it, but then go back and reread one of the classics.

Every generation has a financial bubble and crash. Every generation writes about it. The details may differ, but the lessons are always the same. The current generation can always learn from prior generations.

> *Literature transmits incontrovertible condensed experience...from generation to generation. In this way literature becomes the living memory of a nation. – Alexandr Solzhenitsyn.*

> *Read no history—nothing but biography, for that is life without theory. – Benjamin Disraeli.*

> *In science, read by preference the newest works; in literature, the oldest. The classics are always modern. – Edward Bulwer-Lytton.*

> A word on "investment classics." Since the modern stock market has arguably only existed since the 1600s (starting in the Netherlands), it is mostly books written since then that will have the most relevance today. Narrative styles and conventions might make the more recent (past 100 years) books more readable, but probably not any more informative. Similarly, newer books will certainly explain more recent financial history, but will probably not describe any techniques that have not already been used in the past.

PRIOR GATHERERS OF WISDOM CLEVERER THAN I

I cannot write better than most who have come before me.

> *I quote others only in order the better to express myself. – Michel de Montaigne.*

> *When a thing has been said and well, have no scruple. Take it and copy it. – Anatole France.*

> *The ability to quote is a serviceable substitute for wit. – W. Somerset Maugham.*

I would much rather find and share the more memorable and insightful sayings of others.

> *The next thing to saying a good thing yourself, is to quote one. – Ralph Waldo Emerson.*

> *By necessity, by proclivity, and by delight, we all quote. – Ralph Waldo Emerson.*

Good quotations are memorable because they contain important ideas.

A proverb is a short sentence based on long experience.
– Miguel de Cervantes.

The wisdom of the wise and the experience of the ages are perpetuated by
quotations. – Benjamin Disraeli.

It is a good thing for an educated man to read books
of quotations. – Winston Churchill.

And because they convey the ideas in a succinct fashion.

Do not say a little in many words but a great deal in a few.
– Pythagoras.

It is my ambition to say in ten sentences what others say in a whole book.
– Friedrich W. Nietzsche.

Say all you have to say in the fewest possible words, or your reader will be
sure to skip them; and in the plainest possible words or he will certainly
misunderstand them. – John Ruskin.

Broadly speaking, the short words are best, and the old words best of all.
– Winston Churchill.

If some of these words stick in the reader's mind and come to the fore when considering one's investments, then I will consider this book a success.

Thus Follows This Modest Book

A collection of the most insightful quotations I have found over the years.

I have gathered a posie of other men's flowers, and nothing but the thread
that binds them is mine own. – John Bartlett.

So, too, have I attempted to do in this book. The quotations speak for themselves and have stood the test of time. As to my humble efforts to tie them together into a narrative that makes sense, I ask for the gentle reader's kind indulgence.

Carefully selected.

Almost every wise saying has an opposite one, no less wise, to balance it.
– George Santayana.

This is true in more subjective matters such as politics, art, and religion, where there will rarely be an unequivocal proof to settle the matter. But when it comes to money, investing, and their interplay with human nature, I see fewer opposing views in the quotations I come across.

Mostly verified.

> *Quotations found on the Internet are not always accurate.*
> *– Abraham Lincoln.*

Any errors of any sort in this book are wholly the author's fault.

Provably true.

> *A witty saying proves nothing. – Voltaire.*

No comment.

Curated into a hopefully edifying assembly.

> *Those that know, do. Those that understand, teach. – Aristotle.*

I will cautiously claim to fit somewhere in the middle.

> *I cannot teach anybody anything. I can only make them think.*
> *– Socrates.*

So, too, I hope to stimulate thinking with this book.

With ideas often repeated via several different quotations expressing the same concept.

> *If you have an important point to make, don't try to be subtle or clever. Use a pile driver. Hit the point once. Then come back and hit it again. Then hit it a third time—a tremendous whack. – Winston Churchill.*

My point with the occasional repetition to come is to show that certain ideas have always existed, across time and across cultures. Because of their longevity and recurrence, they are therefore likely to hold truth.

And with enough context and explanation that one is not just mindlessly repeating something that sounds clever.

> *He wrapped himself in quotations—as a beggar would enfold himself in the purple of Emperors. – Rudyard Kipling.*

> *Wise men make proverbs, but fools repeat them. – Samuel Palmer.*

> *I hate quotations. Tell me what you know. – Ralph Waldo Emerson.*

All right. Let me try. With quotations.

PART I
Uncomfortable Topics

Why You Should Want Some Wealth

I begin with some brief words in support of wealth and investing. Here I attempt to explain why you should want some money, what it can do for you, and how much might be enough.

> *Having money is of great help in coping with poverty. – Alphonse Allais.*

> *I always knew I was going to be rich. I don't think I ever doubted it for a minute. – Warren E. Buffett.*

THE ELEPHANT IN THE ROOM

Let's get this out of the way right from the start: money is desirable. You would not be holding this book if you were not at least interested in having some. So let's address this interest first.

> *Money is the most important thing in the world. It represents health, strength, honor, generosity, and beauty as conspicuously as the want of it represents illness, weakness, disgrace, meanness, and ugliness. Not the least of its virtues is that it destroys base people as certainly as it fortifies and dignifies noble people. – George Bernard Shaw.*

> *I have nothing but contempt for the people who despise money. They are hypocrites or fools. Money is like a sixth sense without which you cannot make a complete use of the other five. Without an adequate income half the possibilities of life are shut off. – W. Somerset Maugham.*

> *Anyone pretending he has no interest in money is either a fool or a knave. – Leslie Ford.*

More simply put, why is money desirable?

> *Money is better than poverty, if only for financial reasons.*
> *– Woody Allen.*

> *It is not so good with money as it is bad without it. – Yiddish proverb.*

> *I've been rich and I've been poor. Rich is better. – Sophie Tucker.*

> *I have never been in a situation where having money made it worse.*
> *– Clinton Jones.*

But doesn't money corrupt your soul?

> *It's not the creation of wealth that is wrong, but the love of money for its own sake. – Margaret Thatcher.*

I feel like money makes you more of who you already are. If you're an asshole, you become a bigger asshole. If you're nice, you become nicer. Money is fun to make, fun to spend, and fun to give away.
– Sara Blakely.

Success and failure are both difficult to endure. Along with success come drugs, divorce, fornication, bullying, travel, meditation, medication, depression, neurosis and suicide. With failure comes failure.
– Joseph Heller.

If you are successful, you may win false friends and true enemies. Succeed anyway. – Mother Theresa.

Can money buy you love and happiness?

Certainly there are things in life that money can't buy, but it's very funny—did you ever try buying them without money? – Ogden Nash.

Riches may not bring happiness, but neither does poverty.
– Sophie Irene Loeb.

Money can't buy you happiness but it does bring you a more pleasant form of misery. – Spike Milligan.

If you're given a choice between money and sex appeal, take the money. As you get older, the money will become your sex appeal.
– Katharine Hepburn.

Beauty is potent, but money is omnipotent. – John Ray.

What else can money buy?

They say money isn't everything. That's true—but look at how many things it is. – Robert Orben.

While everyone knows what money cannot buy, there are obvious things that money can buy: a sense of security, a comfortable retirement, and an ability to provide for your family. Even from a religious standpoint, money does not have to be such a bad thing. In fact, if it is used to help others, money can be a very positive force.
– Joel Greenblatt.

Money can buy time for leisure, reflection, and learning.

The most popular labor-saving device is still money. – Phyllis George.

Increased means and increased leisure are the two civilizers of man.
– Benjamin Franklin.

People seem to me to be happiest when they are working for nothing and can afford to do so. – Robert Lynd.

> With no wealth, you are obliged to work at whatever job you can get in order to provide necessities. But with wealth, you can choose what work you do, or even to what degree you work at all. This may be a basic observation, but the freedom you obtain is underestimated.

Money can ensure better legal and political protection.

He who has money need have no fear of the law. – Russian proverb.

Whoever has the gold, makes the rules. – unknown.

I declare justice is nothing but the advantage of the stronger.
– Thrasymachus.

> Please, no naïve arguments about justice being blind or fair. While that might be the theoretical ideal, it is nowhere the practical reality. It is pure common sense that if you can afford better legal representation, you more often get a better outcome (not necessarily fairer—just better for you). As for those who cannot afford to bring a lawsuit if wronged, or defend themselves against one (even frivolous), good luck to them.

Money provides some peace of mind.

There's a certain Buddhistic calm that comes from having...money in the bank. – Tim Robbins.

The mass of men lead lives of quiet desperation. – Henry David Thoreau.

Money, it turned out, was exactly like sex, you thought of nothing else if you didn't have it and thought of other things if you did.
– James Baldwin.

> If money is not important, then why do people worry when they don't have any? Conversely, by ensuring you have some income and some savings, you remove this source of worry and can pass your time more agreeably focused on pursuits of your choosing.

Money provides for your children and family.

A father is a banker provided by nature. – French proverb.

Money isn't everything, but it sure keeps you in touch with your children.
– J. Paul Getty.

Money can buy better healthcare.

Money isn't everything—your health is the other ten percent.
– Lillian Day.

You can be young without money but you can't be old without it.
– Tennessee Williams.

Old age ain't no place for sissies. – Bette Davis.

Or for those unable to afford needed healthcare, a situation increasingly common these days even in the most developed nations.

And, unfortunately, money can buy respect and popularity.

Virtue has never been as respectable in society as money. – Mark Twain.

A fool and his money are soon invited everywhere. – unknown.

The civility which money will purchase, is rarely extended to those who have none. – Charles Dickens.

A perhaps timely aside to the reader: this book does not attempt to judge; this book only attempts to point out things that have always been true and which human nature will most probably maintain true in the future.

In summary:

Everybody loves money. That's why it's called "money."
– Danny DeVito's character, Heist, *David Mamet, 2001, film.*

Randolph Duke: Money isn't everything, Mortimer.
Mortimer Duke: Oh, grow up.
– Trading Places, *Dir. John Landis, 1983, film.*

Wealth is not without its advantages and the case to the contrary, although it has often been made, has never proved widely persuasive.
– John Kenneth Galbraith.

Lack of money is the root of all evil. – George Bernard Shaw.

When you come right down to it, almost any problem eventually becomes a financial problem. – Frederic G. Donner.

When I was young I used to think that money was the most important thing in life. Now that I am old, I know it is. – Oscar Wilde.

Money is power, freedom, a cushion, the root of all evil, the sum of blessings. – Carl Sandburg.

How Much Is Enough?

Certainly more than these gentlemen have.

> *I have enough money to last me the rest of my life, unless I buy something.*
> *– Jackie Mason.*

> *I worked my way up from nothing to a state of extreme poverty.*
> *– Groucho Marx.*

Though people will never agree on how much is enough, most agree that more is better.

> *It isn't necessary to be rich and famous to be happy. It's only necessary to be rich. – Alan Alda.*

> *The only way not to think about money is to have a great deal of it.*
> *– Edith Wharton.*

> *It is difficult if not impossible to find some reasonable limit for acquiring more and more property. – Arthur Schopenhauer.*

And many will agree that after a certain point, more wealth doesn't really matter that much.

> *After a certain point money is meaningless. It's the game that counts.*
> *– Aristotle Onassis.*

> *If you can count your money, you don't have a billion dollars.*
> *– J. Paul Getty.*

> I will attempt to define when you reach this "certain point." It occurs when you have no monetary fears of where your next meal will come from or of being able to afford retirement. You feel secure and comfortable in your home (whether you own or rent). You are able to send your children to the best schools they can get into. You can afford to take a couple of nice vacations a year and/or perhaps have a place in the countryside. You reach it when neither medical emergency, nor divorce, nor malicious lawsuit, nor career-ending injury, will be ruinous for yourself or your family. The definitions and checklist will vary through the ages, and from person to person, and even during your life, but what it always equates to is "peace of mind."

After that, it is just a matter for each person to figure out what minimum amount they need for a happy compromise between their "needs" and their "desires."

> *A wise man will desire no more than what he may get justly, use soberly, distribute cheerfully, and leave contentedly. – Benjamin Franklin.*

The man who has begun to live more seriously within begins to live more simply without. - Ernest Hemingway.

It is good to have what you want, but it is better to want only what you have. - Menedemus.

There is no dignity quite so impressive, and no one independence quite so important, as living within your means. - Calvin Coolidge.

A well-governed appetite is a great part of liberty.
- Lucius Annaeus Seneca.

The greatest wealth is to live content with little. - Plato.

Frugality is a handsome income. - Erasmus.

Defining a minimum amount is less difficult, and it starts with the basics. Once your family has food, shelter, safety, and assured access to healthcare and education, everything else is probably a discretionary luxury.

It is always OK to desire more wealth, but once your basic needs are met, beware turning this desire into an unhealthy obsession.

If a man is proud of his wealth, he should not be praised until it is known how he employs it. - Socrates.

A wise man should have money in his head, but not in his heart.
- Jonathan Swift.

He does not possess wealth; it possesses him. - Benjamin Franklin.

What the object of senile avarice may be I cannot conceive. For can there be anything more absurd than to seek more journey money, the less there remains of the journey? -Marcus Tullius Cicero.

Someone else will always have more, and there will always be that thing you do not have. But do you really need more, or need that extra thing, in order to be happy?

What difference does it make how much you have? What you do not have amounts to much more. - Lucius Annaeus Seneca.

Money never made a man happy yet, nor will it. There is nothing in its nature to produce happiness. The more a man has, the more he wants. Instead of filling a vacuum, it makes one. - Benjamin Franklin.

There is no calamity greater than lavish desires. There is no greater guilt than discontentment. And there is no greater disaster than greed.
- Lao-Tzu.

Before strongly desiring anything, we should look carefully into the happiness of its present owner. – François de La Rochefoucauld.

At the end of the day, once you have met your basic needs, provided for your family, and live in some measure of comfort, then what more do you really need?

The best condition in life is not to be so rich as to be envied nor so poor as to be damned. – Josh Billings.

I am indeed rich, since my income is superior to my expense and my expense is equal to my wishes. – Edward Gibbon.

Happiness resides not in possessions and not in gold, happiness dwells in the soul. – Democritus.

And I repeat the modern caveat: you must meet your basic needs and provide for your family.

Deciding What to Do With Yourself

It is important to carefully choose your career, regardless of how you feel about money. Doing an excellent job at something you like doing is a better path to long-lasting wealth than doing a half-hearted job at something you dislike but that pays well. And why be miserable?

> *No one wants to die. Even people who want to go to heaven don't want to die to get there, and yet, death is the destination we all share. No one has ever escaped it, and that is as it should be, because Death is very likely the single best invention of Life. It's life's change agent. It clears out the old to make way for the new. Right now the new is you, but someday not too long from now, you will gradually become the old and be cleared away. Sorry to be so dramatic, but it is quite true. Your time is limited, so don't waste it living someone else's life. Don't be trapped by dogma, which is living with the results of other people's thinking. Don't let the noise of others' opinions drown out your own inner voice. And most important, have the courage to follow your heart and intuition. They somehow already know what you truly want to become. Everything else is secondary. – Steve Jobs, Stanford University commencement speech, 2005.*

> *You are not here merely to make a living. You are here to enable the world to live more amply, with greater vision, and with a finer spirit of hope and achievement. You are here to enrich the world. You impoverish yourself if you forget this errand. – Woodrow Wilson.*

HAPPINESS LEADS TO WEALTH

Figure out what you enjoy doing.

> *Knowing yourself is the beginning of all wisdom. – Aristotle.*

> *Resolve to be thyself; and know, that he who finds himself, loses his misery. – Matthew Arnold.*

> *What is the goal of life? To be that self which one truly is. – Carl S. Rogers.*

> *Tell me to what you pay attention and I will tell you who you are. – José Ortega y Gasset.*

> *Do what you love. – Henry David Thoreau.*

Focus on what you enjoy doing.

> *It is not enough to be industrious; so are the ants. What are you industrious about? – Henry David Thoreau.*

> *Employ thy time well, if thou meanest to get leisure.*
> *– Benjamin Franklin.*

> *Singleness of purpose is one of the chief essentials for success in life, no matter what may be one's aim. – John D. Rockefeller, Jr.*

> *Definiteness of purpose is the starting point of all achievement.*
> *– Clement Stone.*

> *Know what thou canst work at, and work at it like a Hercules.*
> *– Thomas Carlyle.*

> *Persistency of purpose is a power. It creates confidence in others. Everybody believes in the determined man.*
> *– Orison Swett Marden.*

> *One of the secrets of a successful life is to be able to hold all of our energies upon one point, to focus all of the scattered rays of the mind upon one place or thing. – Orison Swett Marden.*

Become good at what you enjoy doing.

> *What one does easily, one does well. – Andrew Carnegie.*

> *What we hope ever to do with ease, we must learn first to do with diligence. – Samuel Johnson.*

> *The quality of a person's life is in direct proportion to their commitment to excellence, regardless of their chosen field of endeavor.*
> *– Vince Lombardi.*

> *The average person puts only 25% of his energy and ability into his work. The world takes off its hat to those who put in more than 50% of their capacity, and stands on its head for those few-and-far-between souls who devote 100%. – Andrew Carnegie.*

> *Devote your entire willpower to mastering one thing at a time; do not scatter your energies. – Paramehanta Yogananda.*

> *Better a little which is well done, than a great deal imperfectly.*
> *– Plato.*

> *True greatness consists in being great in little things. – Samuel Johnson.*

> *The secret to success is to do common things uncommonly well.*
> *– John D. Rockefeller, Sr.*

Do not always expect immediate, unconditional success. That is not the way things work.

A man would do nothing if he waited until he could do it so well that no one could find fault. – John Henry Newman.

If you live your life fully, you will die only once. But if you are scared of every step, fear will kill you day after day. – Paulo Coelho.

A life spent making mistakes is not only more honorable, but more useful than a life spent doing nothing. – George Bernard Shaw.

Have persistence, tenacity, and confidence in yourself.

If you believe in yourself and have dedication and pride—and never quit, you'll be a winner. The price of victory is high, but so are the rewards. – Bear Bryant.

People who are unable to motivate themselves must be content with mediocrity, no matter how impressive their other talents. – Andrew Carnegie.

What great thing would you attempt if you knew you could not fail? – Robert H. Schuller.

As soon as you trust yourself, you will know how to live. – Johann Wolfgang von Goethe.

Make the most of yourself, for that is all there is of you. – Ralph Waldo Emerson.

The ablest man I ever met is the man you think you are. – Franklin D. Roosevelt.

Bonus tip: Favor professions that you can do at any age and in any physical condition. Having longevity in your profession will maximize your earnings potential.

People who work sitting down get paid more than people who work standing up. – Ogden Nash.

Hard work never killed anybody, but why take a chance? – Edgar Bergen.

That is the basic recipe. Heed the above guidelines, and the rewards should follow.

Do what you love, the money will follow. – Marsha Sinetar.

Nothing great was ever achieved without enthusiasm. – Ralph Waldo Emerson.

Ability will never catch up with the demand for it. – Confucius.

Success is not to be pursued; it is to be attracted by the person you become. – Jim Rohn.

Success usually comes to those who are too busy to be looking for it. – Henry David Thoreau.

If a man has any brains at all, let him hold on to his calling, and, in the grand sweep of things, his turn will come at last. – William McCune.

What we must decide is how we are valuable, rather than how valuable we are. – F. Scott Fitzgerald.

The best way to make money in a business is not to think too much about making it. – Henry Ford.

Starting out to make money is the greatest mistake in life. Do what you feel you have a flair for doing, and if you are good enough at it money will come. – William Rootes.

ACCIDENTAL HAPPINESS IS RARE

Only you can figure out what makes you happy.

There are only two mistakes one can make along the road to truth; not going all the way, and not starting. – Buddha.

Never permit a dichotomy to rule your life, a dichotomy in which you hate what you do so you can have pleasure in your spare time. Look for a situation in which your work will give you as much happiness as your spare time. – Pablo Picasso.

There are three things extremely hard: steel, a diamond, and to know one's self. – Benjamin Franklin.

Trust yourself. You know more than you think you do. – Benjamin Spock.

Yes, Dr. Spock was addressing new mothers regarding care of their babies. But this also applies to what will make you happy.

Having no goals or interests in life will, unsurprisingly, not lead to happiness or wealth.

Of all the unhappy people in the world, the unhappiest are those who have not found something they want to do. – Lyn Yutang.

You have to have a vision. It's got to be a vision you articulate clearly and forcefully. You can't blow an uncertain trumpet. – Theodore Hesburgh.

Life is the art of drawing without an eraser. – John W. Gardner.

*If you don't know what you want, you end up with a lot you don't.
– Chuck Palahniuk.*

*If you don't know where you are going, any road will take you there.
– Lewis Carroll.*

Nor will you find happiness or success through adopting other people's goals or doing what others tell you to do.

The easiest thing to be in the world is you. The most difficult thing to be is what other people want you to be. Don't let them put you in that position. – Leo Buscaglia.

When you are content to be simply yourself and don't compare or compete, everybody will respect you. – Lao Tzu.

You must live your life and your goals before wasting away your time.

If you take too long in deciding what to do with your life, you'll find you've done it. – George Bernard Shaw.

*You can't get away from yourself by moving from one place to another.
– Ernest Hemingway, The Sun Also Rises.*

*Do something instead of killing time, because time is killing you.
– Paulo Coelho.*

You must actively find and create your own happiness.

*People often say that this or that person has not yet found himself. But the self is not something one finds, it is something one creates.
– Thomas Szasz.*

People are always blaming their circumstances for what they are. I don't believe in circumstances. The people who get on in this world are the people who get up and look for the circumstances they want, and, if they can't find them, make them. – George Bernard Shaw.

Change yourself and your fortunes will change. – Portuguese proverb.

Happiness is not a goal; it is a by-product. – Eleanor Roosevelt.

Your work is going to fill a large part of your life, and the only way to be truly satisfied is to do what you believe is great work. And the only way to do great work is to love what you do. If you haven't found it yet, keep looking. Don't settle. As with all matters of the heart, you'll know when you find it. And, like any great relationship, it just gets better and better

as the years roll on. So keep looking until you find it. Don't settle.
– Steve Jobs, Stanford University commencement speech, 2005.

For the past 33 years, I have looked in the mirror every morning and asked myself: "If today were the last day of my life, would I want to do what I am about to do today?" And whenever the answer has been "No" for too many days in a row, I know I need to change something.
– Steve Jobs.

Your Suitability to Invest

To what degree do you want to be involved in your investments? Though the ultimate responsibility for making and maintaining your wealth will always rest with you, it is fair to say that you do not need to personally sign off on every single investment. Of course, to some this is their joy and passion, and they can almost be called professional investors—the only difference is that they are not also doing it on a fee basis for others. But for others without the inclination, stomach, or head for investing, it will be enough to hire one or two professional money managers and review things once a year. How involved do you want to be?

Every natural human impulse seems to be a foe to success in stocks. And that is why success is so difficult. - Fred Kelley.

BEWARE YOUR EMOTIONS

The successful long-term investor needs to know how to stay calm.

I suspect that temperament costs investors more than ignorance. – John Train.

The most important quality for an investor is temperament, not intellect. – Warren E. Buffett.

I believe that uncontrolled basic emotions are the true and deadly enemy of the speculator; that hope, fear, and greed are always present, sitting on the edge of the psyche, waiting on the sidelines, waiting to jump into the action, plow into the game. – Jesse Livermore.

Those who experience unpredictable or frequent or extreme emotional swings should beware. You cannot make thoughtful decisions when either depressed or giddy.

The one absolute requirement of a money manager is emotional maturity. If you don't know who you are, the stock market is an expensive place to find out. – Adam Smith.

To be unduly elated when you win, or unduly depressed when you lose, is a sign that you are carrying too much sail and not enough ballast. – Kodak Magazine, June, 1923.

The stock market is probably not a good place for someone overly greedy.

It would be foolish to overlook the human vice of greed. The successful trader must be able to recognize and control his greed. If you get a buzz from profits and depressed by losses, you belong in Las Vegas, not the markets. – Mark Ritchie.

> The successful investor has to have the self-control to take partial profits early and often. The overly-greedy investor who leaves everything invested hoping for just one more increase will often find the stock moving the other way instead, and will very soon be looking at a loss rather than a gain.

You don't need to avoid being emotional in the rest of your life. Sound investing involves not taking the market personally, and making sure your buy and sell decisions are based on reasoned thought, not emotions.

The investment process is only half the battle. The other weighty component is struggling with yourself, and immunizing yourself from the psychological effects of the swings of markets, career risk, the pressure of benchmarks, competition, and the loneliness of the long distance runner. – Barton Biggs.

A successful trader is rational, analytical, able to control emotions, practical, and profit oriented. – Monroe Trout.

Nothing gives one person so much advantage over another as to remain always cool and unruffled under all circumstances. – Thomas Jefferson.

Unless you can watch your stock holding decline by 50% without becoming panic-stricken, you should not be in the stock market. – Warren E. Buffett.

> In the market, prices of stocks you own will often go down. Can you remain calm and confident that you are right, or will you panic and sell, only to watch the stock bounce back the next day?

Beware Your Intelligence

Overthinking the stock market can be a handicap.

If your IQ is higher than 150 then you are better off selling 30 points to someone else. If you are too bright, you won't make it in investing. You need emotional stability and inner peace to be a good investor and if you think your IQ is higher than it is, then you are in real trouble. – Warren E. Buffett.

Basic intelligence should usually suffice.

To invest successfully over a lifetime does not require a stratospheric IQ, unusual business insights, or inside information. What's needed is a sound intellectual framework for making decisions and the ability to keep emotions from corroding that framework. – Warren E. Buffett.

Everyone has the brainpower to follow the stock market. If you made it through fifth-grade math, you can do it. – Peter Lynch.

Everyone has the brainpower to make money in stocks. Not everyone has the stomach. – Peter Lynch.

Good long-term investing does not rely on complex math.

The key requirements are intellectual curiosity and the ability to keep focused on the topic.

If you are ready to give up everything else—to study the whole history and background of the market and all the principal companies whose stocks are on the board as carefully as a medical student studies anatomy—if you can do all that, and, in addition, you have the cool nerves of a great gambler, the sixth sense of a clairvoyant, and the courage of a lion, you have a ghost of a chance. – Bernard Baruch.

You need to have a passionate interest in why things are happening. That cast of mind, kept over long periods, gradually improves your ability to focus on reality. If you don't have the cast of mind, you're destined for failure even if you have a high IQ. – Charles Munger.

Good long-term investing requires good knowledge of your investments, of what they do and how they make money, and of how the business and technology cycles might affect them.

NOT DOING IT YOURSELF JUST MIGHT BE BEST

As discussed earlier, you should focus on the things you do well.

Do not let what you cannot do interfere with what you can do. – John Wooden.

If you run after two hares, you will catch neither. – Latin proverb.

You cannot expect to be good at everything.

Sometimes it is more important to discover what one cannot do, than what one can do. – Lin Yutang.

Common sense teaches that booksellers should not speculate in hops, or bankers in turpentine; that railways should not be promoted by maiden ladies, or canals by beneficed clergymen ... in the name of common sense, let there be common sense. – Walter Bagehot, Lombard Street.

> Therefore, do not waste time trying to become merely adequate at something you have no real stomach or inclination for, while neglecting the thing you might really have a gift for.

You should also question why you might want to be a hands-on investor.

In all games the difference between the amateur and the professional is that the professional plays the odds, while the amateur, whether he realizes it or not, is among other things a thrill seeker. Investment, too, is part a science and part a game, and just as in poker, you need to sort out your motives. – John Train.

Because the stock market is not necessarily a fun place, or an exciting place, or a cheap hobby.

If you don't know who you are, the stock market is an expensive place to find out. – George Goodman.

You Must Invest and Manage Your Wealth

In the short term, you may be poor or an entrepreneur with every penny sunk into your new venture and nothing to invest elsewhere. But some day, you will have some money to invest, and then these remarks will become more relevant. Your personal responsibility toward matters of money will become unavoidable, and you will have to choose to actively manage or delegate and supervise. You cannot pretend this aspect of your life does not exist or continually delay addressing it.

> *Without ambition one starts nothing. Without work one finishes nothing. The prize will not be sent to you. You have to win it.*
> *– Ralph Waldo Emerson.*

> *Things turn out best for the people who make the best of the way things turn out. – John Wooden.*

> *Each player must accept the cards life deals him or her, but once they are in hand, he or she alone must decide how to play the cards in order to win the game. – Voltaire.*

MONEY MUST BE INVESTED

To protect your savings and purchasing power, your money cannot just sit as cash—it must be invested in ways where it will either appreciate in value, or earn interest, or both.

> *Foul cankering rust the hidden treasure frets*
> *But gold that's put to use more gold begets.*
> *– William Shakespeare,* Sonnets, Venus and Adonis.

> *Just making money is not enough anymore. Now we have to worry about our money making money. – Woody Allen.*

Ever since the invention of the stock market in the 1600s, it has been one of the best places to invest money.

> *If you want to build a realistic retirement nest egg, you have to marry the stock market as soon as you can and stick with it for the rest of your life.*
> *– Jim Jorgensen.*

As with anything, there are some risks...

> *Statistics show that investing your money in the stock market is nearly twice as secure as feeding it to otters. – Dave Barry.*

...But you cannot simply do nothing.

> *Many people take no care of their money till they come nearly to the end of it, and others do just the same with their time.*
> *– Johann Wolfgang von Goethe.*

> *It is easy to dodge our responsibilities, but we cannot dodge the consequences of dodging our responsibilities. – Josiah Stamp.*

> *You can avoid reality, but you cannot avoid the consequences of avoiding reality. – Ayn Rand.*

> *A person often meets his destiny on the road he took to avoid it.*
> *– Jean de La Fontaine.*

> *When you have to make a choice and don't make it, that is in itself a choice. – William James.*

Indeed, there is probably even less safety and security in doing nothing.

> *Security is mostly superstition. It does not exist in nature, nor do the children of men as a whole experience it. Avoiding danger is no safer in the long run than outright exposure. The fearful are caught as often as the bold. – Helen Keller.*

> *There is no security on this earth—only opportunity.*
> *– Douglas MacArthur.*

> *There is no security in life, only opportunity. – Mark Twain.*

> *Standing in the middle of the road is very dangerous; you get knocked down by the traffic from both sides. – Margaret Thatcher.*

> *I do not believe in a fate that falls on men however they act; but I do believe in a fate that falls on them unless they act. – Buddha.*

> *If you don't risk anything, you risk even more. – Erica Jong.*

> The world changes. Changing with it carries risks, but sitting still might cost even more. You may have inherited the local buggy whip monopoly, but if the automobile was just invented, you need to make plans. You may have all your money in cash and think yourself safe, but eventually interest rates will climb and take a big bite out of your purchasing power (especially true for readers in less stable economies). No investment or business can survive without adapting. If you at least try to change with the world, you've got a chance of preserving your wealth.

Therefore, you are always better off sallying forth and taking small, appropriate and well-researched chances.

A ship in the harbor is safe, but that's not what ships are built for.
– William Thayer Shedd.

It is not possible to diversify away all risk in a world economy where
speculative frenzies and the rapid movement of capital make history a
poor guide to the future. – James Surowiecki.

It is better to be adventurous than cautious, because Fortune is a woman.
– Niccolò Machiavelli.

Growth demands a temporary surrender of security. – Gail Sheehy.

> Find investments you have had a chance to take a good look at, where the
> upside is greater than the downside, and where it is big enough to matter
> for you but not big enough to bankrupt you.

And making a habit of investing, or at least keeping informed of investments
made for you by others, will also give you something to do.

The best thing about investing is that it's indoor work with no heavy
lifting. – unknown.

When you're 94, tennis fades, and so does sex, but there's still the market.
– Roy Neuberger.

You Must Supervise Your Finances

One way or another, you must manage your financial affairs, whether you decide
to do it all yourself, or hire/delegate 100% of it away, or some combination of the
two. Choices must be made, and periodic evaluations and adjustments must be
performed. "To not choose, is to choose." And the only person who can do this is you.

You are free to make your choices, but you are prisoner of the
consequences. – Pablo Neruda.

Don't go around saying the world owes you a living. The world owes you
nothing. It was here first. – Mark Twain.

No one saves us but ourselves. No one can and no one may. We ourselves
must walk the path. – Buddha.

Always bear in mind that your own resolution to succeed is more
important than any one thing. – Abraham Lincoln.

To be a money master, you must first be a self-master. – J. P. Morgan.

Would you live with ease / Do what you ought, not what you please.
– Benjamin Franklin.

If need be, you can delegate to others, but you should always remain involved to some degree.

A prince who will not undergo the difficulty of understanding must undergo the danger of trusting. - Lord Halifax.

Nothing is beneath you if it is in the direction of your life.
- Ralph Waldo Emerson.

If you want something done well, do it yourself. - Napoleon Bonaparte.

And you must always monitor.

When an arrow does not hit its target, the marksman blames himself, not another person. A wise man behaves in the same way. - Confucius.

To hold others responsible for failure is a way of escaping one's own responsibility. Responsibility is a heavy burden and a great honor at the same time. Whoever shoulders responsibility must be worthy of it.
- Sheik Mohammed bin Rashid Al Maktoum.

YOUR FINANCES CANNOT WAIT

You cannot delay or hide from making financial choices.

You cannot run away from a weakness. You must sometimes fight it out or perish; and if that be so, why not now, and where you stand?
- Robert Louis Stevenson.

You cannot escape the responsibility of tomorrow by evading it today.
- Abraham Lincoln.

> You cannot hide from other aspects of your life. Why should your financial life be any different?

There are no valid excuses for financial procrastination.

It is folly to fear what one cannot avoid. - Danish Proverb.

We have forty million reasons for failure, but not a single excuse.
- Rudyard Kipling.

I attribute my success to this—I never gave or took any excuse.
- Florence Nightingale.

The world is not interested in the storms you encountered, but did you bring in the ship? - William McFee.

> Since delegating is an option you can at least interview a few financial planners, advisers, or money managers. Ask a few friends with money for some recommendations. Make a few phone calls.

Therefore make your best attempt, for it will always be better than doing nothing.

Do what you can, with what you have, where you are.
– Theodore Roosevelt.

The bravest sight in the world is to see a great man struggling
against adversity. – Lucius Annaeus Seneca.

Facing it, always facing it, that's the way to get through. Face it.
– Joseph Conrad.

Accept the challenges, so that you may feel the exhilaration of victory.
– George S. Patton.

It is not in the stars to hold our destiny but in ourselves.
– William Shakespeare.

Start small. Ask for help. Read books. Speak with people. Slowly learn.

Since your finances are a serious, long-term project, you must get started today.

If you wait, all that happens is that you get older. – Mario Andretti.

A man has made at least a start on discovering the meaning of human
life when he plants shade trees under which he knows full well he will
never sit. – D. Elton Trueblood.

The great French Marshall Lyautey once asked his gardener to plant a
tree. The gardener objected that the tree was slow growing and would not
reach maturity for 100 years. The Marshall replied, "In that case, there is
no time to lose; plant it this afternoon!" – John F. Kennedy.

Care for your wealth and it will grow.

PART 2
Investing Basics

Getting Started

As you begin to think about investing, I offer some initial words of guidance. Aim for more saving, less frivolous spending, and a view toward your longer-term financial picture.

THE BASIC PLAN

Saving money is the first step.

> *The safest way to double your money is to fold it in half and put it back in your pocket. – Frank McKinney ('Kin') Hubbard.*

> *I'm a minimalist. I don't really need much to enjoy a good holiday—just my family and the bare essentials. – Jean Reno.*

The goal is to build and protect your wealth, with investing as the means.

> *In the long run, it's not just how much money you make that will determine your future prosperity. It's how much of that money you put to work by saving it and investing it. – Peter Lynch.*

> *Savings will not make you rich. Only canny investments do that. The role of savings is to keep you from becoming poor. – Jane Bryant Quinn.*

The long-term plan thus involves both saving and investing.

> *A faithfully kept program of savings and conservative investments can give you more money and a better life than that of your neighbors who spend everything they get. This is probably the oldest financial advice in the world, but there are some things you can't improve on.*
> *– Jane Bryant Quinn.*

> Regularly save some money. Once you've saved a little bit, invest it. Repeat.

THINGS TO BEWARE

Don't just think about saving. Get started today, even if you've had good fortune in the past.

> *The road to poverty is paved with the good intentions of those who wanted to save but never got around to it. – William Nickerson.*

If at first you do succeed it can give you a false sense of importance.
– Frank Tyger.

> Start accumulating a reserve. Even though you may be younger and have not yet had a spell of bad luck or difficult times—these should come eventually.

Remember that a lot of spending is really gratuitous or ego-driven, and thus can be decreased.

Many could forego heavy meals, a full wardrobe, a fine house, et cetera; it is the ego they cannot forego. – Mohandas Gandhi.

Too many people spend money they haven't earned, to buy things they don't want, to impress people they don't like. – Will Rogers.

> It is a good practice to first consider whether you really need any contemplated purchase.

Do not spend what you do not (yet) have.

Do not count your chickens before they are hatched. – Aesop.

Do not spend now, relying on future profits, for they very often do not come or are smaller than expected. Whereas, on the contrary, expenses always multiply. – Francesco Guicciardini.

> Do not assume that tomorrow's savings will be sufficient for later needs. What if tomorrow's income is lower? Instead, save something today.

If you really do need something, then buy a quality version that will last, as opposed to a cheap one that you will have to keep replacing.

We're too poor to buy cheap things. – unknown.

Siamo troppo poveri per pagare meno. (We are too poor to pay less).
– Italian peasant proverb.

Buy less, pay more. – Scottish proverb.

> Quality often retains value, whereas poor quality does not. Therefore, if you buy good quality, you can often recoup some value through a sale or donation.

Rather than buying things you do not need with today's excess cash, always keep some in reserve (saved or in liquid investments readily convertible to cash) for the unforeseen emergency expense.

He who buys what he doesn't need must often sell what he does need.
– English proverb.

He who buys what he does not want ends in wanting what he cannot buy. – Mrs. Ethel Alec-Tweedie, 1904.

The point is that you do not want to be forced into selling an otherwise good investment, possibly at a fire sale price, the day you absolutely need some money for an emergency. You always want a buffer of cash so that you can ride out a temporary period where your investments may not be liquid or highly valued.

Think Things Through

In financial matters, mistakes can be very costly. Be thoughtful. Take the time to consider pros and cons, and anticipate why and how things could go right or wrong. Evaluate not only how much you can make but also how much you can lose. Consider both sides of the risk-reward tradeoff, and act deliberately. Few people actually do, so this can be your advantage.

> *What is the hardest task in the world? To think. - Ralph Waldo Emerson.*

> *Thinking is the hardest work there is, which is the probable reason why so few engage in it. - Henry Ford.*

> *By failing to prepare you are preparing to fail. - Benjamin Franklin.*

> *All investments are unforgiving of human error. There are no exceptions. - Harvey Mackay.*

THINK ABOUT WHY, WHAT, AND HOW

Always consider "why" you might want to make a given investment.

> *Erst waegen, dann wagen. (First weigh, then venture). - Count Helmuth Von Moltke, personal motto.*

> *The secret of success is before attempting anything, be very clear about why you are doing it. - Guan Yin Tzu.*

Why does this investment makes sense for you? In the case of a company's stock, it could be that you understand that company's industry. But in other matters, such as buying a vacation home, first consider whether this investment makes sense for your way of life.

Investigate the details, or the "what" of the investment.

> *Even if the stream is shallow, wade it as if it were deep. - Korean Proverb.*

> *Work hard, study the data. Truth is always buried in the details. - Matthew R. Simmons.*

> *The truth is rarely pure and never simple. - Oscar Wilde.*

> *The devil is in the details. - unknown.*

> *God is in the details. - Ludwig Mies van der Rohe.*

What happened to make the investment cheap (or merely "reasonable") in the first place? What is the challenge or problem involved and what can be changed or fixed? What is the likelihood of successfully overcoming the challenge or solving the problem?

Then, of course, consider the "how" aspects of the investment under consideration.

Give me six hours to chop down a tree and I will spend the first four sharpening the axe. – Abraham Lincoln.

Make preparations in advance. You never have trouble if you are prepared for it. – Theodore Roosevelt.

What's the use of running if you're not on the right road? – German proverb.

Think of the going out before you enter. – Arabian proverb.

How will the investment become more valuable? How long will this take? How will you exit once things prove out, or if you should change your mind, or if you end up needing the money elsewhere?

KEEP THESE GOALS IN MIND

Always do the best job you can.

People forget how fast you did a job—but they remember how well you did it. – Howard W. Newton.

If most of us are ashamed of shabby clothes and shoddy furniture, let us be more ashamed of shabby ideas and shoddy philosophies. – Albert Einstein.

Do the things that are necessary and useful, as opposed to superfluous "make-work."

I have discovered that all human evil comes from this, man's being unable to sit still in a room. – Blaise Pascal.

A hundred lifetimes may not be enough to rectify the mistake made in one short morning. – Chinese proverb.

It is human nature to think wisely and act foolishly. – Anatole France.

You do not have to make a trade or new investment every day. You do not have to rebalance your portfolio every month. There is no minimum quantity of investing transactions.

Be comfortable doing nothing, sometimes.

If there's nothing to do, do nothing. – James Tisch, favorite saying.

Lethargy bordering on sloth remains the cornerstone of our investment style. – Warren E. Buffett.

The true secret of success in the investment and speculative world is not so much which good securities to buy, but rather which investments to avoid. – Morton Shulman.

Sometimes your best investments are the ones you don't make. – Donald Trump.

> Being comfortable standing still while others are rushing about is a very useful skill.

Saying "no" initially, declining to act or to invest, buys you more time to think about it.

The wise avoid the headlong rush: when the moment passes the way will still be open. – Chen Zi'ang.

One-half of the troubles of this life can be traced to saying "yes" too quickly and not saying "no" soon enough. – Josh Billings.

When, against one's will, one is high pressured into making a hurried decision, the best answer is always "no," because "no" is more easily changed to "yes," than "yes" is changed to "no." – Charles E. Nielson.

> You are never forced to enter into an investment. You can always delay or say no. Never let someone else's schedule rob you of your time to think.

ACT ONLY WITH UNDERSTANDING

An investment opportunity or choice may seem tempting, but there is rarely a need to decide immediately. An ill-considered decision is often worse than no decision.

People cannot stand too much reality. – Carl Jung.

We humans cannot bear very much reality. – T. S. Elliot.

Neurosis is the inability to tolerate ambiguity. – Sigmund Freud.

> Investment opportunities are usually not as clear as others may make them out to be.

Sleep on it. Think it through beforehand. Do not act in haste.

Light seems brighter in the dark and action is discerned more clearly in tranquility. – Su Shi.

Think like a man of action, act like a man of thought. – Henri Bergson.

Make haste slowly. – Caesar Augustus.

Never mistake motion for action. – Ernest Hemingway.

Real action is in silent moments. – Ralph Waldo Emerson.

Think urgently. Act slowly.

Do not be afraid to reconsider an action or prior decision.

Second thoughts are even wiser. – Euripides.

Time is the wisest counselor. – Pericles.

Never let laziness or your ego stand in the way of correcting a poor decision (hopefully before it is too late).

You will never have perfect knowledge or clairvoyance.

Nothing in this world can one imagine beforehand, not the least thing. Everything is made up of so many unique particulars that cannot be foreseen. – Rainer Maria Rilke.

So always take the time to reasonably think through a problem, and one of two things will become clear. Either you reach a point where you have considered all the angles enough to feel you understand the risks and can be comfortable with a decision, or the situation remains too unclear to justify a decision.

Thinking is essential in order to prevent the "avoidable" mistakes.

When a man picks up a stick thinking any stick will do, it's usually a boomerang. – G. K. Chesterton.

Remember this, whoever lives a life of chance will in the end find himself a victim of chance. The right way is to think, to examine, and to consider every detail carefully, even the most minute. – Francesco Guicciardini.

Whatever failures I have known, whatever errors I have committed, whatever follies I have witnessed in private and public life have been the consequence of action without thought. – Bernard M. Baruch.

People always call it luck when you've acted more sensibly than they have. – Anne Tyler.

Spend the time to think things through before acting. You will avoid the obvious mistakes and increase your success rate.

Being Patient

Success will require patience. If you are confident that a particular investment's basic premise is correct, and if you have double and triple checked, then you must be patient while waiting for the market to concur. The market is fickle and follows no one's schedule.

Adopt the pace of nature: Her secret is patience. – Ralph Waldo Emerson.

DOING A LITTLE WORK...

Success in investing, as in almost anything else, does not happen overnight.

Everybody wants to be somebody; nobody wants to grow.
– Johann Wolfgang von Goethe.

It does not matter how slowly you go so long as you do not stop.
– Confucius.

Do not strive for things occurring to occur as you wish, but wish the things occurring as they occur, and you will flow well. – Epictetus.

Most people would succeed in small things if they were not troubled with great ambitions. – Henry Wadsworth Longfellow.

Success is a consequence and must not be a goal. – Gustave Flaubert.

Learning to invest, and seeing your investments bear fruit, will take time.

Success requires some work.

Hell hides behind pleasure, paradise hides behind work and trouble.
– Muhammad.

The dictionary is the only place where success comes before work.
– Vince Lombardi.

And once you have put in some work, you usually see some rewards.

There are no secrets to success. It is the result of preparation, hard work, and learning from failure. – Colin L. Powell.

I do not know anyone who has got to the top without hard work. That is the recipe. It will not always get you to the top, but should get you pretty near. – Margaret Thatcher.

I never knew an early-rising, hard-working, prudent man, careful of his earnings, and strictly honest who complained of bad luck.
– Henry Ward Beecher.

Work hard, apply your principles, and be patient. If you are doing the right things, success will follow.

...BRINGS A FEW OPPORTUNITIES...

If you study investing, you will learn to recognize opportunities.

The secret of success in life is for a man to be ready for his opportunity when it comes. - Benjamin Disraeli.

I'll study and get ready, and then the chance will come. - Abraham Lincoln.

You gotta be ready when luck comes around. - Ernest Hemingway.

Then, inevitably, you will eventually find opportunities.

In the fields of observation chance favors only the prepared mind. - Louis Pasteur.

Chance does nothing that has not been prepared beforehand. - Alexis de Tocqueville.

And the more time you spend looking, the more opportunities you will find.

The two most powerful warriors are patience and time. - Leo Tolstoy.

He that can have patience can have what he will. - Benjamin Franklin.

There are always attractive investments out there. It is just a question of finding them.

There is very little chance or luck in this process.

No victor believes in chance. - Friedrich W. Nietzsche.

Chance is a word void of sense; nothing can exist without a cause. - Voltaire.

While every investment outcome has some element of chance, luck, or randomness, your investing track record smoothes this out over time. It's like poker or backgammon, where any one game may depend on luck, but where the net result of a hundred games is due to skill.

You have to actively work to find the opportunities.

All successful men have agreed in one thing—they were causationists. They believed that things went not by luck, but by law; that there was not a weak or cracked link in the chain that joins the first and last of things. - Ralph Waldo Emerson.

Luck plays little role in successful investing. It is only through learning to recognize what makes a good opportunity and actively devoting the time to evaluating potential opportunities that you will eventually find the attractive ones.

...That Will Reward Over Time

Once you find a good investment, stick with it as long as it remains a good investment.

If the job has been correctly done when a common stock is purchased, the time to sell it is—almost never. – Philip A. Fisher.

Our favorite holding period is forever. – Warren E. Buffett.

This is the ideal scenario.

In my opinion, the greatest misconception about the market is the idea that if you buy and hold stocks for long periods of time, you'll always make money. – Victor Sperandeo.

But sometimes, or eventually, the story changes. Buggy whips were a pretty safe investment until the automobile came along. Camera film was resilient too until the digital camera arrived (look up Kodak's story). Nothing will last forever, so monitor your investments for any new development that impacts their long-term health.

Stay with your investment ideas for as long as they make sense, without much care to what is fashionable or what the market may be doing.

In the long run, most people will find themselves better fixed if they will invest not on the basis of large returns and high interest rates, but on the soundness of the company, its prospects for the future, and hold what they buy for permanent investment. Trying to "beat the market" is a losing game for the vast majority. – A. P. Giannini.

I don't think it makes sense for an institutional investor with as long an investment horizon as Yale's to structure a portfolio to perform well in a period of financial crisis. That would require moving away from equity-oriented investments that have served institutions with long time horizons well. – David Swensen.

In 30 years in this business, I do not know anybody who has done it successfully and consistently, nor anybody who knows anybody who has done it successfully and consistently. Indeed, my impression is that trying to do market timing is likely, not only not to add value to your investment program, but to be counterproductive. – John C. Boggle.

I've never considered it a legitimate goal to say you're going to invest at the bottom. There is no price other than zero that can't be exceeded on the downside, so you can't really know where the bottom is, other than in retrospect. That means you have to invest at other times. If you wait until the bottom has passed, when the dust has settled and uncertainty has been resolved, demand starts to outstrip supply and you end up competing with too many other buyers. So if you can't expect to buy at the bottom and it's hard to buy on the way up after the bottom, that means you have to be willing to buy on the way down. – Howard Marks.

> Do not be tempted into chasing the fashionable "flavor du jour" investments that everyone else may be pursuing as there is no "fashionable and trendy" winning investment strategy. Do not agonize whether you are buying at the absolute bottom or selling at the absolute top; that is impossible and, besides, a further price dip should be considered an opportunity to buy more.

Indeed, attempting to forecast or predict which way the market will move is asking for disappointment.

If you would live by the crystal ball, learn to eat shattered glass – various.

Everyone has a plan until they get punched in the face. – Mike Tyson.

No one on Wall Street has ever figured out how to time stocks' swings perfectly. Most people, in fact, fail miserably at timing. – Tom Petruno.

I used to be bullish, then I was bearish. Now I'm brokish. – Milton Berle.

Something about "the best laid plans of mice and men" comes to mind.

Stay invested, for the long term, with worthy stocks.

Whatever method you use to pick stocks or stock mutual funds, your ultimate success or failure will depend on your ability to ignore the worries of the world long enough to allow your investments to succeed. It isn't the head but the stomach that determines the fate of the stock-picker. – Peter Lynch, Beating the Street.

What always impresses me is how much better the relaxed, long-term owners of stocks do with their portfolios than the traders do with their switching of inventory. The relaxed investor is usually better informed and more understanding of essential values; he is more patient and less emotional; he pays smaller annual capital gains taxes; he does not incur unnecessary brokerage commissions; and he avoids behaving like Cassius by "thinking too much." – Lucien O. Hooper.

The most important message of this book is to stay invested in stocks. This is extremely difficult for many investors, especially during bear markets. As a result, they jump into and out of even the best funds as market conditions change, dramatically lowering their returns. It does little good to purchase the right stocks or funds if the next time the market trembles you find yourself scurrying to the safety of money market assets. – Jeremy J. Siegel, Stocks for the Long Run.

Throughout all my years of investing, I've found that the big money was never made in the buying or selling, the big money was made in the waiting. – Jesse Livermore.

If an investment is selling for less than its true potential worth, then others will also eventually recognize this and bid up the price. If your thesis is correct, then you just have to wait for the market to realize this— and weather any downturns along the way.

Making Investment Decisions

Following is some guidance regarding the methodology of making investment decisions. Simplify as much as possible. Understand as much as is relevant. Keep your emotions as neutral as possible. Do not worry too much about mistakes. Then, decide whether or not to put your money at risk.

Wealth is the product of man's capacity to think. – Ayn Rand.

The value of an idea lies in using it. – Thomas A. Edison.

START BY SIMPLIFYING

Simplify and reduce any question down to its essential components.

No problem can be solved until it is reduced to some simple form. The changing of a vague difficulty into a specific, concrete form is a very essential element in thinking. – J. P. Morgan.

Make everything as simple as possible, but no simpler. – Albert Einstein.

If a problem is too big and too complex, keep breaking it into smaller parts until these become solvable. While you may oftentimes want to understand everything about a potential investment before investing, all you need to find is one or two negatives to rule out a potential investment, and then start spending your time more productively on the next potential idea.

Eliminate extraneous and irrelevant details.

Our life is frittered away by detail… Simplify, simplify.
– Henry David Thoreau.

Small minds are much distressed by little things. Great minds see them all but are not upset by them. – François de La Rochefoucauld.

A wise man sees as much as he ought, not as much as he can.
– Michel de Montaigne.

Out of clutter, find simplicity. From discord, find harmony. In the middle of difficulty lies opportunity. – Albert Einstein.

Imagine you're evaluating the stock of a company that makes widgets. All that matters is how this company (and thereby its stock) will become worth more money in the future. Historical details from ten years ago are probably not relevant, nor is an exhaustive list of all the variations of widgets currently made.

Envision trying to explain the situation to a child or to a non-financial person.

Wise men hear and see as little children do. – Lao-Tzu.

*A truly great man never puts away the simplicity of a child.
– Chinese proverb.*

All children are artists. The problem is how to remain an artist once he grows up. – Pablo Picasso.

Summarize the problem, choice to be made, or opportunity available. Start with the core issues.

*If you can't explain it simply, you don't understand it well enough.
– Albert Einstein.*

*A wise man begins in the end; a fool ends in the beginning.
– English proverb.*

If you have anything of importance to tell me, for God's sake begin at the end. – Sara J. Duncan.

> If sufficiently attractive, an investment case should be simple to understand. The range of choices, or courses of action, should be few. Something that takes too long to explain is likely dressed up with too much "hot air" to be truly attractive.

At this point, the right course of action should be clear.

Rid oneself of trivial knowledge and the greater knowledge will be plain to see. – Zhuang Zhou.

Once the facts are clear, the decision jumps at you. – Peter F. Drucker.

The more you simplify the more you can manage. – Xunzi.

SEEK UNDERSTANDING

When investing, you cannot improvise or hope for lucky guesses.

*Investment must be rational; if you can't understand it, don't do it.
– Warren E. Buffett.*

Always take a little time to reflect on what you are about to do.

Question attentively, and then meditate at leisure over what you have learned. – Confucius.

Yet once we act, we forfeit the option of waiting until new information comes along. As a result, not-acting has value. The more uncertain the

outcome, the greater may be the value of procrastination.
– Peter L. Bernstein, Against the Gods*.*

> There is very rarely a need to act immediately on an investment idea. A mistake due to an overly hasty decision is much worse than a missed opportunity due to a thoughtful and deliberate decision.

Wait until you reasonably think you understand the investment and its associated risks.

To know that we know what we know, and to know that we do not know what we do not know, that is true knowledge. – Copernicus.

I am never afraid of what I know. – Anna Sewell.

> Many successful investors limit their activity to types of businesses or industries that they feel they have some understanding of, and ignore the rest. You do not have to invest everywhere.

This way, if things go wrong, at least you will understand why. You will also be better prepared to intervene or exit the investment sooner rather than later, thus better preserving your money.

I say we never know where we are going, but we sure as heck ought to know where we are. – Howard Marks.

I want to be able to understand my mistakes. This means I only do things I completely understand. – Warren E. Buffett.

> Buffett ignored technology and the Internet through the 1990s, to some ridicule. When the Internet bubble finally burst, his former critics were not to be found. Do not get caught up in things you do not understand, no matter the confidence of your peers.

TAME YOUR EMOTIONS

Remove all emotion from your investing deliberations. Whether or not you personally like a company's management, product, or the style of their corporate logo should not matter unless it is relevant to how much money they will make in the future.

Buy stocks the way you buy groceries, not the way you buy perfume.
– Benjamin Graham.

Your investments—all those lines on your monthly statements—are not your friends, do not have feelings, and do not care whether or not you buy or sell them. Avoid animism and the pathetic fallacy.

You can't be sentimental about your investments and make money from them. – Tyler G. Hicks.

Investing is most intelligent when it is most businesslike.
– Warren E. Buffett quoting Benjamin Graham.

Only ever buy and sell investments based on their future prospects. How much money you have made or lost on them in the past, good or bad, has no bearing on the decision you are making today.

Keep emotion out of your stock decision-making process. Love your spouse, your children, but don't love your stocks. Just because they have been good to you in the past is no guarantee they will be good to you in the future. – Anne E. Brown.

Don't hang onto a stock for sentimental reason or to escape payment of the capital gains tax. When a time to sell is indicated—sell! You'll make mistakes, of course—everybody does; success in this business is in being 90 percent right 70 percent of the time!
– Ira U. Cobleigh and Peter J. Deangelis.

Do not make rash or spur-of-the-moment investment decisions.

Don't drink and trade. – unknown.

Conversely, do not overthink your investment decisions, or excessively worry about them once made.

Keep cool: it will be all one a hundred years hence.
– Ralph Waldo Emerson.

> Once you have done your homework, senseless worry serves little purpose.

DON'T WORRY ABOUT MISTAKES

When you make a certain number of investment decisions, some of them are bound to eventually reveal themselves as mistakes. Don't let these inevitable misses bother you.

If you're not making mistakes, you're not trying hard enough.
– Vince Lombardi.

A mistake in judgment isn't fatal, but too much anxiety about judgment is. – Pauline Kael.

The only man who never makes a mistake is the man who never does anything. – Teddy Roosevelt.

You will contemplate many investments in your career. For any given one, after a reasonable amount of investigation, learn to make a decision and move on.

Take time to deliberate, but when the time for action has arrived, stop thinking and go on. – Napoleon Bonaparte.

But the good big decisions, they don't take any time at all. If they take time, you're in trouble. – Warren E. Buffett.

> Spend the time to get your facts straight and determine what is merely opinion, conjecture, or extraneous information. Once you have done all that, the right decision should become clear even if it is "I will never know enough about this opportunity to fully evaluate it, thus I will pass."

Do not agonize over your decisions.

In any moment of decision, the best thing you can do is the right thing, the next best thing is the wrong thing, and the worst thing you can do is nothing. – Theodore Roosevelt.

There is no more miserable human being than one in whom nothing is habitual but indecision. – William James.

Patience has its limits. Take it too far, and it's cowardice.
– George Jackson.

> These days, we call it "decision paralysis" or its close cousin "analysis paralysis." In dealing with investments and, in order to be honest with yourself, you must learn to make decisions. "Yes" it absolutely appears to be a good investment. Or, "No" it does not appear attractive. Or, even, "This one is too complex, I pass." Oftentimes, it is making this third decision that will save one from mediocre investments and frauds.

If you have done your homework on the way into an investment, and you are monitoring it to the best of your ability, then you have done your duty. Some of your investments will still fail. At least you know this and are prepared.

We ought to do everything both cautiously and confidently at the same time. – Epictetus.

Hope for the best, but prepare for the worst. – English proverb.

Expect the best. Prepare for the worst. Capitalize on what comes.
– Zig Ziglar.

Plans are worthless, but planning is everything.
– General Dwight D. Eisenhower.

> Do your homework diligently; choose to act or not, and then move on to the next task.

Decision Making Summary

For investing, quality decision making is essential.

The ability to make a decision is another characteristic of a winner in money matters. I have found over and over again that those who succeed in making large sums of money reach decisions very promptly and change them, if at all, very slowly. I have also found that people who fail to make money reach decisions very slowly, if at all, and change them frequently and quickly. – Venita VanCaspel.

Quickly figure out the major issues, make the decision, and minimize second-guessing.

For catching good investment ideas in a timely manner, efficient decision making is essential.

Great ideas have a very short shelf life. – John M. Shanahan.

Once you have a new idea, waste no time in doing the necessary homework.

For successfully managing your wealth, competent decision making is essential.

Nothing is more difficult, and therefore more precious, than to be able to decide. – Napoleon Bonaparte.

Once you've done your research and learned all that you reasonably can or that is essential, make a decision. "Invest" or "Don't Invest." And if it is too complicated, uncertain, or all-or-nothing to spend more time on, then don't invest. Saying "I don't know," "let me think about it more," or "give me another week or two" constitutes procrastination.

Being Wary of General Rules

It's best to avoid groupthink, and learn to recognize when an investment might present an exception to the general rules. Every situation is unique. There is usually something to learn, and some profit to be made, from not travelling with the herd.

When everyone thinks alike, everyone is likely to be wrong.
– Humphrey Neill, The Art of Contrary Thinking.

OVERLY BROAD RULES ARE TOO OFTEN USELESS FOR INVESTING

It is really very simple. Do not trust generalizations.

All generalizations are dangerous, even this one. – Alexandre Dumas.

All generalizations, including this one, are false. – Mark Twain.

Especially when contemplating individual stocks.

Do not engage in generalizations.

To generalize is to be an idiot. – William Blake.

Nothing is so useless as a general maxim.
– Thomas Babington Macaulay.

Anything that can be "put in a nutshell" should remain there.
– Bertrand Russell.

Generalizations are not very useful for vetting or eliminating investments because they eliminate the interesting exceptions.

Be wary whence come generalizations.

Platitude: an idea (a) that is admitted to be true by everyone, and (b) that is not true. – H. L. Mencken.

Common sense is the collection of prejudices acquired by age eighteen.
– Albert Einstein.

Everyone is a prisoner of his own experience. No one can eliminate prejudices—just recognize them. – Edward R. Murrow.

Since you will never rid yourself of all prejudices, it is valuable to be aware of them, and thus be in a position to compensate for these out-of-date conceits when circumstances call for it.

Be suspicious when the general is used to justify the specific.

Crafty men deal in generalizations. – unknown.

Every situation is unique and there are exceptions to every rule. Think everything through for yourself and come to your own conclusions.

More often than not, generalizations have little basis in fact.

A lie told often enough becomes the truth. – Vladimir I. Lenin.

If an idiot were to tell you the same story every day for a year, you would end by believing it. – Horace Mann.

Repetition does not transform a lie into a truth. – Franklin D. Roosevelt.

The more people who believe in something, the more apt it is to be wrong. The person who's right often has to stand alone.
– Soren Kierkegaard.

Question generalizations especially when most people believe that something is beyond reproach—part of accepted knowledge which "right-thinking" people "should" believe.

Traditional wisdom is long on tradition and short on wisdom.
– Warren E. Buffett.

Nothing is so firmly believed as that which we least know.
– Michel de Montaigne.

The greater the ignorance the greater the dogmatism. – William Osler.

And even worse, generalizations are often wrong despite being wrapped in the cloak of local culture, religion, or anything else one is not supposed to question.

Prejudices are what fools use for reason. – Voltaire.

Prejudice springs from ignorance. – Chinese proverb.

Dogma does not mean the absence of thought, but the end of thought.
– G. K. Chesterton.

Faith: Not wanting to know what is true. – Friedrich W. Nietzsche.

Therefore, three things to beware. First, beware all things you take for granted.

The greatest obstacle to discovery is not ignorance—it is the illusion of knowledge. – Daniel J. Boorstin.

The greatest enemy of knowledge is not ignorance. It is the illusion of knowledge. – Stephen Hawking.

It ain't so much the things we don't know that get us into trouble. It's

*the things we know that just ain't so. – variously Mark Twain, Artemus
Ward, Kin Hubbard, Will Rogers, Charles Kettering, Eubie Blake, Yogi
Berra, or Josh Billings.*

You cannot take anything for granted when contemplating the future of
an investment.

Second, always beware that you may lack some essential piece of knowledge or
be unaware of some important ramification or contingency. A rule or belief may
seem fine on its face, but always look for circumstances where it may fail, as such
a realization could be profitable.

*To be ignorant of one's ignorance is the malady of the ignorant.
– Amos Bronson Alcott.*

*Nothing in all the world is more dangerous than sincere ignorance and
conscientious stupidity. – Dr. Martin Luther King, Jr.*

It is worse still to be ignorant of your ignorance. – Saint Jerome.

*Nothing is more terrible than ignorance in action.
– Johann Wolfgang von Goethe.*

The future is always changing. What can change that will put this
investment at risk? What new development might occur that is outside
of today's basic assumptions and generalizations?

Third, and lastly, whenever dismissing a belief as erroneous or faulty, beware you
are not merely replacing it with some other trendy mass-market consensus belief
that itself may be erroneous.

*A great many people think they are thinking when they are merely
rearranging their prejudices. – William James.*

Spotting the Error Can Lead to Profit

The first step is to always test any rule, belief, or thesis.

*It is wrong always, everywhere, and for everyone, to believe anything
upon insufficient evidence. – William James.*

*In all affairs it's a healthy thing now and then to hang a question mark
on the things you have long taken for granted. – Bertrand Russell.*

*One's first step in wisdom is to question everything—and one's last is to
come to terms with everything. – Georg Christoph Lichtenberg.*

Check any rule, belief or thesis. More often than not, there will be exceptions, special cases, and situations where the rule just does not apply.

A wise man recognizes the convenience of a general statement, but he bows to the authority of a particular fact. – Oliver Wendell Holmes, Sr.

You are young, my son, and, as the years go by, time will change and even reverse many of your present opinions. Refrain therefore awhile from setting yourself up as a judge of the highest matters. – Plato.

It is not enough that you form, and even follow the most excellent rules for conducting yourself in the world; you must, also, know when to deviate from them, and where lies the exception. – Fulke Greville.

The young man knows the rules, but the old man knows the exceptions. – Oliver Wendell Holmes, Jr.

In investing, there are always exceptions.

Note that not knowing the exceptions can be very costly.

No [investment] rule always works. – Howard Marks.

In theory, there is no difference between theory and practice. But in practice, there is. – Yogi Berra.

Theories usually lose you money. The more you believe your theory, the more you will lose. – Henry Clasing.

Conversely, and of most interest to us here, successful investing involves finding these exceptional situations, especially when unknown to others. You then have the opportunity to act on these discoveries and thereby profit.

The art of being wise is the art of knowing what to overlook. – William James.

The cleverly expressed opposite of any generally accepted idea is worth a fortune to somebody. – F. Scott Fitzgerald.

To conclude this section, I offer three more thoughts: First, always start with a blank slate.

The only true wisdom is in knowing you know nothing. – Socrates.

Approach every new investment idea with as open and blank a mind as possible. Do your research, do your due diligence, think it through, and discuss it with people you respect who are knowledgeable in the field. Then think it through for yourself and reach your own conclusions.

Second, remember that the silliest pagan superstitions of the ancients were once regarded with the same seriousness and general acceptance of many of society's current dogmas.

There is nothing so absurd but some philosopher has said it. – Cicero.

And third, logically, consider that what is new and heretical today, may just be the next great truth waiting to dawn.

All this worldly wisdom was once the unamiable heresy of some wise man. – Henry David Thoreau.

The heresy of one age becomes the orthodoxy of the next. – Helen Keller.

Every generation will inevitably see the rise of some new technology or custom. Figure out what big changes are occurring during your life, and then profit from them.

Finding Your Own Path

Finding your own path involves independence of thought, responsibility, not relying on others, and making one's own investment decisions.

> *To repeat what others have said, requires education; to challenge it, requires brains. - Mary Pettibone Poole.*

> *If you believe everything you read, better not read. - Japanese proverb.*

> *The wisest men follow their own direction. - Euripides.*

THINK. FOR. YOURSELF.

Whether picking individual stocks or simply picking someone to manage your money for you, successful investors think for themselves.

> *The road to success in investing is paved with independence of spirit, decisiveness and the courage of one's conviction. - Peter L. Bernstein.*

> *Self-trust is the first secret of success. - Ralph Waldo Emerson.*

> *Be your own torch and your own refuge... Seek refuge in no others but only in yourself. - The Mahaparinibbana Sutta.*

> No one else will really know what you need, so you must decide.

Independence in thought brings independence in all else.

> *The strongest man in the world is he who stands most alone.*
> *- Henrik Ibsen.*

> *One man with courage is a majority. - Thomas Jefferson.*

> *Do we not realize that self-respect comes with self-reliance?*
> *- Abdul Kalam.*

> *Whoso would be a man must be a nonconformist.*
> *- Ralph Waldo Emerson.*

> *Every man who is truly a man must learn to be alone in the midst of all others, and if need be against all others. - Romain Rolland.*

> Those who think for themselves rarely need someone else to tell them what to do.

It's not so much that your thought or idea must be original, it's that it should be what you figure out for yourself and have reason to believe correct.

Nothing that is worth knowing can be taught. – Oscar Wilde.

All truly wise thoughts have been thought already thousands of times; but to make them truly ours, we must think them over again honestly, till they take root in our personal experiences.
– Johann Wolfgang von Goethe.

When you have arrived at a conclusion through your own thought process, you will more fully understand and trust your conclusion.

Only when we forget what we were taught do we start to have real knowledge. – Henry David Thoreau.

Rough work, iconoclasm, but the only way to get at truth.
– Oliver Wendell Holmes.

Whatever you think, be sure it is what you think. – T. S. Eliot.

There are two requirements for success in Wall Street. One, you have to think correctly; and secondly, you have to think independently.
– Benjamin Graham.

> Editorial clarification: Here, Graham is talking about success in choosing investments. He is most assuredly not talking about how smooth-talking investment bankers go about generating their often-obscene fees.

GET ADVICE, BUT DON'T NECESSARILY FOLLOW IT

Beware simply parroting other people's opinions.

Most people are other people. Their thoughts are someone else's opinions, their lives a mimicry, their passions a quotation. – Oscar Wilde.

There are many people who reach their conclusions about life like schoolboys; they cheat their master by copying the answer out of a book without having worked out the sum for themselves. – Soren Kierkegaard.

Learned we may be with another man's learnings: we can only be wise with wisdom of our own. – Michel de Montaigne.

Don't follow the advice of others, rather, learn to listen to the voice within yourself. – Dogen.

When we ask for advice, we are usually looking for an accomplice.
– Marquis de la Grange.

The wise pursue understanding; fools follow the reports of others.
– Tibetan proverb.

Even if your three most respected peers tell you that something is a good investment idea, you should still do enough basic work to convince yourself. Since everyone makes mistakes, it is only by doing your own work that you can best avoid the mistakes of others. Of course, ideas from people you respect often provide fertile ground to begin work, but let the work be your own. And if there is a mistake to be made, let it be your own as well.

Constant reliance on someone else's advice is never a good idea...

Don't walk in front of me, I may not follow. Don't walk behind me, I may not lead. Walk beside me and be my friend. - Albert Camus.

The man who goes alone can start today; but he who travels with another must wait till that other is ready. - Henry David Thoreau.

...Unless the person is your stylist or interior decorator.

In matters of style, swim with the current; in matters of principle, stand like a rock. - Thomas Jefferson.

Nor can you reliably succeed by making a carbon copy of other people's ideas and methods.

Do not seek to follow in the footsteps of the men of old, seek what they sought. - Matsuo Basho.

I have no faith in their paths, but believe that every man must make his own path. - Black Hawk.

Do not go where the path may lead, go instead where there is no path and leave a trail. - Ralph Waldo Emerson.

Traveler, there is no path. Paths are made by walking.
- Antonio Machado.

In business or in life, don't follow the wagon tracks too closely.
- H. Jackson Brown, Jr.

All know the way, few actually walk it. - Bodhidharma.

Ultimately, you must be your own person and rely only on yourself. Otherwise, your investing decisions become a committee decision, and no committee ever made a wise decision.

This said, it never hurts to ask for, and listen to, advice given by people you respect. However, you should treat this advice as just another input into your reasoning process and make up your own mind as to how much of it you agree with.

It takes humility to seek feedback. It takes wisdom to understand it, analyze it, and appropriately act on it. - Stephen Covey.

Believe nothing, no matter where you read it, or who said it, even if I have said it, unless it agrees with your own reason and your own common sense. - Gautama Buddha.

Nobody can give you wiser advice than yourself. - Marcus Tullius Cicero.

One of the advantages of being a captain, Doctor, is being able to ask for advice without necessarily having to take it. - Captain Kirk, Star Trek, TV show, "Dagger of the Mind" episode.

You are the captain of your investment ship.

Exercise your skepticism. There is never any rush to believe something.

Don't follow any advice, no matter how good, until you feel as deeply in your spirit as you think in your mind that the counsel is wise. - Joan Rivers.

Skepticism is the chastity of the intellect, and it is shameful to surrender it too soon or to the first comer: there is nobility in preserving it coolly and proudly through long youth, until at last, in the ripeness of instinct and discretion, it can be safely exchanged for fidelity and happiness. - George Santayana.

BEWARE THE CONSENSUS—CONSIDER THE CONVERSE

In investing, you can never get rich just by copying everyone else.

No one can possibly achieve any real and lasting success, or get rich in business, by being a conformist. - J. Paul Getty.

It is impossible to produce a superior performance unless you do something different from the majority. - John Templeton.

The most money is always made from anticipating a company's good performance (or any other event) before it happens and before everyone else realizes it will happen. Once everyone has figured out that a company will do well, there's probably not much more money to be made from its stock.

Market prices are the sum total of known facts, opinions, sentiment, and expectations. The point of investing on the basis of contrary opinion is to take advantage of unexpected change. - John C. Hathaway, May 2011 market letter.

Things are almost never clear on Wall Street, or when they are, then it's too late to profit from them. – Peter Lynch.

What everyone knows isn't worth knowing. – Gerard Loeb.

Markets are constantly in a state of uncertainty and flux and money is made by discounting the obvious and betting on the unexpected. – George Soros.

You make money by buying something before everyone else buys it, not after.

So if your investment idea is already known to most people, beware.

Whenever you find yourself on the side of the majority, it is time to pause and reflect. – Mark Twain.

If an idea is fashionable, that is by itself a pretty good reason to regard it with extreme skepticism. – Paul Krugman.

A fashion is nothing but an induced epidemic. – George Bernard Shaw.

A public opinion poll is no substitute for thought. – Warren E. Buffett.

The stock of the greatest company in the world is crap if every investor already thinks it is the greatest company in the world. – Andy Kessler, Running Money.

Once you realize "everybody already knows" about something, start by considering the opposite.

The one who follows the crowd will usually get no further than the crowd. The one who walks alone is likely to find himself in places no one has ever been. – Albert Einstein.

Take the course opposite to custom and you will almost always do well. – Jean-Jacques Rousseau.

If they give you ruled paper, write the other way. – Ray Bradbury.

Only dead fish swim with the stream. – unknown.

Eagles don't flock. – H. Ross Perot.

History has shown that in every age and in every field of human knowledge, many of the views which almost everyone accepted as true and never bothered to think about further, were in time proven completely wrong. – Philip A. Fisher.

When popular opinion is nearly unanimous, contrary thinking tends to be most profitable. The reason is that once the crowd takes a position, it creates a short-term, self-fulfilling prophecy. But when a change occurs, everyone seems to change his mind at once. – Gustave Le Bon.

Then, start thinking about things only tangentially related, out of the box, dismissed or ignored.

Sometimes having a new idea simply means stopping having an old idea. – Edwin Land.

Close both eyes to see with the other eye. – Rumi.

Imagination is more important than knowledge. Knowledge is limited. Imagination encircles the world. – Albert Einstein.

You can make a living from fairly competent investing. But to make a lot of money, you must see something that others have not yet seen.

Think different. Think crazy. This will not always work, but at least you are looking where few others are looking.

The best things and best people rise out of their separateness; I'm against a homogenized society because I want the cream to rise. – Robert Frost.

Logic will get you from A to B. Imagination will take you everywhere. – Albert Einstein.

There is no great genius without a mixture of madness. – Aristotle.

Look for that different take on things, not yet considered by others, but investable now and that will become valuable once others realize it.

Genius, in truth, means little more than the faculty of perceiving in an unhabitual way. – William James.

Talent hits a target no one else can hit; Genius hits a target no one else can see. – Arthur Schopenhauer.

Discovery consists of seeing what everybody has seen, and thinking what nobody has thought. – Albert Szent-Gyorgi.

Imagination rules the world. – Napoleon Bonaparte.

Work on imagining what will come next.

A Rant on Mass-Media "News"

Mass media exists to entertain and sell advertising.

Journalists: People who have nothing to say and know how to say it. – Karl Kraus.

The advertisement is the most truthful part of a newspaper.
– Thomas Jefferson.

It's amazing that the amount of news that happens in the world every
day always just exactly fits the newspaper. – Jerry Seinfeld.

> By all means read the popular press, even the investment advice therein.
> But recognize it for what it is: how the average person perceives the
> investment landscape. We call this the public consensus. And it is usually
> late and wrong.

Mass media does not exist to inform (except as a second-derivative comment on
what titillates the masses).

There is much to be said in favor of journalism in that by giving us the
opinion of the uneducated, it keeps us in touch with the ignorance of the
community. – Oscar Wilde.

Newspaper editors are men who separate the wheat from the chaff, and
then print the chaff. – Adlai E. Stevenson.

The public have an insatiable curiosity to know everything, except what
is worth knowing. – Oscar Wilde.

People who read the tabloids deserve to be lied to. – Jerry Seinfeld.

Mass media does not relate important news—or at least, not a calm, sober,
intelligent, non-partisan, analysis into the what, why and wherefore of the
important news.

Trying to determine what is going on in the world by reading newspapers
is like trying to tell the time by watching the second hand of a clock.
– Ben Hecht.

If you do not read the newspaper, you are uninformed. If you do read the
newspaper, you are misinformed. – Mark Twain.

The man who reads nothing at all is better educated than the man who
reads nothing but newspapers. – Thomas Jefferson.

You will very rarely learn anything actionable from following the news.

If it is in the headlines, it's in the stock price. – Bill Miller.

Though I listen to the noise to make sure there's no new information that
I need to know, I don't worry about most of it. – James S. Chanos.

> A caveat: You will almost never find anything useful in the immediate
> contents of the news. However, by keeping yourself informed, this could

well lead to valuable secondary conclusions, where upon reading one or more bits of news, you cleverly figure out an investable implication or expectation that was not directly stated in the news.

In fact, the news is most often more of a distraction than anything else.

Everybody gets so much information all day long that they lose their common sense. – Gertrude Stein.

Therefore, it is best to mostly ignore popular media.

I do not take a single newspaper, nor read one a month, and I feel myself infinitely the happier for it. – Thomas Jefferson.

I picked up the newspaper from the mailbox, but it contained nothing of any importance, only the things that journalists had decided we should know, feel involved in, and have an opinion about. – Paulo Coelho, The Witch of Portobello.

I find television very educational. Every time someone switches it on I go into another room and read a good book. – Groucho Marx.

The individual who has experienced solitude will not easily become a victim of mass suggestion. – Albert Einstein.

A RANT ON STOCK MARKET "RESEARCH"

To begin with, most "research" is just wishful thinking, albeit dressed up in charts and numbers.

Fake realism is the escapist literature of our time. And probably the ultimate escapist reading is that masterpiece of total unreality, the daily stock market report. – Ursula K. LeGuin.

To the list of famous oxymorons—military intelligence, learned professor, deafening silence, and jumbo shrimp—I'd add professional investing. – Peter Lynch.

Accounting is but an aid to business thinking, not a substitute for it. – Warren E. Buffett.

We seldom saw any Wall Street research and laughed at most of what we did see. – Peter L. Bernstein.

You might reasonably ask, then why do brokerage firms go to the trouble of writing their reports, publishing them, and giving interviews in the press and on television?

The entire purpose of the vast enterprise known collectively as "the stock market" is, from the point of view of the men who run it, to churn up the greatest possible amount of buying and selling, so as to generate the greatest possible number of commissions. – Nicolas Darvas.

> Wall Street firms earn some fees when you have your investment account with them. But they earn more, through commissions, when they can get you to buy and sell.

Advisers—most of the time—have no real knowledge as to whether something will rise or fall.

It is either going to trade higher, or it will make a new low.
– apocryphal Wall Street proverb, originator unknown.

Question: "Do you know what the markets (or a given stock) will do today?"
Answer: "They will fluctuate." – J. P. Morgan.

> This is, under most circumstances, the only possible honest answer.

There is no such thing as a real hot market or stock tip; most of the time it is a product of wishful thinking. Sometimes, though, it might be true insider information (illegal to trade on), could be wrong anyway, and will usually get you into a lot of trouble.

Here is what to do with hot tips. If you get a hot tip, make a note of it and pretend to be very interested. But don't buy. If the thing takes off, listen a little more closely the next time this fellow has a tip. If it gets mauled, look bitter the next time you see him. He will assume that you bought the stock; he will feel guilty; and he will buy you a very nice lunch.
– Andrew Tobias.

Get inside information from the president and you will probably lose half your money. If you get it from the chairman of the board, you will lose all of your money. – Jim Rogers.

I have probably purchased fifty "hot tips" in my career, maybe even more. When I put them all together, I know I am a net loser. – Charles Schwab.

The odds of anyone calling you on the phone with good investment advice are about the same as winning Lotto without buying a ticket.
– Joel Greenblatt.

> The same applies to all those stock market tips and "investment opportunities" sent these days via robo-personalized email.

Give a cold shoulder to cold callers. Never invest in anything based on a phone call from someone you don't know or whose office is a post office box. - Nancy Dunnan.

I always pass on good advice. It is the only thing to do with it. It is never of any use to oneself. - Oscar Wilde.

Always remember that just because someone works in investing, that does not necessarily make them an investing wizard. They, too, are human, with their own mix of emotional foibles and sometimes-erroneous beliefs.

It makes me shudder. Lots of people drive to their broker's office in Rolls-Royces to get financial advice from somebody who came to work in a bus. - Milton Berle.

Personally, I like the "A" train. And occasionally a taxi.

Pay no attention to that man behind the curtain! The Great Oz has spoken! - The Wizard of Oz, 1939.

So what if the speaker is some big respected investment adviser? If they were really that smart and that successful in the market, then long ago they would have retired to their own private island. And the rare exceptions, the smart ones who are still working, remember that their picks are still wrong just short of half the time.

Ignoring Other Peoples' Opinions

Ignore what other people think. It is OK to hear what they have to say, but not OK to blindly rely on them. It is essential that you always make sure you think for yourself.

> *Too often we hold fast to the clichés of our forebears. We subject all facts to a prefabricated set of interpretations. We enjoy the comfort of opinion without the discomfort of thought. – John F. Kennedy.*

> *One should as a rule, respect public opinion in so far as is necessary to avoid starvation and to keep out of prison, but anything that goes beyond this is voluntary submission to an unnecessary tyranny, and is likely to interfere with happiness in all kinds of ways. – Bertrand Russell.*

OPINIONS DO NOT MATTER

What is Right, or Wrong, matters.

> *You're neither right nor wrong because other people agree with you. You're right because your facts are right and your reasoning is right—and that's the only thing that makes you right. And if your facts and reasoning are right, you don't have to worry about anybody else.*
> *– Benjamin Graham.*

> *The truth is the truth even if nobody believes it, and a lie is still a lie even if everybody believes it. – A. B. Fulton Sheen.*

> *The truth is incontrovertible; malice may attack it, ignorance may deride it, but in the end, there it is. – Winston Churchill.*

> *The sky is no less blue because the blind man does not see it.*
> *– Danish proverb.*

> The world is full of metaphorically "blind people," those who will not see what you might see in an investment and those you will not be able to convince that you are right. If they are not raising any new information or risks you have not already considered, then you should not worry about what they think. If all the data has been put on the table, then it is merely a difference of opinion or interpretation, and there will always be that.

We should therefore not care (much) about what others believe.

It never ceases to amaze me: we all love ourselves more than other people, but care more about their opinions than our own.
– Marcus Aurelius.

Never explain—your friends do not need it and your enemies will not believe you anyway. – Elbert Hubbard.

Few people are capable of expressing with equanimity opinions which differ from the prejudices of their social environment. Most people are even incapable of forming such opinions. – Albert Einstein.

Be content with your own convictions.

It is easy in the world to live after the world's opinion; it is easy in solitude to live after our own; but the great man is he who in the midst of the crowd keeps with perfect sweetness the independence of solitude.
– Ralph Waldo Emerson.

He then remains equally calm when the majority is on his side as when he finds himself in a minority for he has done his part: he has expressed his convictions; he is not lord of minds and attitudes.
– Johann Wolfgang von Goethe.

If you are standing upright, do not fear a crooked shadow.
– Chinese proverb.

AFTER ALL, NOBODY KNOWS ANYTHING

Seriously, nobody really knows anything, anyway.

Nobody knows anything. – William Goldman.

Everybody is ignorant, only on different subjects. – Will Rogers.

But unfortunately, most pretend they do know something.

When facts are few, experts are many. – Donald Gannon.

Opinions are like assholes; everyone has one. – Simone Elkeles.

Any fool can criticize, condemn and complain, and most fools do.
– Benjamin Franklin.

Do not let other peoples' unsolicited criticism bother you, and do not waste your time critiquing others who may not necessarily welcome it.

The whole problem with the world is that fools and fanatics are always so certain of themselves, but wiser people so full of doubts.
– Bertrand Russell.

Have doubts. They are good for your mental and financial health.

Especially economists. (Small exception granted to serious hands-on investors who retain some humility.)

An economist's guess is liable to be just as good as anybody else's.
– Will Rogers.

An economist is an expert who will know tomorrow why the things he predicted yesterday didn't happen today. – unknown.

If economists could manage to get themselves thought of as humble, competent people on a level with dentists, that would be splendid.
– John Maynard Keynes.

When it comes to forecasting, there are only two kinds of economists, those who don't know and those who don't know that they don't know.
– Ray Marshall.

I believe that the general growth in large [financial] institutions has occurred in the context of an underlying structure of markets in which many of the larger risks are dramatically—I should say, fully—hedged.
– Alan Greenspan, US Congressional hearing, 2000.

So sayeth the chief banker of the United States just as the whole "Dot-Com" bubble was starting to implode, with most technology-darling stocks about to descend by at least half.

We've never had a decline in house prices on a nationwide basis. So, what I think what is more likely is that house prices will slow, maybe stabilize, might slow consumption spending a bit. I don't think it's going to drive the economy too far from its full employment path, though,
– Ben Bernanke, July 1, 2005.

So sayeth the next chief banker of the United States just before the whole housing market started a 30% decline, the worst in at least three generations and a decline possibly continuing as of this writing (2013).

[Economists' advice] is something like patent medicine—people know it is largely manufactured by quacks and that a good percentage of the time it won't work, but they continue to buy the brand whose flavor they like.
– Barbara Bergman.

The only function of economic forecasting is to make astrology look respectable. – Ezra Solomon.

And most mathematicians.

I have hardly ever known a mathematician who was capable of reasoning. – Plato.

A mathematician is a blind man in a dark room looking for a black cat, which isn't there. – Charles Darwin.

> This is often because mathematicians, like finance professors and other academics, tend to lose track of the "big picture" context. They may be very good at identifying a mathematical relationship "in general" or "on average," but they are mostly incapable of evaluating randomness, human vicissitudes, and outlier events.

Or anyone touted as an "expert" or "guru" or "successful."

Do not be bullied out of your common sense by the specialist; two to one, he is a pedant. – Voltaire.

Expert: a man who makes three correct guesses consecutively.
– Laurence J. Peters.

There is nothing so stupid as an educated man, if you get off the thing that he was educated in. – Will Rogers.

Learned fools are the greatest fools. – German proverb.

With the increasing specialization in modern times, professional losers are now commonplace. – Victor Niederhoffer.

My definition of a guru is someone who is lucky enough to be quoted in the right publication at the right time saying the right thing.
– Herb Greenberg.

Do not be fooled into believing that because a man is rich he is necessarily smart. There is ample proof to the contrary.
– Julius Rosenwald.

Scholars at Duke University studied 11,600 forecasts by corporate chief financial officers about how the Standard & Poor's 500-stock index would perform over the next year. The correlation between their estimates and the actual index was less than zero. – David Brooks.

Or anyone else touted as a "scholar" or "academic" or "scientist."

A scholar is a person who may have spent a long period of time learning, but this does not mean he has learned anything or that he is clever enough to do so. – George C. Lichtenberg.

Much learning does not teach understanding. – Heraclitus.

If all it took to beat the markets was a Ph.D. in mathematics, there'd be a hell of a lot of rich mathematicians out there. – Bill Dries.

I love farmers—too much "education" has not distorted their common sense. - Baron de Montesquieu.

We should rather examine, who is better learned, than who is more learned. - Michel de Montaigne.

When a distinguished but elderly scientist states that something is possible, he is almost certainly right. When he states that something is impossible, he is probably wrong. - Arthur C. Clarke.

There are many who know many things, yet are lacking in wisdom. - Democritus.

Men can acquire knowledge but not wisdom. Some of the greatest fools ever known were learned men. - Spanish proverb.

Beware overly-qualified academics offering the latest "solution," latest new trendy theory on how to make money, or anything else. They are probably really out flogging a book or pushing for tenure.

There are many people who claim to be teachers of others who should themselves be taught first of all. - Leo Tolstoy, A Calendar of Wisdom.

Stay away from the overly popular "gurus."

And especially any "conventional view" held by "the masses."

A thing does not therefore cease to be true because it is not accepted by many. - Spinoza.

He that knows least commonly presumes most. - Thomas Fuller, Gnomologia.

Why is it that those who are the quickest to judge are often those in possession of the fewest facts? - John Wooden.

Ignorance more frequently begets confidence than does knowledge: it is those who know little, not those who know much, who so positively assert that this or that problem will never be known by science. - Charles Darwin.

There are people whose watch stops at a certain hour and who remain permanently at that age. - Charles Sainte-Beuve.

Since the masses are always eager to believe something, for their benefit nothing is so easy to arrange as facts. - Charles-Maurice de Talleyrand.

It is the proof of a bad cause when it is applauded by the mob. - Lucius Annaeus Seneca.

Where all men think alike, no one thinks very much. – Walter Lippmann.

The conventional view serves to protect us from the painful job of thinking. – John Kenneth Galbraith.

> While you might learn something by understanding (and either integrating or dismissing) whatever data the other person is using to form their opinion, beyond that you should not care about their opinion.

If a million people say a foolish thing, it is still a foolish thing.
– Anatole France.

The fact that an opinion has been widely held is no evidence whatever that it is not utterly absurd. – Bertrand Russell.

Instead, be not afraid to critique everything for yourself and make up your own mind.

In real life, illusions can only transform our life for a moment, but in the domain of thoughts and the intellect, misconceptions may be accepted as truth for thousands of years, and make a laughingstock of whole nations, mute the noble wishes of mankind, make slaves from people and lie to them. These misconceptions are the enemies with which the wisest men in the history of mankind try to struggle. The force of the truth is great, but its victory is difficult. However, once you receive this victory, it can never be taken from you. – Arthur Schopenhauer.

LESS DEBATE. MORE ACTION.

Most people are not worth debating with, so do not thus waste your time.

Never engage in a battle of wits with an unarmed opponent. – William Shakespeare (popular paraphrase of original in Romeo and Juliet *play).*

Wise men do not argue with idiots. – Japanese proverb.

Talk sense to a fool and he calls you foolish. – Euripides.

It is impossible to defeat an ignorant man in an argument.
– William G. McAdoo.

Most thoughtful people do not waste time debating.

Consistent winners tell virtually no one their activities in the marketplace... Consistent losers tell anyone who will listen the details of their market activities, to the point of campaigning for their point of view. – Henry Classing.

You should abstain from arguments. They are very illogical ways to convince people. Opinions are like nails; the stronger you hit them, the deeper inside they go. – Decimus Junius Juvenalis.

Opinion has caused more trouble on this little earth than plagues or earthquakes. – Voltaire.

In an argument, you are not arguing for truth but for yourself.
– Thomas Carlyle.

> Having an informed debate, even if spirited, about the merits of an investment idea is still useful if the participants are sticking to the facts, as one might still learn something from someone with a contrary way of interpreting these facts. But if it is an "I'm right, you're wrong" argument, then that is no longer a civil exchange of ideas. You are only wasting time you could better spend in an informed exchange and getting yourself and someone else annoyed. Not useful.

Instead, thoughtful people focus on "doing."

It's not enough to simply have the insight to see something apart from the rest of the crowd, you also need to have the courage to act on it and to stay with it. It's very difficult to be different from the rest of the crowd the majority of the time, which by definition is what you're doing if you're a successful trader. – Bill Lipschutz.

Against criticism a man can neither protest nor defend himself; he must act in spite of it, and then it will gradually yield to him.
– Johann Wolfgang von Goethe.

No man is a free man until he learns to do his own thinking and gains the courage to act on his own personal initiative. – Andrew Carnegie.

Few people think more than two or three times a year; I have made an international reputation for myself by thinking once or twice a week.
– George Bernard Shaw.

Others have seen what is and asked why? I have seen what could be and asked why not? – Pablo Picasso.

> Do not spend time trying to convince others that your current investment is a good idea. Instead, spend that time more productively by thinking about what your next investment will be.

Closing Opinion on Opinions

If you still want another opinion, at least get an experienced, realistic one.

Idealism increases in direct proportion to one's distance to the problem.
– John Galsworthy.

Ask opinions of those individuals who spend their time studying and
learning. – Taisou.

Receive an old man's counsel and a learned man's knowledge.
– Greek proverb.

And, I would specify, get an opinion from someone with hard-won practical knowledge, not a theoretical academic.

You will find that thoughtful, conservative advisers will often be in agreement.

The views of men of wise counsel are much the same. – Liu Bei.

But even then, wise people can still be wrong, or still disagree.

Wise men are not wise at all times. – Ralph Waldo Emerson.

Nothing will ever be attempted if all possible objections must
first be overcome. – Samuel Johnson.

No matter how well you perform there's always somebody of intelligent
opinion who thinks it's lousy. – Laurence Olivier.

Remember to beware easy, "everybody knows" so-called truths or facts.

A lie gets halfway around the world before the truth has a chance to put
its pants on. – Winston Churchill.

Remember to avoid those seeking to debate for the sake of debating.

One who is too insistent on his own views, finds few to agree with him.
– Lao Tzu.

Reminder: "Debate" is a club activity done in school for fun, and not something that will ever affect the truth, what is right, or what a given outcome will be.

Also remember to ignore any personal attacks from a frustrated debater.

I always cheer up immensely if an attack is particularly wounding
because I think, well, if they attack one personally, it means they have not
a single political argument left. – Margaret Thatcher.

The only thing you should ever care about is being eventually correct.

The four most beautiful words in our common language: I told you so.
– Gore Vidal.

This brings us back to always having the courage to figure out, and hold, your own opinions.

There's only one kind of woman...or man, for that matter. You either believe in yourself or you don't. – Captain Kirk, Star Trek *TV show.*

The important thing is not what they think of me, but what I think of them. – Queen Victoria.

I care not what others think of what I do, but I care very much about what I think of what I do. That is character! – Theodore Roosevelt.

What you think about yourself is much more important than what others think of you. – Marcus Annaeus Seneca.

Hearing what others think is fine, so long as it does not take up too much of your time. But then, make up your own mind, and ignore what others think.

PART 3
Delegation, Depth & Risk

Hiring Investment Help

Having read the prior chapters and being a smart and competent individual, you may still decide you do not wish to handle the details of investing your money. Or perhaps you do not want to be solely responsible for all of it. This is fine. If anything, it is probably wise to have an external manager or two with whom you can compare your investment choices and ensure that your family's wealth is not dependent on one person. Therefore, I offer some advice on choosing a good money manager.

In case you did not happen to read the book jacket or Foreword, in the interest of full disclosure, I must here remind the reader that I work by day as a money manager. This next chapter covers what I do professionally and touches on how my income is earned. And while I do genuinely think that most people should employ some form of money manager or seek outside assistance—having seen too many well-intentioned amateurs make too many costly rookie mistakes—I am clearly biased in this matter. Therefore, please add a grain of salt and continue to think critically for yourself while you indulge me on what I have to say in this chapter.

IT HELPS TO HAVE HELP

You will never have all the answers.

> *No man is wise enough by himself. – Titus Maccius Plautus.*

> *A man who is his own lawyer has a fool for a client. – Proverb.*

Getting better results often requires some outside help.

> *To achieve satisfactory investment results is easier than most people realize; to achieve superior results is harder than it looks.*
> *– Benjamin Graham.*

> *To go fast, go alone; to go far, go together. – Chinese proverb.*

Successful people always look to surround themselves with skilled people and to rely on these people.

> *Men too involved in details usually become unable to deal with great matters. – François, duc de La Rochefoucauld.*

> Do not be this person. Instead...

> *I use not only all the brains I have but all I can borrow.*
> *– Woodrow Wilson.*

I have seen that in any great undertaking it is not enough for a man to depend simply upon himself. – Lone Man, Teton Sioux.

The secret of success lies not in doing your own work, but in recognizing the right man to do it. – Andrew Carnegie.

Do you really have the time, temperament, and desire to manage the entirety of your wealth?

I wish to have as my epitaph: "Here lies a man who was wise enough to bring into his service men who knew more than he." – Andrew Carnegie.

If so, consider delegating investment responsibility for some or all of your wealth to an outside manager.

SEEK THE UNCONVENTIONAL, THOUGHTFUL, INDEPENDENT

Outstanding managers do not get their outstanding returns by taking the exact same approach as all the other managers out there.

Anybody who is any good is different from anybody else.
– Felix Frankfurter.

Perhaps it is better to be irresponsible and right than responsible and wrong. – Winston Churchill.

In fact, you want someone who will take a somewhat different approach from yours (or from your other manager if hiring two), so that all of you do not fall to the same mistakes at the same time.

If a man does not keep pace with his companions, perhaps it is because he hears a different drummer. Let him step to the music he hears, however measured or far away. – Henry David Thoreau.

And those who were seen dancing were thought to be insane by those who could not hear the music. – Friedrich W. Nietzsche.

Give preference to managers who ask important, insightful questions about your needs and situation. You should want someone eager to do more than simply pool your money with that of many others and invest it all the same way.

Judge a man by his questions rather than by his answers. – Voltaire.

The wise man doesn't give the right answers, he poses the right questions.
– Claude Levi-Strauss.

A wise man's questions contain half the answer.
– Solomon ben Yehuda ibn Gabirol.

Allow for some unconventional tastes or unorthodox behavior. After all, this is precisely what you are looking for—independent thinkers unafraid of going against the crowd.

It has been my experience that folks who have no vices have very few virtues. – Abraham Lincoln.

The problem with people who have no vices is that generally you can be pretty sure they're going to have some pretty annoying virtues. – Elizabeth Taylor.

It is with rivers as it is with people: the greatest are not always the most agreeable nor the best to live with. – Henry Van Dyke.

In the whole of human history there has never existed a single person whose conduct was always perfect. Understanding this, the wise don't try to be perfect. – Lao Tzu.

Avoid those who invest conventionally, like all their peers, avoiding the least bit of controversy.

Never be wrong on your own. – John Maynard Keynes.

Worldly wisdom teaches that it is better for reputation to fail conventionally than to succeed unconventionally. – John Maynard Keynes.

A sound banker, alas, is not one who foresees danger and avoids it, but one who, when he is ruined, is ruined in a conventional and orthodox way along with his fellows, so that no one can really blame him. – John Maynard Keynes.

Avoid any investment firm where all investment decisions are made by committee.

I've searched all the parks in all the cities and found no statues of committees. – G. K. Chesterton.

A committee is a group of men who keep minutes and waste hours. – Milton Berle.

What is a committee? A group of the unwilling, picked from the unfit, to do the unnecessary. – Richard Long Harkness.

At firms where the managers are limited to making investments from a pre-approved list and obliged to use allocation guidelines, you will end up paying bespoke fees for a cookie-cutter, uninspired approach.

Avoid large bank trust departments, asset management divisions of large investment banks, etc.

[In 1968, while I was at the SEC, World Bank head Robert McNamara] asked me what I thought about investment bankers, and I told him the truth—which was that I was trying to indict most of them under the Sherman Act. He asked me what I thought of commercial bankers, and I said I thought they sailed around in little ships on Long Island Sound in the summertime and wore white buck shoes. – Eugene Rotberg.

Banking may well be a career from which no man really recovers. – John Kenneth Galbraith.

Whose bread I eat, his song I sing. – German proverb, 12th century.

He who pays the piper calls the tune. – Proverbs.

> A reason to avoid trust departments of large banks is because their motivation is to keep the trust fees flowing and keep the assets invested in the bank's own products, or with the bank's own advisers, as much as possible. They will never do anything controversial or disagree with you on an investment matter—whereas you should really want the opposite. As for the asset management divisions of large investment banks, these are notorious dumping grounds for investment products that the bank could not sell to its institutional investors, such as random lots of illiquid bonds, riskier bets dumped into some fund sold to the retail clientele, and the like.

At all costs, avoid asset allocators, investment consultants, advisers, and their ilk.

Cleverness is not wisdom. – Euripides.

A consultant is someone who takes the watch off your wrist and tells you the time. – unknown.

Pension consultants have not made a difference in terms of adding value for clients. They are not able to prove that they choose better money managers. – Charles Ellis.

> Beware. The thicker their presentation or brochure, or the greater their quantity of complicated graphs, the less they truly understand their subject and the more they are actively trying to hoodwink you.

FAVOR THE SMALLER, DEDICATED, INVOLVED MANAGER

You want someone who knows you, who caters to you, and whose secretary and partner also do the same.

Everyone needs a small-town banker. Especially in a big town. – Jane Bryant Quinn.

You want a true relationship with your money manager. Not a close personal friendship, but a relationship with someone who actually knows who you are when you call. Certainly avoid the fake, big-firm "relationship manager" who has to look you up in the computer when you call and gets replaced every six months.

I always have believed deeply in the importance of people and personal relationships. I still am as convinced as ever that successful long-term financial relationships are far more a matter of personal knowledge and interpersonal relationships than of just supposedly "objective" numbers and technology. – David Rockefeller.

You can get very good service from the one-man shop, and you certainly want only one decision maker, but it is better to work with a manager who has at least a partner or two plus a few talented junior professionals. This way, there can be a little diversification of investment ideas and a few people to fall back on should your manager ever get hit by the proverbial bus.

Deliberation is the work of many men. Action, of one alone. – Charles de Gaulle.

If you're looking for the most important thing that we look for in a money manager selection process, it's continuity of good managers. It's the common denominator of success in money management—a dedicated group of professionals who have worked together for long periods of time. So that when they do fall into the tank, they work themselves out of it together. And if you have confidence in that group of people, then you don't terminate them when they go into the tank. You know that in due course they'll get out. – George Russell, Jr.

The first method for estimating the intelligence of a ruler is to look at the men he has around him. – Niccolò Machiavelli, The Prince.

Behind every able man, there are always other able men. – Chinese proverb.

Favor managers who are actively involved in their business and involved with their clients. Favor the manager who is actually doing the work and is available on the phone when you call.

If you wish a job done promptly and well, get a busy man to do it. The idle man knows too many substitutes and shortcuts. – Andrew Carnegie.

He who is slowest in making a promise is the most faithful in respecting it. – Jean Jacques Rousseau.

If you want work well done, select a busy man; the other kind has no time. – Elbert Hubbard.

If your investment adviser plays golf, ask him what his handicap is. If it is under six, be careful; the chances are he is either lying or spending far too much time on the golf course. – Bennett W. Goodspeed.

Author's note to prospective clients: My golf game is awful.

Look for the manager whose own money is largely invested alongside his clients' money, in the same funds, the same products, and the same stocks.

Whenever you purpose to consult with anyone about your affairs, first observe how he has managed his own; for he who has shown poor judgment in conducting his own business will never give wise counsel about the business of others. – Isocrates.

An example of a really responsible system is the system the Romans used when they built an arch. The guy who created the arch stood under it as the scaffolding was removed. It's like packing your own parachute. – Charles Munger.

Invest with managers who co-invest a fair percentage of their net worth and who have ownership stakes in the investment firm. These are people incentivized to work hard for their own (and your) long-term benefit.

The really large corporate trust or asset manager has never had a chance—both performance-wise, and in terms of building a real relationship—against the smaller dedicated manager.

Generally speaking, I think [money manager] size does have a negative impact, but there are firms—they're rare—where size has not had a great impact. – George Russell, Jr.

DO NOT BE (MUCH) IMPRESSED BY PERFORMANCE

Measuring and tracking must be done, but intelligently.

You can't manage what you can't measure. – William Hewlett.

It is much more difficult to measure nonperformance than performance. – Harold S. Geneen.

Regardless of their overall situation, most managers will be able to show you some period, or some segment of their assets, or some particular account, during which their performance was good.

The thing that is most interesting to me is that every one of the managers is able to give me a chart that shows me that he was in the first quartile or

*the first decile. I have never had a prospective manager come in and say,
"We're in the fourth quartile or bottom decile." – John English.*

Also, beware the manager who has only recently had good performance. It might
be fleeting, and it might be the only reason they just happen to be out marketing
to you right now.

*Don't be overly impressed with investment firms that have had highly
successful investment performance records within the recent past. You
might be giving money to an organization that is so happily riding the
last trend that they will be the last to admit when the trend is ending.
– Bennett W. Goodspeed.*

*Money managers have created their own nightmare by saying, "Boy, look
at the February we had." They call about March 3rd. – Robert G. Kirby.*

*Most investment managers would produce better returns for their clients
if they completely ignored current market price. – Robert G. Kirby.*

*Ninety percent of what passes for brilliance or incompetence in investing
is the ebb and flow of investment style—growth, value, small, foreign.
– Jeremy Grantham.*

Success makes a fool seem wise. – H. G. Bohn.

Trend is not destiny. – Paul Valéry.

> Anyone can get lucky over a recent short period of time. It does not mean
> anything.

Look for performance over at least five years so that it covers at least one bad
period in the markets.

*Even the best investment managers do not always have great results.
There is no man for all seasons in this business. – John English.*

*Investment opportunities change over the long term. You want a pilot
who can fly even if the weather changes. – Shelby White.*

*Judge a person not by his ability to make money, but by his ability to
retain it. – Chinese proverb.*

> Making money and preserving it, over a long period of time, is hard to
> attribute to luck.

Evaluate over the long term, and favor the manager who presents results this way.

*I think the fact that I don't look at the stock market every hour is very
helpful, and the fact that I don't look at the relative performance [of*

different funds]. Because you can't manage a portfolio as if you're running a race every five minutes. - Gerald Tsai.

It's a good discipline to often say, "I don't really care what goes on in the market today." When you do that you can actually get something useful done. - James Montier.

The years see what the days will never know. - Chinese proverb.

Favor the manager who still does OK despite a temporary period of poor performance. All managers will almost certainly go through these periods from time to time—you want the manager who has shown he can do OK despite it.

Being a professional ... is making fewer mistakes than others, as few as possible. - Françoise Giroud.

A professional is someone who can do his best work when he doesn't feel like it. - Alistair Cooke.

If you want to know what a man is really like, take notice how he acts when he loses money. - New England proverb.

Good long-term performance is indeed a good sign.

First-class investment performance cannot be measured on a quarterly or annual basis. Outstanding investors don't work that way. - Charles Ellis.

There's no luck to professional portfolio investing: you can no more pile up a superlative record by luck or accident than you can win a chess tournament by luck or accident. - John Train.

Beware Overly Glossy Marketing

Beware the glib tongue, the smooth talker who always seems to know all the answers.

A dog is not considered a good dog because he is a good barker. A man is not considered a good man because he is a good talker. - Gautama Siddhartha.

Some people do not become thinkers simply because their memories are too good. - Friedrich W. Nietzsche.

A great memory does not make a mind, any more than a dictionary is a piece of literature. - John Henry Cardinal Newman.

Beware of those who laugh at nothing or at everything.
- Arnold H. Glasow.

Have a care, therefore, where there is more sail than ballast.
- William Penn.

Indeed, the good investor by definition usually cares little what other people think, and thus is probably not a very smooth operator around clients. Look for this guy.

Beware the person or team full of certainty and lacking any doubt.

Only fools and charlatans think they know and understand everything.
- Anton Pavlovich Chekhov.

Believe those who are seeking the truth. Doubt those who find it.
- André Gide.

He who is looking for wisdom is already wise; and he who thinks that he has found wisdom is a stupid man. - Eastern proverb.

A wise man has doubts even in his best moments. Real truth is always accompanied by hesitations. If I could not hesitate, I could not believe.
- Henry David Thoreau.

Instead, someone who is a good investor is usually worrying about something.

Beware the managers willing to promise the sun, moon and stars, and effusing on how great and wonderful they are.

Many promises impair confidence. - Latin proverb.

When a man speaks of his strength, he whispers his weakness.
- John Barrymore.

It is what people actually did in the stock market that counted—not what they said they were going to do. - Jesse Livermore.

An investor who claims to foresee nothing but smooth sailing is either naïve or intentionally misleading you.

Beware any results that are not audited.

Trust, but verify. - Ronald Reagan.

Notice those topics they are not discussing.

The cruelest lies are often told in silence. - Robert Louis Stevenson.

Pay as much attention to what they say as to what they do not say...but which you would normally have expected them to say.

Beware the manager unable to take responsibility for poor performance or unable to admit ever making a real, serious mistake.

He that is good for making excuses is seldom good for anything else.
– Benjamin Franklin.

When a man is wrong and won't admit it, he always gets angry.
– Haliburton.

No persons are more frequently wrong, than those who will not admit they are wrong. – François de La Rochefoucauld.

Those who never retract their opinions love themselves more than they love the truth. – Joseph Joubert.

> Any manager with at least a decade in the business has at some point made a real mistake. If he is unable to admit this regarding the past, how will he behave when he makes a mistake with your account?

Do not be impressed by a back story, however fascinating, that has nothing to do with investing.

Don't trust anyone cute, or more generally, anyone who gets press because his life (as opposed to his work) makes a good story. Mr. A grew up middle class in the 'burbs, got good grades in college, and has turned out to be a very good investment analyst. Mr. B grew up in Greenland, spent four years in the French Foreign Legion, climbs the Himalayas, and claims to be able to beat the market. Guess who gets profiled in Greed magazine? – Paul Krugman.

Do not be impressed by fancy titles, degrees, or sales literature. Be impressed by what your manager actually does for you over the course of the year. Did they protect your money, execute your transfers, return your phone calls, and generally make themselves available to help?

It does not matter what your title is, it's about what you do. One should not look at titles, but rather at achievements.
– Sheik Mohammed bin Rashid Al Maktoum.

As I grow older, I pay less attention to what men say. I just watch what they do. – Andrew Carnegie.

I have always thought the actions of men the best interpreters of their thoughts. – John Locke.

Trust only movement. Life happens at the level of events, not words. Trust movement. – Alfred Adler.

Eyes are more accurate witnesses than ears. – Heraclitus.

In fact, actively avoid those who seem to put too much weight on their credentials. Such managers are dangerous because they are either hiding a lack of real-world common-sense knowledge, or they think they know everything.

> *There is usually only a limited amount of damage that can be done by dull or stupid people. For creating a truly monumental disaster, you need people with high IQs. – Thomas Sowell.*

>> Having a few awards or professorships can give some managers a false sense of confidence, of knowing all the answers—which can increase the severity of the eventual stumble. Look up the story of Long-Term Capital Management (LTCM), a hedge fund that had two Nobel Prize-winning economists amongst its partners.

Similarly, beware excessive use of jargon and complicated words. This implies that the manager either likes to hear himself speak, or is hiding a lack of practical knowledge behind an excess of theory.

> *Why did it take Alan Greenspan ten years to get around to marrying his girlfriend? Because it took her ten years to figure out what he was talking about. – Richard Russell.*

>> Well-known economist Alan Greenspan was Chairman of the U.S. Federal Reserve Board from 1987 to 2006. He infamously missed the housing bubble inflation during his watch.

Seek Candid, Direct, and Thus (Hopefully) Trustworthy

In financial matters, the inexperienced, non-financial client is, actually, sometimes wrong. Which is why, in this field, such clients should especially seek a manager who will occasionally contradict them.

> *Le client n'a jamais tort. (The customer is never wrong). – César Ritz.*

>> With all due respect to my dedicated clients: Not always, and not in this business.

Saying "yes" to clients all the time is a great way to gather new clients. This is good for the money manager, and big firms often like this strategy precisely because it is an easy way to grow assets. It is easier, in fact, than actually growing the assets of existing clients—which turns out to be unfortunate in the longer run for the first group of clients.

> *To be successful an advisory service must tell people what they want to hear, not necessarily what the truth is. – Nicolas Darvas.*

No, dear client, you cannot expect a 20% return on your assets forever. Not legitimately, not from me, and not from anyone else. Sorry. Look for the manager who is not afraid to tell you that.

He who dares not offend cannot be honest. – Thomas Paine.

Fear not those who argue but those who dodge.
– Marie Ebner von Eschenbach.

I don't want any yes-men around me. I want everyone to tell me the truth—even though it costs him his job. – Samuel Goldwyn.

Look for the manager who would prefer to lose a client than to subvert what he believes to be correct.

I would rather lose half our shareholders...than lose half of our shareholders' money. – Jean-Marie Eveillard.

Some interesting background: During the rise of the Internet bubble in the late 1990s, this highly regarded fund manager avoided these stocks. Feeling left out, many of Eveillard's clients were upset and withdrew money, presumably to move it to more aggressive (compliant?) managers. Within a few years, Internet, technology and related funds proceeded to lose 50% or more of client monies.

See what a prospective manager has to say about other managers.

You can tell more about a person by what he says about others than you can by what others say about him. – Leo Aikman.

Ask your potential manager who else he would recommend, if not him.

If you are a "smaller" client (under a million dollars in 2013), look for signs that you might not be all that important to your prospective manager.

You can easily judge the character of a man by how he treats those who can do nothing for him. – James D. Miles.

And for the men out there, be sure to bring your wife to these meetings.

Women are never disarmed by compliments. Men always are. That is the difference between the sexes. – Oscar Wilde.

Beware flattery from a manager who wants you as a client (and re-read the first few points above).

Remember, you do not necessarily want the manager who has more brains. You want the manager who has more integrity.

Ability without honor is useless. – Cicero.

No amount of ability is of the slightest avail without honor.
– Andrew Carnegie.

Beware those proclaiming their trustworthiness.

No one who deserves confidence ever solicits it. – John Churton Collins.

The greatest liar is he who talks most of himself. – West African proverb.

The louder he talked on his honor, the faster we counted our spoons.
– Ralph Waldo Emerson.

Beware those glossing over the truth, omitting all the small hiccups.

Whoever is careless with the truth in small matters cannot be trusted
with important matters. – Albert Einstein.

Beware the paranoid types, or those whose contracts are too long and have too many clauses. They are likely more interested in protecting themselves than in ever doing what is right by you.

He who mistrusts most should be trusted least. – Greek proverb.

Trust everybody, but yourself most of all. – Danish proverb.

Trust no one who doesn't trust you. – Wade Hudson.

Eventually, you will just have to start trusting somebody.

The best way to find out if you can trust somebody is to trust them.
– Ernest Hemingway.

It is more shameful to distrust our friends than to be deceived by them.
– François, duc de La Rochefoucauld.

Trust men and they will be true to you; treat them greatly and they will
show themselves great. – Ralph Waldo Emerson.

And remember, there is nothing wrong with checking their work.

Trust everyone, but cut the cards. – Finley Peter Dunne.

How prone to doubt, how cautious are the wise! – Homer.

Caution is the eldest child of wisdom. – Victor Hugo.

With wisdom, doubt grows. – Johann Wolfgang von Goethe.

Great doubts, deep wisdom. Small doubts, little wisdom.
– Chinese proverb.

> Even the most honest manager is not immune from making some sort of accounting or bookkeeping error, therefore you should check your accounts regularly.

Do Not Begrudge the Management Fee

A good adviser adds value, and you will mostly get what you pay for.

Good council has no price. – Giuseppe Mazzini.

You seldom improve quality by cutting costs, but you can often cut costs by improving quality. – Karl Albrech.

> Adviser A may charge 0.5% (50 basis points, or "bps") more for her annual asset management fee than Adviser B. However, if Adviser A consistently returns 1% more (100 bps) than Adviser B, you will in effect gain a 50 bps greater return by using Adviser A. In other words, by paying fifty cents to Adviser A, you will get a dollar back. What a bargain!

Beware free advice.

Free advice is worth the price. – Robert Half.

What you get free costs too much. – Jean Anouilh.

In investing, everyone has an opinion. But if they were right that often, they would also be wealthy. Are they?

The cheapest commodity in the world is investment advice from people not qualified to give it. – Louis Engel.

Possibly the only thing worse than an amateur investor is an amateur investment adviser. – Nicolas Darvas.

Always consider how the people involved in a transaction are being paid, and follow the money to discover their motivations.

If you are not paying for it, you're not the customer; you're the product being sold. – unknown.

> The trading commissions may be cheap, but is your broker making it up on overly-wide spreads (excessive separation between the bid and the ask prices)? Is your broker proposing investment products you might not want, or products of questionable suitability but that happen to pay fat fees and commissions (at your expense), or are you being otherwise limited in your selections?

Unlike a money manager, a broker might not charge an asset management fee. But that is because he makes money on commissions. So remember that a broker's incentive is not so much to build your wealth, but to keep generating trades.

They're not interested in truth or what's best for the client, but in making the sale with the least amount of work. – James S. Chanos.

A stockbroker is someone who invests other people's money until it's all gone. – Woody Allen.

To recap, and along the lines of "follow the money"—always understand who is getting paid, how, and why. This will help ensure that their long-term motivation is aligned with your best interests.

The iron rule of nature is: you get what you reward for. If you want ants to come, you put sugar on the floor. – Charles Munger.

THEN LEAVE THEM ALONE

Once you have allocated some money to a manager and discussed your general parameters and expectations, give him some room to work. Try not to call and question every trade he makes.

The best executive is the one who has sense enough to pick good men to do what he wants done, and self-restraint enough to keep from meddling with them while they do it. – Theodore Roosevelt.

Never tell people how to do things. Tell them what to do and they will surprise you with their ingenuity. – George S. Patton.

Hire good people, then let them work.

By letting it go it all gets done. The world is won by those who let it go. But when you try and try, the world is beyond the winning. – Lao Tzu.

You must delegate some things. Trying to be a control freak will only create friction and problems.

Your managers will, of course, make some mistakes. Do not chide them too much. After all, they probably got a few things right as well.

I am not given to prediction: one's foresight is forgotten, only one's errors are well remembered. – John Kenneth Galbraith.

When you are right no one remembers; when you are wrong no one forgets. – Irish proverb.

And as long as your money managers are doing a good job, being conscientious, and giving good service, be thankful and encouraging to them.

I have yet to find the man, however exalted his station, who did not do better work and put forth greater effort under a spirit of approval than under a spirit of criticism. – Charles Schwab.

As with your car repair shop or plumber, being nice always brings you even better service.

Research, Questioning, and Learning

If you are going to buy a stock or bond, invest in a mutual fund or a hedge fund, or hire a money manager—really, if you are considering any sort of investing activity—then you need to have done a little research first. Otherwise, you are merely gambling. Research can be of the very deep sort that a financial analyst might do, or it can be as cursory as reading a few magazine articles. What is important is that you know something about the investment and form your own opinion.

> *One of life's most painful moments comes when we must admit that we didn't do our homework, that we are not prepared. – Merlin Olson.*

> *Look for the truth; it wants to be found. – Blaise Pascal.*

> *The truth is out there. –* X-Files *television show tagline, 1990s.*

DO A LITTLE RESEARCH

Start by making just a small effort to understand the basics about your investments.

> *All wish to be learned but no one is willing to pay the price. – Juvenal.*

> *No man was ever wise by chance. – Lucius Annaeus Seneca.*

> All it takes is spending a little time to read about investable subjects that intrigue you.

Continue by regularly asking some very simple questions.

> *I keep six honest serving-men*
> *(They taught me all I knew);*
> *Their names are What and Why and When*
> *and How and Where and Who.*
> *– Rudyard Kipling.*

> With the answers to these basic questions, you will be well on your way to understanding for yourself the facts about any potential investment.

Even minimal research can make all the difference.

> *Investing without research is like playing stud poker and never looking at the cards. – Peter Lynch.*

Start With a Blank Slate

Though you might be curious about some investment or industry, never assume you already know how things will play out.

It is a capital mistake to theorize before one has data. Insensibly one begins to twist facts to suit theories, instead of theories to suit facts.
– Arthur Conan Doyle, The Adventures of Sherlock Holmes.

It is always better to have no ideas than false ones; to believe nothing, than to believe what is wrong. – Thomas Jefferson.

The wise man does not set his mind either for anything or against anything; what is right, he will follow. – Confucius.

Starting out with a hypothesis is acceptable, but always doubt it, always check it.

If a man will begin with certainties, he shall end in doubts; but if he will be content to begin with doubts, he shall end in certainties.
– Francis Bacon.

The only man who behaved sensibly was my tailor; he took my measurement anew every time he saw me, while all the rest went on with their old measurements and expected them to fit me.
– George Bernard Shaw.

Beware assumptions you take for granted, because they may not be true, or remain true.

Preconceived notions are locks on the doors of wisdom. – Merry Browne.

The most useful piece of learning for the uses of life is to unlearn what is untrue. – Antisthenes.

Always remember that things change.

Whatever you do know, recognize that it is incomplete, that you can learn more, and that someone else out there invariably will know more about any given topic.

The fool doth think he is wise, but the wise man knows himself to be a fool. – William Shakespeare, As You Like It.

I am the wisest man alive, for I know one thing, and that is that I know nothing. – Socrates.

Knowledge is proud that he has learned so much; Wisdom is humble that he knows no more. – William Cowper.

Education is an admirable thing, but it is well to remember from time to time that nothing worth knowing can be taught. – Oscar Wilde.

Recognizing the limits of what you know is valuable.

An education isn't how much you have committed to memory, or even how much you know. It's being able to differentiate between what you do know and what you don't. - Anatole France.

The more you learn, the more you realize how limited your knowledge really is.

Knowing when to seek expertise, and who to consult, is also valuable.

Knowledge is of two kinds. We know a subject ourselves, or we know where we can find information upon it. - Samuel Johnson.

ASK QUESTIONS, THEN LISTEN

It is almost certain there will be something you will not understand about some new investment idea.

He who asks a question may be a fool for five minutes; he who never asks a question remains a fool forever. - Chinese proverb.

There are no foolish questions and no man becomes a fool until he has stopped asking questions. - Charles Proteus Steinmetz.

The fool wonders; the wise man asks. - Benjamin Disraeli.

Use your questions to cut to the crux of whether or not an idea will be successful.

It is better to know some of the questions than all of the answers. - James Thurber.

The right question is usually more important than the right answer to the wrong question. - Alvin Toffler.

Ignore trivial background information. Focus on what will make this a good investment or not.

Hesitate to assume you already know all the answers.

The more urgently you want to speak, the more likely it is that you will say something foolish. - Leo Tolstoy.

A stupid person should keep silent. But if he knew this, he would not be a stupid person. - Muslih-ud-Din Saadi.

He who knows does not speak. He who speaks does not know. - Lao-Tzu.

And freely admit ignorance if you are not sure.

> *Blessed are they who have nothing to say and who cannot be persuaded to say it. – James Russell Lowell.*

> *I was gratified to be able to answer promptly, and I did. I said I didn't know. – Mark Twain.*

> *He must be very ignorant for he answers every question he is asked. – Voltaire.*

Because if you are doing most of the talking, you are probably talking too much.

> *Wise men talk because they have something to say; fools because they have to say something. – Plato.*

> *Fools have no interest in understanding; they only want to air their own opinions. – Proverbs 18:2.*

> *Most people have to talk so they won't hear. – May Sarton.*

> *Outside noisy, inside empty. – Chinese proverb.*

When you are talking too much, the other people will not get a chance to say something that you did not know or that might not have occurred to you.

> *It takes a great man to be a good listener. – Calvin Coolidge.*

> *Listen! Or your tongue will make you deaf. – Cherokee proverb.*

> *You don't learn anything by talking. – unknown.*

> *Only speak when your words are better than your silence. – Arabic proverb.*

> *The quieter you become, the more you can hear. – Baba Ram Dass.*

So focus on listening—it is valuable work!

> *It is the province of knowledge to speak and it is the privilege of wisdom to listen. – Oliver Wendell Holmes.*

> *Courage is what it takes to stand up and speak; courage is also what it takes to sit down and listen. – Winston Churchill.*

> *I like to listen. I have learned a great deal from listening carefully. Most people never listen. – Ernest Hemingway.*

Always let the other person talk.

BE SUSPICIOUS OF STATISTICS

Statistics, like quotations, are not always of impeccable pedigree.

Oh, people can come up with statistics to prove anything, Kent. 40% of all people know that. – Homer Simpson character, The Simpsons, *TV show, "Homer the Vigilante" episode.*

Statistics can be cited out of context, taken from a poor sample, or misapplied.

If you torture the data long enough, it will confess to anything.
– various.

Statistics can be derived via methodologies so complex as to be meaningless.

Don't do equations with Greek letters in them. – Warren E. Buffett.

Beware of geeks bearing formulas. – Warren E. Buffett.

> A good investment idea usually does not require complex math.

Even when patently wrong, there will always be some small situation, some exception, in which the statistics do seem to apply.

He uses statistics as a drunken man uses lamp-posts—for support rather than illumination. – Andrew Lang.

On average, everyone has one testicle and one breast. – unknown.

Even a stopped clock is right twice a day. – Marie von Ebner-Eschenbach.

> People will inevitably notice these seeming links in the data, but that does not mean there is an actual link or that the relationship will still be true tomorrow.

So remember to always be suspicious.

Statistics are like a bikini. What they reveal is suggestive, but what they conceal is vital. – Aaron Levenstein.

There are three kinds of lies: lies, damned lies, and statistics.
– Benjamin Disraeli.

Always rely on your own judgment first and foremost.

Statistics are no substitute for judgment. – Henry Clay.

> If something sounds too good to be true, then it probably is. Or, if it cannot be explained to the average person, then stay away.

SEPARATE FACT FROM OPINION

In any debate or inquisition into a prospective investment, there will always be certain immutable facts.

> *A fact is a fact and is always the same. An opinion may vary with what you had for dinner. – Charles F. Kettering.*

Be sure of your facts, and avoid taking facts out of context.

> *There is nothing more deceptive than an obvious fact. – Arthur Conan Doyle,* The Adventures of Sherlock Holmes.

Because it is easy to repurpose a fact.

> *There are no facts, only interpretations. – Friedrich W. Nietzsche.*

> *Generally, the theories we believe we call facts, and the facts we disbelieve we call theories. – Felix Cohen.*

> *Everything we hear is an opinion, not a fact. Everything we see is a perspective, not the truth. – Marcus Aurelius.*

Or to find some idiot attesting that something false is instead true.

> *Every absurdity has a champion to defend it. – Oliver Goldsmith.*

Or to find some greater idiot willing to die for some false idea.

> *A thing is not necessarily true because a man dies for it. – Oscar Wilde.*

If you want to be right and make money, you cannot cherry-pick your facts.

> *Facts do not cease to exist because they are ignored. – Aldous Huxley.*

> *People inevitably start out with an opinion; to ask them to search for the facts first is even undesirable. They will simply do what everyone is far too prone to do anyhow: look for the facts that fit the conclusion they have already reached. – Peter F. Drucker,* The Essential Drucker.

Nor will it be profitable to maintain a view that is not supported by the facts.

> *Every man has a right to his opinion, but no man has a right to be wrong in his facts. – Bernard Baruch.*

> For example, as of this writing, it is fashionable in some areas of the United States to be dismissive of the notions of climate change and sea level rise. Causal analyses may indeed be open for debate, but the rising average water level is not. So no matter what you want to believe, think twice before investing in any coastal home sitting right at sea level.

What matters is whether your investment hypothesis is correct and makes you money—not whether it conforms to some ideal or aesthetic you might prefer.

It doesn't matter how beautiful your theory is, it doesn't matter how smart you are. If it doesn't agree with experiment, it's wrong.
- Richard Feynman.

AVOID EXCESSIVE INFORMATION

When researching an investment, be aware that it is easy to drown in data.

There are no answers in this business. There's just a hell of a lot of information. - George Russell, Jr.

> Very true. I spend most of my time reading, and now, with the Internet, there is no lack of information or data sources. The challenge is to focus on what is most useful.

Recognize that only some of that data might have real meaning, be useful for analysis, and lead to conclusions.

Where is the wisdom we have lost in knowledge? Where is the knowledge we have lost in information? - T. S. Eliot.

The biggest difficulty with mankind today is that our knowledge has increased so much faster than our wisdom. - Frank Whitmore.

Knowledge cuts up the world. Wisdom makes it whole.
- Brazilian proverb.

Information is not knowledge. - Albert Einstein.

> With any piece of information about an investment, ask "why is this important?"

Focus on what might be relevant; ignore or avoid everything else.

Information is a source of learning. But unless it is organized, processed, and available to the right people in a format for decision making, it is a burden, not a benefit. - William Polland.

Do not become archivists of facts. Try to penetrate to the secret of their occurrence, persistently search for the laws which govern them.
- Ivan Pavlov.

> Find the qualities, conditions or attributes that will make this investment succeed or fail. Gather these elements and focus your thinking on these elements. Ignore most else.

Be aware of intangibles, like quality of management, reputation, honesty, motivation, etc.

> *Things that matter most must never be at the mercy of things that matter least. – Johann Wolfgang von Goethe.*

> *Not everything that counts can be counted, and not everything that can be counted counts. – Albert Einstein.*

> *The truth is more important than the facts. – Frank Lloyd Wright.*

> You can ask about these things, but remember that the answers are usually subjective.

Beware overly long investment pitches.

> *Speeches that are measured by the hour will die with the hour.*
> *– Thomas Jefferson.*

> *This report, by its very length, defends itself against the risk of being read.*
> *– Winston Churchill.*

> I am a firm believer that any good investment idea can be fully described in one paragraph. Everything else is supporting information. And if the idea promoter cannot do so, they either do not fully understand the idea or they are trying to "baffle you with bullshit," as the saying goes.

Recognize that there will often be an intangible, un-measurable aspect to any investment.

> *Those who understand only what can be explained understand very little.*
> *– Marie von Ebner-Eschenbach.*

And finally, recognize that you will never have complete information.

> *The man who insists upon seeing with perfect clearness before he decides, never decides. – Henri Frederic Amiel.*

> Conversely, if perfect information existed, then either the market would already know it or you would be about to commit the crime of insider trading. All investments involve a bet, a leap of faith, an assumption, or an instinct that you will be correct.

FOCUS ON VALUABLE INFORMATION

Finding the right information will make you rich.

> *As a general rule, the most successful man in life is the man who has the best information. – Benjamin Disraeli.*

It is not having "the most information," but "the best information." In investing, this means having figured out what will make an investment succeed or fail.

But first, realize that this does not mean reacting to the latest news about a stock or investment.

> *Market efficiency is a description of how prices in competitive markets respond to new information. The arrival of new information to a competitive market can be likened to the arrival of a lamb chop to a school of flesh-eating piranha, where investors are—plausibly enough— the piranha. The instant the lamb chop hits the water, there is turmoil as the fish devour the meat. Very soon the meat is gone, leaving only the worthless bone behind, and the water returns to normal. Similarly, when new information reaches a competitive market there is much turmoil as investors buy and sell securities in response to the news, causing prices to change. Once prices adjust, all that is left of the information is the worthless bone. No amount of gnawing on the bone will yield any more meat, and no further study of old information will yield any more valuable intelligence. – Robert C. Higgins,* Analysis for Financial Management.

What everyone else already knows is usually of little investable value.

Nor does it mean randomly gathering as much information as you can about a prospective investment. That can lead to a lot of work for very little return.

> *A weak mind is like a microscope, which magnifies trifling things, but cannot receive great ones. – Lord Chesterfield.*

> *Education... has produced a vast population able to read but unable to distinguish what is worth reading. – George Macaulay Trevelyan.*

> *Knowledge without wisdom is a load of books on the back of an ass. – Japanese proverb.*

> *Most of the learning in use, is of no great use. – Benjamin Franklin.*

Rather, if you apply basic common-sense business principles to investment categories you know something about, you stand a decent chance at success.

> *The man who grasps principles can successfully select his own methods. The man who tries methods, ignoring principles, is sure to have trouble. – Ralph Waldo Emerson.*

> *An amateur who devotes a small amount of study to companies in an*

industry he or she knows something about can outperform 95% of the
paid experts who manage the mutual funds, plus have fun in doing it.
– Peter Lynch.

> Start with businesses or industries you feel you can understand, and then apply common sense.

It is more a matter of knowing what to look for and where to look.

And though it is obviously more difficult to get superior information on
a company, the crux of the matter is superior judgment, to know what to
look for, recognize it when you see it and know how to weigh it.
– Peter Vermilye.

People who consistently make money in their investments succeed
because of their understanding—more than because of information. They
apply basic principles of the real world to their investments, rather than
allowing specific information to direct them. – Harry Browne.

> Once you have a basic understanding of a business, the rest is mere common sense.

The whole point is to put yourself in a position, thanks to your knowledge and experience, so that you will be earlier than others to recognize and act on emerging attractive investments, before these ideas get discovered by everyone else.

The secret of all victory lies in the organization of the non-obvious.
– Marcus Aurelius.

All truths are easy to understand once they are discovered; the point
is to discover them. – Galileo Galilei.

Buy on the rumor, sell on the news. – Wall Street proverb.

> This means that you have to buy when things are still uncertain. Once things are certain, prices will reflect that. Then, not only is it too late to buy, but now it's probably time to sell since there are no more uncertainties whose discoveries could push the stock price higher.

Learn from Others

Learning from others provides invaluable knowledge.

It is great folly to wish to be wise all alone.
– François de La Rochefoucauld.

If you think education is expensive, try ignorance. – Derek Bok.

Spend time with people who are knowledgeable about industries that interest you.

Focus particularly on those with real-world experience relating to the investments you are contemplating, rather than theorists or ivory-tower academics.

It isn't quite the same thing to comment on the bull ring and to be in the bull ring. – Spanish proverb.

Ask the experienced rather than the learned. – Arabian proverb.

Is there anyone so wise as to learn by the experience of others? – Voltaire.

You do not need to be a genius. You just want to surround yourself with geniuses.

A dwarf standing on the shoulders of a giant may see farther than the giant himself. – Robert Burton.

He that walks with the wise will be wise. – Book of Proverbs.

Most investing wisdom already exists. You just need to seek out those who know and listen to them—something that most people have trouble doing.

A single conversation across the table with a wise man is worth a month's study of books. – Chinese proverb.

Human beings, who are almost unique in having the ability to learn from the experience of others, are also remarkable for their apparent disinclination to do so. – Douglas Adams.

We will learn an enormous amount in a very short time, quite a bit in the medium term and absolutely nothing in the long term. That would be the historical precedent. – Jeremy Grantham. [On expected investor reaction to the 2008 real estate and stock market implosion.—Ed.]

Speak with people who have been investing longer than you.

Avoid being the "unconscious incompetent," the first person in the following quotation.

There are four kinds of people: Those who know not, and know not that they know not. These are foolish. Those who know not, and know they know not. These are simple, and should be instructed. Those who know, and know not that they know. These are asleep; wake them. Those who know, and know that they know. These are the wise; listen to them. – Arab proverb.

And remember that your learning will come from many sources.

> *People learn 25% from their teacher, 25% from listening to themselves, 25% from their friends, and 25% from time. – Paulo Coelho,* The Witch of Portobello.

Take the time, and make the effort, to tap all of these sources.

Investments and Risk

It is important to know how to consider risk and to determine how much risk you can take on. Though risk cannot be avoided or ignored, it can be better understood and thus reduced.

The public...demands certainties... But there are no certainties.
– H. L. Mencken.

The three most important words in investing... Margin of Safety.
– Warren E. Buffett.

YOU CANNOT AVOID RISK

...In any aspect of life.

Just try and stay out of my way. Just try! I'll get you, my pretty, and your little dog, too! – Wicked Witch of the West, The Wizard of Oz, *1939.*

To be alive at all involves some risk. – Harold MacMillan.

> If you stay at home, you risk losing touch with friends and family, losing perspective on the world, and not getting enough sunshine, exercise, or whatever. If you go out, you risk getting hit by a bus. Invest only in government and corporate bonds and you still risk the "black swan" of a government default, or you more likely face purchasing power loss if inflation outpaces your coupon rate. The correct approach lies in minimizing and optimizing the risks you do choose to take.

And especially in investing.

October: This is one of the peculiarly dangerous months to speculate in stocks. The others are July, January, September, April, November, May, March, June, December, August and February. – Mark Twain.

To survive, or even get ahead a little, you must therefore take some risks.

Behold the turtle. He makes progress only when he sticks his neck out.
– James Bryant Conant.

The sure way to miss success is to miss the opportunity. – Victor Chasles.

You miss one hundred percent of the shots you never take.
– Wayne Gretsky.

In every success story, you find someone has made a courageous decision.
– Peter F. Drucker.

Risk is really just another word for "probability." So what are the odds of success or failure?

You cannot manage outcomes, you can only manage risk.
– Peter Bernstein.

All knowledge resolves itself into probability. – David Hume.

Life is a school of probability. – Walter Bagehot.

Figure out how likely it is your investment will succeed or fail.

Estimate how much you can thereby gain or lose.

Do you dare to stay out? Do you dare to go in?
How much can you lose? How much can you win?
– Dr. Seuss, Oh, The Places You'll Go.

The chance of gain is by every man more or less overvalued, and the chance of loss is by most men undervalued. – Adam Smith.

Take calculated risks. That is quite different from being rash.
– George S. Patton.

Success comes to those who can recognize and correctly value risk.
– Sidney Weinberg.

In nature, there are neither rewards nor punishments; there are consequences. – Robert Greene Ingersoll.

Wisdom consists of the anticipation of consequences. – Norman Cousins.

Therefore, it is always more important to know what you might lose, rather than what you might gain.

Set the allowance against the loss and thou shalt find no loss great.
– Francis Quarles.

Carnegie never wanted to know the profits, he always wanted to know the cost. – Charles Schwab.

Always know the downside. Of your money at risk, how much could become lost?

Never expose oneself to excessive, intolerable, or debilitating losses.

What folly is it to play a game which you can lose incomparably more than you can win? – Francesco Guicciardini.

Before you attempt to beat the odds, be sure you could survive the odds beating you. – Larry Kersten.

Only a fool tests the depth of the water with both feet. – African proverb.

> In other words, focus on those opportunities where there is more upside than downside. Only make bets that you can afford to lose, and can survive losing.

Because, despite your best guess at the odds and probabilities, those are averages—not a guarantee of a particular outcome in any particular investment situation. In any one specific investment, things could always end up far off on the undesirable tail side of the distribution of possible outcomes.

Fate laughs at probabilities. – Edward Bulwer-Lytton.

The laws of probability, so true in general, so fallacious in particular.
– Edward Gibbon.

Which is why you should not only be prepared to occasionally lose, but should even expect to occasionally lose.

There is a Wheel on which the affairs of men revolve, and its mechanism is such that it prevents any man from being always fortunate.
– Andrew Carnegie.

A change in fortune hurts a wise man no more than a change of the moon. – Benjamin Franklin.

> Don't get upset. Losing is within the range of probable outcomes, even if it was only a small chance. Therefore, if this happens despite correctly doing your homework, accept it as one of the vagaries of life. If you did make any mistake in estimation, learn from it for the next time. But otherwise, move on.

YOU CAN ONLY TRY TO REDUCE RISK

Try to make sure that, no matter what goes wrong, you can still get all (or most) of your initial investment back.

An investment operation is one which upon thorough analysis promises safety of principal and an adequate return. Operations not meeting these requirements are speculative. – Benjamin Graham.

I am more concerned with the return OF my money than the return ON my money. – Will Rogers. [Emphasis added—Ed.]

Confronted with the challenge to distil the secret of sound investment into three words, we venture the motto, "margin of safety."
– Benjamin Graham.

When investing in any sort of business, look for a business opportunity good enough that it will not matter if management is incompetent. (This applies to common stocks, private equity, placements, partnerships, venture capital, acting as a silent partner, angel investing—basically anything to do with a business).

> *You should invest in a business that even a fool can run, because someday a fool will. – Warren E. Buffett.*

> *Our conclusion is that, with few exceptions, when management with a reputation for brilliance tackles a business with a reputation for poor fundamental economics, it is the reputation of the business that remains intact. – Warren E. Buffett.*

In investing, there is no "right" level of risk, nor can investment risk be "scientifically" calculated.

> *There is no way any professor of economics or minister of the church can tell you what your risk tolerance should be. – Paul Samuelson.*

> A side note on the absurdity of some modern risk calculation practices: currently, the "risk" of a stock (or other security) is usually determined via a formula that takes, as one key element, the "beta", or measurement of the security's past price deviation around an average or a benchmark. In other words, the past is held to have predictive value over future prices. And yet, these people providing the seeming reassurance of a "scientific" measure or estimate of future risk are the same people with the disclaimer "past performance is no predictor of future results" boldly emphasized on the back pages of their research reports.

Don't worry too much about your investments. Work hard to find good ones, then move on to something more productive.

> *The reason why worry kills more people than work is that more people worry than work. – Robert Frost.*

> *It is important to distinguish between respect for the market and fear of the market. While it is essential to respect the market to assure preservation of capital, you cannot win if you are fearful of losing. Fear will keep you from making correct decisions. – Howard Seidler.*

> Learn what can go wrong. Go in with your eyes open, then don't worry too much more about it.

Always strive to make smart, well thought-out investments. Only accept risks when you think you have fully studied and understand the risk, and when you can survive should the worst outcome occur.

Rule #1: Don't lose money.
Rule #2: Don't forget Rule #1.
– Warren E. Buffett.

Risk is the chance of loss, and for most of history it was viewed as that.
There is a chance I'm going to lose. But in the capitalist system, risk is also
an opportunity. Nothing ventured, nothing gained is as important to
keep in mind as the fear that if I don't manage my affairs, I can get wiped
out. – Peter L. Bernstein.

As long as you have fully considered your investments in this manner, there is not much more you can do.

Investing vs. Speculating vs. Gambling

When putting your money at risk, which of these three terms might best characterize the bet being made: investing, speculating, or gambling? Are you taking a reasoned risk or wishfully wagering on a whim? Is this part of a methodical investment program or an unproven get-rich-quick scheme?

> *If you bet on a horse, that's gambling. If you bet you can make three spades, that's entertainment. If you bet cotton will go up three points, that's business. See the difference? – William F. ('Blackie') Sherrod.*

> *When I was young people called me a gambler. As the scale of my operations grew, I became known as a speculator. Now I am called a banker. But I have been doing the same thing all the time. – Ernest Cassel.*

> *If you can't spot the sucker in the first half hour at the table, then you are the sucker. –* Rounders, *Levien and Koppelman, 1998, film.*

WHO IS AWARE OF THE RISK?

Subscribers to all three of the above characterizations could be making the exact same bet. The differentiating (and defining) factor, however, is to what degree each is aware of the risks.

> *A "speculator" is one who runs risks of which he is aware and an "investor" is one who runs risks of which he is unaware. – John Maynard Keynes.*

> *The most realistic distinction between the investor and the speculator is found in their attitude toward stock-market movements. The speculator's primary interest lies in anticipating and profiting from market fluctuations. The investor's primary interest lies in acquiring and holding suitable securities at suitable prices. – Benjamin Graham.*

> *The term speculation has, in my opinion, gained an unearned negative connotation. People think of speculators as the people who drive prices up in shady stock transactions, real estate deals, and so forth. But in reality, all market speculators do is focus their attention on intermediate price movements, trying to profit by their buying and selling activity. Speculators provide crucial liquidity to the markets and in most cases facilitate the orderly transfer of assets to their best use. – Victor Sperandeo.*

Investment and speculation are said to be two different things, and the prudent man is advised to engage in one and avoid the other. This is something like explaining to the troubled adolescent that Love and Passion are two different things. He perceives that they are different but they don't seem quite different enough to clear up his problems.
– Fred Schwed, Where Are the Customers' Yachts?

Seek investment situations where the probability of success is greater than the probability of failure.

The gambler is the one most obliviously (or purposefully) undergoing the risk.

The roulette table pays nobody except him that keeps it. Nevertheless a passion for gaming is common, though a passion for keeping roulette tables is unknown. – George Bernard Shaw.

Gambling is taking a risk when the odds are against you, like playing the lottery or pumping silver dollars into a slot machine. Speculating is taking a risk when the odds are in your favor. – Victor Sperandeo.

Going to Vegas or Monte Carlo, or regularly playing your local lottery, is considered by some (including this author) as a tax on people who are bad at math. The odds are simply against you. Do not gamble. However, even this author will grant the occasional dispensation when large lottery jackpots come up and the total spent is less than the cost of a good martini. You can think of this as buying the entertainment value of the temporary fantasy that you might actually win.

Insanity is repeating the same mistake and expecting a different result.
– various.

No, you are not more likely to win the lottery playing your birthday numbers on your birthday than on any other day. Nor are you likely to make your fortune by pursuing the stocks they just talked about on the daily finance show.

Consistency is the last refuge of the unimaginative. – Oscar Wilde.

No, you do not have to "be in it to win it," so stop playing lottery and save or buy some stocks instead.

Gambling is the child of avarice, the brother of iniquity, and the father of mischief. – George Washington.

An occasional small-stakes poker game with friends is fine. Spending your days in the casino, or at the track, is not.

THERE IS NO ABSOLUTE CERTAINTY OR SAFETY

Accept therefore that there is no such thing as a safe bet. There is always an element of risk, and things may not work out as planned. Remember this, and always consider that the bet may not pay off.

I always avoid prophesying beforehand, because it is a much better policy to prophesy after the event has already taken place.
- Winston Churchill.

Those who have knowledge, do not predict. Those who predict, do not have knowledge. - Lao Tzu.

Forethought we may have, undoubtedly, but not foresight.
- Napoleon Bonaparte.

Prediction is very difficult, especially about the future. - Niels Bohr.

You can never be 100% certain of anything.

Doubt is therefore good.

Doubt is not a pleasant condition, but certainty is absurd. - Voltaire.

Assumptions keep us awake nights. - Earl Shorris.

Certainty is to be feared and suspected.

Risk comes from not knowing what you are doing. - Warren E. Buffett.

Fools rush in where angels fear to tread. - Alexander Pope, An Essay on Criticism.

There is no such thing as a sure thing.

Hopes and wishes are to be avoided at all costs.

Expectation is the root of all heartache. - William Shakespeare.

He that lives upon hope will die fasting. - Benjamin Franklin.

Talk of the year ahead and the devil laughs. - Japanese proverb.

The trouble with most people is that they think with their hopes or fears or wishes rather than with their minds. - Will Durant.

Hope is not an investment strategy. - unknown.

Their judgment was based more upon blind wishing than upon any sound prediction; for it is a habit of mankind to entrust to careless hope what they long for, and to use sovereign reason to thrust aside what they do not desire. - Thucydides.

You may like a company's products and hope their stock succeeds, but do not confuse those warm feelings with a sober assessment of the risk/reward situation.

BE WARY OF SHORTCUTS

Get-rich-quick schemes are more likely to bring heartburn than riches.

It is by attempting to reach the top at a single leap that so much misery is caused in the world. – William Cobbett.

Even if one does get lucky, holding on to fortune is a separate challenge.

What we obtain too cheap, we esteem too lightly. – Thomas Paine.

It is better to deserve honors and not have them than to have them and not deserve them. – Mark Twain.

Wealth and rank are what people desire, but unless they are obtained in the right way they may not be possessed. – Confucius.

Often, those who make a fortune too quickly are the fastest to lose it.

Speculators often prosper through ignorance; it is a cliché that in a roaring bull market knowledge is superfluous and experience is a handicap. But the typical experience of the speculator is one of temporary profit and ultimate loss. – Benjamin Graham.

Whatever fortune has raised to a height, she has raised only to cast it down. – Lucius Annaeus Seneca.

There is scarcely an instance of a man who has made a fortune by speculation and kept it. – Andrew Carnegie.

Success has made failures of many men. – Cindy Adams.

The wise person will never confuse luck with earned success.

Luck has never made a man wise. – Seneca the Younger.

Shallow men believe in luck, wise and strong men in cause and effect. – Ralph Waldo Emerson.

There are no coincidences, either in life or in one's fate. A man creates his own destiny. – Abel Villemain.

On this earth, in the final analysis, each of us gets exactly what he deserves. But only the successful recognize this. – Georges Simenon.

Beware the person (or company) who clearly had one unearned lucky break in finding success. Luck does not make this person wise, nor will luck stay around to make sure this person stays successful.

The wise person will never confuse a lucky investment outcome with a safely repeatable investment outcome.

In my opinion, especially in good times, far too many people can be overheard saying, "Riskier investments provide higher returns. If you want to make more money, the answer is to take more risk." But riskier investments absolutely cannot be counted on to deliver higher returns. Why not? It's simple: if riskier investments reliably produced higher returns, they wouldn't be riskier! – Howard Marks.

Worry less about high returns. Find the unbalanced return in which the probability of a positive result is greater than the probability of a negative result, and in which the value of the potential winnings exceeds the value of what you might lose.

PART 4
Flavors & Fluctuations

Ideas You Might Not Like

A successful investor picks investments that go up. It does not matter whether you feel an affinity for the company behind the stock in question, whether you personally like the management team, whether you like the person who came up with the investment idea, or whether your neighbor agrees with the idea. What matters is being right about which way the investment will move.

Judge a tree from its fruit; not from the leaves. – Euripides.

OPEN YOUR MIND

With any new investment idea, always start with a blank slate, having no preconceptions.

He who knows nothing is closer to the truth than he whose mind is filled with falsehoods and errors. – Thomas Jefferson.

The wise man does not set his mind either for anything or against anything; what is right, he will follow. – Confucius.

Unless you're tolerant, you can't have an open mind. If you don't have an open mind, you can't be a good investor. You've got to let everything in and be willing to digest it. – Mark Mobius.

Don't let your prejudices get in the way of making money.

Always look at things from a different point of view.

The real voyage of discovery consists not in seeing new landscapes but in having new eyes. – Proust.

The greatest obstacle to discovery is not ignorance but the illusion of knowledge. – Daniel Boorstin.

Indeed, always consider the opposing point of view as well.

It is the mark of an educated mind to be able to entertain a thought without accepting it. – Aristotle.

The test of a first-rate intelligence is the ability to hold two opposed ideas in the mind at the same time, and still retain the ability to function. One should, for example, be able to see that things are hopeless and yet be determined to make them otherwise. – F. Scott Fitzgerald.

Playing devil's advocate with your investment ideas is a good exercise.

Remember that a good investment idea need not be elegant, pretty, or complex.

Don't judge a book by its cover. – American proverb.

It does not matter whether the cat is black or white, only that it catches mice. – Deng Xiaoping.

Whether or not you like or respect whoever originated the investment idea is immaterial.

We often refuse to accept an idea merely because the tone of voice in which it has been expressed is unsympathetic to us.
– Friedrich W. Nietzsche.

The greatest lesson in life is to know that even fools are right sometimes.
– Winston Churchill.

A man may learn wisdom even from a foe. – Aristophanes.

And whether or not you yourself would buy the company's products does not matter.

Nobody ever went broke underestimating the taste of the American public. – H. L. Mencken.

No one in this world has ever lost money by underestimating the intelligence of the great masses of the plain people. – H. L. Mencken.

Just because you do not like hamburgers is not a valid reason to avoid investing in McDonald's. The question is whether the company has a sunny future, not whether you will ever patronize their product. Disassociate your personal tastes from an objective assessment of an investment opportunity. You do not want to rule out potentially good opportunities merely because you might never personally use the product in question. Keep an open mind.

BE PREPARED TO CHANGE YOUR MIND

If you are a reasonable investor, you will regularly discover things to change your mind.

We learn something every day, and lots of times it's that what we learned the day before was wrong. – Bill Vaughan.

The foolish and the dead alone never change their opinions.
– James R. Lowell.

Only the wisest and the stupidest of men never change. – Confucius.

The smart person accepts. The idiot insists. – Greek proverb.

A wise man changes his mind; a fool, never. – Spanish proverb.

It is surprising how most people regularly resist changing their minds.

Faced with the choice between changing one's mind and proving there is no need to do so, almost everyone gets busy on the proof.
– John Kenneth Galbraith.

Since most people are stubborn, there is a benefit to being contrarian, to considering another outcome.

Admitting an error, sooner rather than later, is a good way to get in on a good investment idea while it is still cheap or to minimize or avoid further loss on a bad investment idea.

A stumble may prevent a fall. – English proverb.

No matter how far you have gone on a wrong road, turn back.
– Turkish proverb.

Every great mistake has a halfway moment, a split second when it can be recalled and perhaps remedied. – Pearl S. Buck.

A man who has committed a mistake and does not correct it, is committing another mistake. – Confucius.

Focus on protecting your wealth, not on protecting your ego.

Recognizing a mistake and moving on is the financially smart thing to do.

A man should never be ashamed to own that he has been in the wrong, which is but saying, in other words, that he is wiser today than he was yesterday. – John Maynard Keynes.

Once we realize that imperfect understanding is the human condition, there is no shame in being wrong, only in failing to correct our mistakes.
– George Soros.

Any man worth his salt will stick up for what he believes right, but it takes a slightly better man to acknowledge instantly and without reservation that he is in error. – Andrew Jackson.

Refusing to recognize when you are in error can be dangerous to your investing longevity.

It is not the strongest of the species that survives, nor the most intelligent, but the one most responsive to change. – Charles Darwin.

Failure has nothing to do with knowledge, it is resistance to change.
– Ron Pannosi.

However, when changing one's mind, only do so after full reflection, and when convinced it is the right thing to do.

To change and to improve are two different things. – German proverb.

All change is not growth, as all movement is not forward.
– Ellen Glasgow.

It's not about the argument. It's about the investment.

It is an intelligent man who knows when he has lost an argument.
– unknown.

The man who questions opinion is wise; the man who quarrels with fact is a fool. – Frank A. Garbutt.

> The secret is being able to tell the difference between opinion and fact. It's helpful to remember that this is not debate club in high school. Investing is not about your ability to argue a stock's merits with friends— the market is not listening and does not care. Investing is only about whether or not you are actually right about whether an investment will go up or down in value.

Therefore, be prepared to change your mind when necessary.

No liberal man would impute a charge of unsteadiness to another having changed his opinion. – Cicero.

When the facts change, I change my mind. What do you do, sir?
– John Maynard Keynes.

> Always re-examine your assumptions, and do not be tied to initial opinion—as per the just-quoted very successful investor.

Buy Early, Buy Cheap, Be Contrarian

To be successful at investing you need to buy before the crowd becomes interested, avoid paying too much, and sell once the crowd gets excited.

Nine-tenths of wisdom consists in being wise in time.
– Theodore Roosevelt.

RECOGNIZE VALUE BEFORE EVERYONE ELSE

Be the first to recognize when any sort of investment opportunity—a stock, a business, a piece of land, a minerals right, a painting, anything, really—will become worth more in the future than it is today.

Strike when the iron is hot. – English proverb.

To see things in the seed, that is genius. – Lao Tzu.

The first man gets the oyster, the second man gets the shell.
– Andrew Carnegie.

> The most money is made by getting in on things early. Though, of course, this is difficult to do.

By realizing, before everyone else, that something could well be worth more tomorrow, you can buy it cheaply today from the majority of market participants who have not yet figured this out.

The secret of success is to know something nobody else knows.
– Aristotle Onassis.

In the kingdom of the blind, the one-eyed man is king.
– Desiderius Erasmus, Adages.

Knowledge of the truth before the next man, in peace or war, lay behind every correct decision in history and was the source of all great reputations. – Ian Fleming, Thunderball.

> Profit comes from seeing the discrepancy before everyone else.

Such investment opportunities may initially appear small or overly discounted by others. It is important to recognize those opportunities that will probably be worth much more tomorrow and in which the difference will eventually become significant enough to require a materially higher valuation.

Small opportunities are often the beginning of great enterprises.
– Demosthenes.

One dog barks because it sees something; a hundred dogs bark because they heard the first dog bark. – Chinese proverb.

Do not wish for quick results, nor look for small advantages. If you seek quick results, you will not reach the ultimate goal. If you are led astray by small advantages, you will never accomplish great things. – Confucius.

Spend your time looking for the better investment opportunities.

RECOGNIZE THAT "VALUE" IS ALWAYS BASED ON FUTURE PERCEIVED VALUE

Always remember that how an investment performed last year is irrelevant to its future value.

Investing is like baseball. If you want to score runs, don't study the scoreboard, study the playing field. – Warren E. Buffett.

The investor of today does not profit from yesterday's growth. If past history was all there was to the game, the richest people would be librarians. – Warren E. Buffett.

Remember that current prices are mostly based on how people think and feel today about an investment's near-term future prospects.

Stocks are bought on expectations, not facts. – Gerald M. Loeb.

You make most of your money in a bear market, you just don't realize it at the time. – Shelby Cullom Davis.

Buy cheap and sell dear. – Baron Rothschild.

The best situation is one not yet recognized by others, but where there are precedents to be drawn.

Look for the future that has already happened. – Peter F. Drucker.

Find investments in which similar situations have had a positive conclusion.

The value to you, or opportunity for gain, should always be based on what you think the investment will be worth in the future, not just the short-term future but over the longer run or over the course of an economic cycle.

To know values is to know the meaning of the market. – Charles Dow.

It is too simple to say that a stock is worth whatever people will pay for it, because what people are willing to pay for it depends, in turn, on what they think it is worth. It is a circular definition, used as a rationalization of financial foolishness rather than as a rational way to appraise value. – Andrew Tobias.

Only a fool thinks price and value are the same. – Antonio Machado.

Price is what you pay. Value is what you get. – Warren E. Buffett.

It isn't as important to buy as cheap as possible as it is to buy at the right time. – Jesse Livermore.

> If you have realized that something will still be worth more in the future than today's price indicates, then it matters little that today's price is higher than yesterday's price or higher than last week's price. What matters is the future potential for profit, not past potential foregone.

Investing wisely is a long-term game, and it is not always easy.

Investment based on genuine long-term expectations is so difficult today as to be scarcely practicable. – John Maynard Keynes, 1936.

It is the long-term investor...who will in practice come in for the most criticism... For it is the essence of his behavior that he should be eccentric, unconventional, and rash in the eyes of average opinion. – John Maynard Keynes.

Only buy something that you'd be perfectly happy to hold if the market shut down for 10 years. – Warren E. Buffett.

> You must be prepared to ignore other's opinions and market prices, for a while.

GET OUT BEFORE EVERYONE ELSE

Just as you will very rarely buy into some good investment idea at the absolute lowest price bottom, it is a fool's game to think you can get out at the absolute highest price top.

Fishing for tops and bottoms is an expensive trait. Usually, so many mistakes are made along the way that little or no money is left for the anticipated trend when it does actually show up. – Henry Clasing.

Don't try to buy at the bottom and sell at the top. It can't be done except by liars. – Bernard Baruch.

Better to sell and take what profit you can once everyone else starts to like your investment.

Bulls make money and bears make money, but pigs get slaughtered.
– old Wall Street proverb.

If you have bet correctly (whether as a "bull" that something will go up, or as a "bear" that something will go down), and started to see some profit, you should not be shy about taking some profits out. The greedy "pig," who keeps the full bet on for too long, can often lose that profit opportunity.

I never buy at the bottom and I always sell too soon. – Baron Rothschild.

Never buy at the bottom, and always sell too soon. – Jesse L. Livermore.

Once everyone else starts to agree with your investment, it is probably time to sell it.

Once You Start to Have Some Money

Let me offer some words of encouragement for the beginning investor just starting to put some money into the market.

The first twenty million is always the hardest. – Po Bronson.

To turn $100 into $110 is work. To turn $100 million into $110 million is inevitable. – Edgar Bronfman.

Start Investing Wisely

As you start to have a little money, the best way to make more is to start by investing that initial amount.

Put not your trust in money, but put your money in trust.
– Oliver Wendell Holmes, Sr.

The best time to invest is when you have money. – John Templeton.

Then keep your money in the market despite the inevitable ups and downs to come. This is just what the market naturally does. Over the short term, you cannot worry about this and panic every time the market moves up or down five or ten percent.

If you want to make money in the stock market, never be out of the stock market. – Jim Jorgensen.

History has shown the biggest risk is not being in the market when it drops, but being out of the market when it rises. – Jim Jorgensen.

> It is impossible to time the market—to know in advance if a given day or month will be an up (or down) day or month, and to invest (or disinvest) accordingly. If it was possible to do this, then someone out there would be very, very rich, and would have written a book or two about how to do it. It is therefore better to pick good investments that should do well in any environment than to worry too much about what the overall market is doing. Remember that it is a market of individual stocks, not a single monolithic stock market.

Yes, the occasional downs will sometimes hurt when looking at your monthly statement. But remember that over the long term, a good investment will see its value recognized.

You won't learn to hold your own in the world by standing on guard, but
by attacking and getting well hammered yourself.
– George Bernard Shaw.

To be in the game, you have to endure the pain. – George Soros.

> Most of your best investments, at some point, will go down. Or you will
> have bought them just a bit too early, before their ultimate bottom. Grin
> and bear it—that's the nature of the market.

Beware a sudden rise in your income—it is not necessarily sustainable. Do not
spend it all at once, especially not on transient pleasures and consumable goods
(such as vacations or dining out extravagantly), because this level of income
might not still be there tomorrow. If you need a treat, buy something durable.
And always re-invest some of your winnings.

When prosperity comes, do not use all of it. – Confucius.

When you have money, think of the time when you had none.
– Japanese proverb.

> If you created your own wealth, then you should remember how hard
> it was to make it, and value it accordingly. If you did not make it, but
> instead won it or inherited it, or the market suddenly went up, then
> reflect deeply for a moment on how hard it would be to make it, and thus
> how fortunate you are to be at this point. Value it, and act cautiously to
> ensure that you keep it.

Be prepared for sudden, unexpected shortfalls in your income or unexpected and
unplanned expenses.

The superior man, when resting in safety, does not forget that danger
may come. When in a state of security he does not forget the possibility
of ruin. When all is orderly, he does not forget that disorder may come.
Thus this person is not endangered, and his states and all their clans are
preserved. – Confucius.

Do not rely on your present good fortune; prepare for the year when it
may leave you. – Chinese proverb.

Do not boast about tomorrow, for you do not know what a day may
bring forth. – Book of Proverbs.

To be surprised is to die. – Arabian proverb.

> Your investments will not always go up. Good health is a blessing. Jobs are
> not forever. Accidents (and liability) can occur. Thieves and scam artists
> abound. Therefore, take some precautions: have at least two accounts.

Have adequate insurance and an umbrella policy. Have enough in cash or bonds or liquid equivalents for you to subsist on for two to three years. Prepare for the worst, while hoping for the best.

Treat your money with the respect it deserves. The job of ensuring you still have this money tomorrow is very serious business. Your money is what enables your current standard of living. Your money provides you with that buffer of security that many do not have. This is valuable. Safeguard it.

A fool and his money are soon parted. – unknown.

There was a time when a fool and his money were soon parted, but now it happens to everybody. – Adlai Stevenson.

I've noticed that people who don't respect money don't have any. – J. Paul Getty.

Managing money usually requires more skill than making it. – Roy L. Smith.

To manage your money, to protect it, and to have it grow so as to at least match inflation and maintain its purchasing power, you (or your money manager) have to keep finding new investments and making investment decisions. This is hard work, and not all ideas will work out.

REMEMBER THAT YOU ARE FALLIBLE

You were not a know-it-all when you were poor, so why would you suddenly be one now, just because you have a little money? Though this is a most common fallacy, try not to succumb to it.

Nothing is harder to direct than a man in prosperity; nothing more easily managed than one in adversity. – Plutarch.

One way to stay grounded is to make sure you work with people of strong character who are not afraid to occasionally tell you that you are wrong.

Good leadership requires you to surround yourself with people of diverse perspectives who can disagree with you without fear of retaliation. – Doris Kearns Goodwin.

Honest differences of views and honest debate are not disunity. They are the vital process of policy-making among free men. – Herbert Hoover.

Find the investment manager, the accountant, the lawyer, the assistant, the spouse, and others who will not only give you good advice, but also dare to tell you "no."

Beware when everyone seems to agree with you.

Whenever people agree with me I always feel I must be wrong.
– Oscar Wilde.

> Because either they are "yes-men" only trying to flatter you and curry favor for themselves (beware!), or because your view parallels the consensus view of the masses (not always wrong, but rarely a way to make any serious money, and often a good way to lose a lot of it).

Stick to your original principles.

Misfortunes occur only when a person is false to his genius.
– Henry David Thoreau.

Ability can take you to the top, but it takes character to keep you there.
– Zig Ziglar.

> Overconfidence, thinking that just because you had a little success you are now smarter than others in the market, or somehow fated to be lucky, or that you can take shortcuts, or that some petty rules no longer apply to you—these moral failings have proven the downfall of many once-fortunate people.

And do the best you can with what you have.

Don't measure yourself by what you have accomplished, but by what you should have accomplished with your ability. – John Wooden.

Go as far as you can see; when you get there, you'll be able to see farther.
– Thomas Carlyle.

> Learning to invest is a never-ending journey. Keep at it—you will succeed!

Price Fluctuations

As you start to invest, you will quickly realize that nothing ever goes straight up in a smooth line. Values go up and down randomly, often for reasons we will never know, on a daily basis. The successful investor learns to take a longer-term view and ignores this short-term "noise."

The market can do anything. – Jesse Livermore.

TURBULENCE IS ONLY HUMAN

People make markets, and people are emotional, erratic, error-prone, and sometimes irrational.

Markets are people, not places. – Dr. Julius Klein.

The stock market is people. – Bernard Baruch.

The stock market is not an abstract animal. It's a lot of people out there making decisions. And whenever you make one or don't make one, you're making a bet against what all those other people are doing. – Peter L. Bernstein.

A market is the combined behavior of thousands of people responding to information, misinformation and whim. – Kenneth Chang.

> By 2013, this global market would comprise millions of entities, with many being disembodied robotic algorithms residing on some computer—of which a certain percent will have coding errors, random malfunctions and various other behavioral issues.

The emotional aspect often pushes price swings beyond what would be considered pure, rational, fair value.

Markets invariably move to undervalued and overvalued extremes because human nature falls victim to greed and/or fear. – Bill Gross, Everything You've Heard About Investing Is Wrong!

The fact that people will be full of greed, fear, or folly is predictable. The sequence is not predictable. – Warren E. Buffett.

The stock market is an index of how investors feel about the future, not the present. In other words, it is a barometer, not a thermometer. – John Train.

The market is always making mountains out of molehills and
exaggerating ordinary vicissitudes into major setbacks.
– Benjamin Graham.

Ignore today's furor. It will often be forgotten by next week.

Anything can be a catalyst for a price move.

The thing that most affects the stock market is everything.
– James Playsted Wood.

But these little price moves do not necessarily mean anything.

The stock market has called nine of the last five recessions.
– Paul A. Samuelson.

If there is a 50-50 chance that something can go wrong, then 9 times out
of ten it will. – Paul Harvey.

Ignore your investment's daily price fluctuations as most of these are random or un-attributable. Focus instead on what will move your investment's price for the next five years.

BUT IF YOU STILL THINK YOU ARE RIGHT, STAY INVESTED

Reminder: absent any material new information, short-term moves are usually not meaningful.

In the short term, the market is a voting machine. In the long term,
it's a weighing machine. Weight counts eventually. But votes count
in the short term. And it's a very undemocratic way of voting.
– Warren E. Buffett.

Often there is no correlation between the success of a company's
operations and the success of its stock over a few months or even a few
years. In the long term, there is a 100% correlation between the success
of the company and the success of its stock. This disparity is the key to
making money; it pays to be patient, and to own successful companies.
– Peter Lynch.

And the smart investor should ignore these short-term moves.

Some pundits advise selling if a stock declines 10% from your cost.
Ridiculous! Either you understand the company or you don't. If you
don't, you shouldn't own it. If you do, and if the decline is a typical

market jiggle, then the logical maneuver is, if anything, to buy a bit more. If you're going to sell every time the stock goes down, you will never win, any more than a general who always retreats when the enemy advances. – John Train.

I've always detested "stop orders"... Show me a portfolio with 10% stops, and I'll show you a portfolio that's destined to lose exactly that amount. When you put in a stop, you're admitting that you're going to sell the stock for less than it's worth today. – Peter Lynch.

A stop order is a direction to your broker to automatically sell out a stock if it declines to a certain price. I see very, very few instances where this makes sense, perhaps only for professional investors as part of some complex strategy that probably will not see great success anyway. To wit, you should only make investments where you have a high level of confidence, and only sell them if you discover an unforeseen problem with your thesis. A random 10% price decline is not proof of a problem with your thesis—if anything, it is an opportunity to buy some more.

If you remain convinced your thesis is correct, then you should wait for validation.

Sound investing can make you very wealthy if you're not in too big a hurry. – Warren E. Buffett.

If the business does well, the stock eventually follows. – Warren E. Buffett.

Knowing the truth one is not afraid no matter what happens. – Lao Tzu.

You may have to fight a battle more than once to win it. – Margaret Thatcher.

Things refuse to be mismanaged long. – Ralph Waldo Emerson.

If you are right, the value you see will eventually be realized.

View your daily stock ticker as nothing more than an entertaining sideshow.

Mr. Market is very obliging indeed. Every day he tells you what he thinks your interest is worth and furthermore offers to buy you out or to sell you an additional interest on that basis. Sometimes his idea of value appears plausible and justified by business developments and prospects as you know them. Often, on the other hand, Mr. Market lets his enthusiasm or his fears run away with him, and the value he proposes seems to you a little short of silly. – Benjamin Graham.

I'd be a bum on the street with a tin cup if the markets were always efficient. – Warren E. Buffett.

The market is the worst giver of advice—it's prone to tell you what you should have done, not what you should do. - Vitaliy N. Katsenelson.

As far as I'm concerned, the stock market doesn't exist. It is there only as a reference to see if anybody is offering to do anything foolish. - Warren E. Buffett.

> And if the market is offering things at foolish prices, if anything, that may signal an opportunity to buy a bit more of what you like.

PRACTICE SAFE INVESTING AND DAILY ZEN

Never have a position that is too big a piece of your total wealth, or too large, or too levered (bought with borrowed money) to withstand more time or greater fluctuations than might be expected.

The market can stay irrational longer than you can stay solvent. - John Maynard Keynes.

Surrender to the reality that volatility exists or volatility will introduce you to the reality that surrender exists. - Ed Seykota.

> With some options, or levered positions, as your market obligation grows you may be subject to a "margin call," which occurs when your brokerage requires you to deposit extra money to ensure you can meet your growing market obligations. If you are unable to put in more money, then your position gets sold out, regardless of current price, regardless of whether this might create a loss for you, and regardless of your wishes.

Otherwise, if you have done your homework on an investment and double-checked and triple-checked, then try to be an optimist...

For myself I am an optimist—it does not seem to be much use being anything else. - Winston Churchill.

I can imagine no more comfortable frame of mind for the conduct of life than a humorous resignation. - W. Somerset Maugham.

If I had no sense of humor, I would long ago have committed suicide. - Mahatma Gandhi.

When you are losing, wear a winning face. - French proverb.

Instead of worrying, a strong man wears a smile. - Japanese proverb.

In times like these, it helps to recall that there have always been times like these. - Paul Harvey.

Nothing in the affairs of men is worthy of great anxiety. – Plato.

Hakuna matata. (There are no worries). – Swahili proverb.

There is no trouble so great or grave that cannot be much diminished by a nice cup of tea. – Bernard-Paul Heroux.

Keep Calm and Carry On. – 1939 British WWII morale boosting poster.

And find something else to worry about or to work on.

When I look back on all the worries I remember the story of the old man who said on his deathbed that he had had a lot of trouble with his life, most of which never happened. – Winston Churchill.

If you see ten troubles coming down the road, you can be sure that nine will run into the ditch before they reach you. – Calvin Coolidge.

How much pain they have cost us, the evils which have never happened. – Thomas Jefferson.

The greatest mistake you can make in life is to be continually fearing you will make one. – Elbert G. Hubbard.

Worry is interest paid on trouble before it becomes due. – William Ralph Inge.

Never let the future disturb you. You will meet it if you have to, with the same weapons of reason which today arm you against the present. – Marcus Aurelius.

When nothing can be done about the way things are, the wise stop worrying about the situation. – Lao Tzu.

The wise man thinks about his troubles only when there is some purpose in doing so. – Bertrand Russell.

On a regular basis, you should turn off the quote screen and go take a walk outside or read a good book instead. This will help keep you sane and balanced.

Investing Failures

Having covered random volatility in the prior chapter, I now turn to how you can, and inevitably will, permanently lose money. When this happens you want to catch the mishap early, avoid having it ruin you, learn something from it, and move on.

Real risk was not volatility; real risk was stupid investment decisions.
– Dr. Mike Burry, quoted by Michael Lewis in The Big Short.

FAILING IS INEVITABLE

Since it is impossible to always be right, accept that you will have your share of investment (and other) failures.

No man can always be right. So the struggle is to do one's best, to keep the brain and conscience clear, never be swayed by unworthy motives or inconsequential reasons, but to strive to unearth the basic factors involved, then do one's duty. – Dwight D. Eisenhower.

Nobody can be lucky all the time;
* so when your luck deserts you in some fashion*
don't think you've been abandoned in your prime,
* but rather that you're saving up your ration.*
– Piet Hein.

I'm sorry to say so
but, sadly, it's true
that Bang-ups
and Hang-ups
can happen to you.
– Dr. Seuss, Oh, The Places You'll Go.

Indeed, the continued sprinkling of failures is a sign that you are still striving.

A man's life is interesting primarily when he has failed—I well know.
For it's a sign that he tried to surpass himself. – Georges Clemenceau.

Anyone who has never made a mistake has never tried anything new.
– Albert Einstein.

Lord, grant that I might always desire more than I can accomplish.
– Michelangelo.

So keep working.

LEARN FROM YOUR FAILURES

Failure provides the best opportunity to adjust your aim and methods.

> *Nothing stands out so conspicuously, or remains so firmly fixed in the memory, as something you have blundered. – Marcus Tullius Cicero.*

> *Do not weep; do not wax indignant. Understand. – Spinoza.*

> *The season of failure is the best time for sowing the seeds of success. – Paramahansa Yogananda.*

> *Failure is simply the opportunity to begin again more intelligently. – Henry Ford.*

Indeed, to neglect reflecting on one's failure and learning from it is a grave error.

> *It is error only, and not truth, that shrinks from inquiry. – Thomas Paine.*

> *Any man can make mistakes, but only an idiot persists in his error. – Cicero.*

But be careful to not draw too many assumptions from the experience.

> *We should be careful to get out of an experience only the wisdom that is in it—and stop there; lest we be like the cat that sits down on a hot stove-lid. She will never sit down on a hot stove-lid again—and that is well; but also she will never sit down on a cold one anymore. – Mark Twain.*

What we learn through these experiences will usually be remembered and serve us well.

> *The world breaks everyone and afterward many are stronger at the broken places. – Ernest Hemingway.*

> *After crosses and losses men grow humbler and wise. – Benjamin Franklin.*

> *He knows not his own strength that hath not met adversity. – Ben Johnson.*

> *I know not any thing more pleasant, or more instructive, than to compare experience with expectation, or to register from time to time the difference between idea and reality. It is by this kind of observation that we grow daily less liable to be disappointed. – Samuel Johnson, letter to Bennet Langton.*

Of course, it is always best to watch, observe, and learn from the mistakes of others. And to read history books!

Learn from the mistakes of others. You cannot live long enough to make them all yourself. – Eleanor Roosevelt.

From the errors of others a wise man corrects his own. – Publilius Syrus.

Wise men learn more from fools than fools from wise men. – Cato.

Read. Think. Study. Reflect. Try not to be the one who learns by making avoidable mistakes. Those who are wise learn from those who have gone before them, rather than by making all the avoidable rookie mistakes themselves.

Because learning from others is always better than learning at one's own expense.

Experience is one thing you can't get for nothing. – Oscar Wilde.

Experience keeps a dear school, yet fools will learn in no other. – Benjamin Franklin.

So, learn what is relevant from a failed attempt, and be better prepared for next time.

Good judgment comes from experience, and experience comes from bad judgment. – Barry LePatner.

Experience is not what happens to you, it is what you do with what happens to you. – Aldous Huxley.

A learning experience is one of those things that says, "You know that thing you just did? Don't do that." – Douglas Adams.

Experience is not a kind teacher, but it is always a truthful one. – Chinese proverb.

Experience is the name everyone gives to their mistakes. – Oscar Wilde, Lady Windermere's Fan.

The only source of knowledge is experience. – Albert Einstein.

Failure teaches you what does not work. Understanding the failure helps you get closer to figuring out what does work.

REBOUND FROM YOUR FAILURES

A failed investment and some lost money is never really the end of the world.

Never confuse a single defeat with a final defeat. – F. Scott Fitzgerald.

Stumbling is not the same thing as falling. – Portuguese proverb.

When you reach the end of your rope, tie a knot in it and hang on.
- Thomas Jefferson.

Success seems to be largely a matter of hanging on after others have let go. - William Feather.

However long the night, the dawn will break. - African proverb.

> If you are smart, resourceful and motivated, you can always make more money.

Unless you completely lose the will to try again.

A setback is a setup for a comeback. - Willie Jolley.

There are no hopeless situations; there are only people who have grown hopeless about them. - Clare Boothe Luce.

He who loses wealth loses much; he who loses a friend loses more; but he that loses courage loses all. - Miguel de Cervantes.

Or unless you immediately rush out and do something really stupid.

Guard particularly against being overeager to trade in order to win back prior losses. Vengeance trading is a sure recipe for failure.
- Jack D. Schwager.

The stock market demands conviction as surely as it victimizes the unconvinced. - Peter Lynch.

It is a characteristic of wisdom not to do desperate things.
- Henry David Thoreau.

> You should avoid making "double or nothing" bets, as this is one of the fastest ways to end up with "nothing," no matter the size of one's initial worth. You should also avoid investing in an entity that is undergoing a large "bet the farm" type of transition. These are binary (all-or-nothing) bets, and the only time this might be appropriate is when making a number of similar such bets all at once, with the expectation that, though some may fail, enough will succeed so that overall you will end up with a net gain. And even though you should be very wary of doing this, you might still make the occasional such bet (and be clear that this is a bet, not an investment) where you have done some research, have an understanding of the field, and feel very strongly that success will ensue.

So remember that many people finally become successful once they run out of ways to fail, or once events eventually turn in their favor (as they always will).

Success is how high you bounce when you hit bottom. - George S. Patton.

Most great people have attained their greatest success just one step beyond their greatest failure. – Napoleon Hill.

Careful analysis of 178 men who are known to be successful disclosed the fact that all had failed many times before arriving. – Napoleon Hill.

When you get into a tight place and everything goes against you, until it seems as though you could not hang on a minute longer, it is then when you should never give up, for that is just the place and time when the tide will turn. – Harriet Beecher Stowe.

Never give up.

MOVE ON FROM YOUR FAILURES

So you lost money on that last investment. Really, so what?

It's no use crying over spilt milk. – W. Somerset Maugham, Of Human Bondage.

Not even the gods can undo what has been done. – Plutarch.

There is no distance on this earth as far away as yesterday. *– Robert Nathan.*

No one is afraid of yesterday. – Renata Adler.

A great calamity is as old as the trilobites an hour after it has happened. – Oliver Wendell Holmes, Sr.

Forget past mistakes. Forget failures. Forget everything except what you're going to do now and do it. – William Durant.

Forget yesterday's failure or loss. Worry only about what today might bring, and how today might affect your investments.

Dwelling on a loss serves no purpose, and in hindsight everyone has perfect vision.

Reflect upon your blessings, of which every man has many—not on your past misfortune, of which all men have some. – Charles Dickens.

The easiest thing to do, whenever you fail, is to put yourself down by blaming your lack of ability for your misfortunes. – Washington Irving.

When the ship has sunk, everyone knows how she could have been saved. – Italian proverb.

It is really foolish to be unhappy now because you may be unhappy at some future time. – Lucius Annaeus Seneca.

Write it on your heart that every day is the best day in the year.
– Ralph Waldo Emerson.

Never let yesterday use up too much of today. – Will Rogers.

Do not dwell on any loss (or gain, for that matter). By all means try to understand why it happened, but only as an academic exercise in the never-ending quest to better one's self and one's insight and one's decision-making process. What is happening today, and what might happen tomorrow, is much more important (and promising).

What is important is sticking to it.

Success is often nothing more than moving from one failure to the next without loss of enthusiasm. – Winston Churchill.

Great works are performed not by strength but by perseverance.
– Samuel Johnson.

Success is not final, failure is not fatal; it is the courage to continue that counts. – Winston Churchill.

One man has enthusiasm for 30 minutes, another for 30 days, but it is the man who has it for 30 years who makes a success of his life.
– Edward B. Butler.

No person who is enthusiastic about his work has anything to fear from life. – Samuel Goldwyn.

Nothing is ever lost. It is just in a pocket you have yet to check.
– Robert W. Kleinschmidt.

A man is not finished when he's defeated; he's finished when he quits.
– Richard M. Nixon.

Vitality shows in not only the ability to persist but the ability to start over.
– F. Scott Fitzgerald.

Focus exclusively on your long-range goals, and don't worry about what is past.

You must have long range goals to keep you from being frustrated by short range failures. – Charles C. Noble.

Every worthwhile accomplishment, big or little, has its stages of drudgery and triumph; a beginning, a struggle, and a victory. – Ghandi.

Whether today met with success or failure, do not dwell on it for too long. What is much more important is what is to come tomorrow.

LEARN TO RECOGNIZE A FAILED INVESTMENT

The earlier you can catch a mistake, the better.

Every fire is the same size when it begins. – Seneca Indian proverb.

A small hole can sink a big ship. – Russian proverb.

Tackle difficulties when they are easy. Accomplish great things when they are small. Handle what is going to be rough when it is still smooth. Control what has not yet formed its force. Deal with a dangerous situation while it is safe. Manage what is hard while it is soft. Eliminate what is vicious before it becomes destructive. – Lao Tzu.

Neglect mending a small fault, and it will soon be a great one. – Benjamin Franklin.

The wise man does at once what the fool does finally. – Niccolò Machiavelli.

For want of a nail the shoe is lost; for want of a shoe the horse is lost; for what of a horse the rider is lost. For want of a rider the message was lost. For want of a message the battle was lost. For want of a battle the kingdom was lost. And all for the want of a horseshoe nail. – proverb.

> Catch mistakes, problems and bad investments early, before they can grow and snowball into something much larger and much more costly to repair or recover from.

When you discover your formerly attractive investment has a fatal flaw, or when you realize you don't understand it as well as you initially thought you did, then it is usually better to cut your losses and move on.

Always leave a sinking ship. There's no virtue in hanging on to losers. And stocks don't have feelings. – Nancy Dunnan.

One of the hardest things in this world is to admit you are wrong. And nothing is more helpful in resolving a situation than its frank admission. – Benjamin Disraeli.

When a man is wrong and won't admit it, he always becomes angry. – various.

Weak people never give way when they ought to. – Cardinal de Retz.

If you can't take a small loss, sooner or later you will take the mother of all losses. – Jack D. Schwager.

Protect your capital, or as much as you have left. Live to (fight and) invest another day.

> *He who fights and runs away will live to fight another day.*
> *– Demosthenes.*

> *The bamboo which bends is stronger than the oak which resists.*
> *– Japanese proverb.*

> *My principle is to survive first and make money afterwards.*
> *– George Soros.*

> *There are some defeats more triumphant than victories.*
> *– Michel de Montaigne.*

> > Ending an investment with a small loss may be a great recovery from a potential loss of everything.

Ask yourself: Is there any opportunity lurking in this defeat?

> *I always tried to turn every disaster into an opportunity.*
> *– John D. Rockefeller, Sr.*

> > You may have lost money on this investment. But, in the process, did you discover something else that you could bet on? What force caused you to lose? Is there a bet you could make using that force? And always consider the inverse, or where an opposite action might take you.

Looping back to the beginning of this chapter, remember that you will inevitably have failed investments. Keep these three goals in mind. First, aim to avoid the failures in the first place; second, minimize the failures as soon as they reveal themselves to be such; and third, try to end the day with just a few more winners than losers.

> *If six out of ten of my stocks perform as expected, then I'm thankful. Six out of ten is all it takes to produce an enviable record on Wall Street.*
> *– Peter Lynch.*

> > So being right just slightly more than half the time is actually a pretty good investment decision record.

> *A long list of losers from my own portfolio constantly reminds me that the so-called "smart money" is exceedingly dumb about 40% of the time.*
> *– Peter Lynch.*

> > Again, you will have your share of mistakes.

> *If a speculator is correct half of the time, he is hitting a good average.*
> *Even being right three or four times out of 10 should yield a person a*

fortune if he has the sense to cut his losses quickly on the ventures where he has been wrong. – Bernard Baruch.

Maximize the winners, minimize the losers. Hard in practice, but possible. So keep trying!

Be Persistent

To recover from discussing failure, here follows a brief pause to visit the land of motivational quotations. I make no attempt here to compete with the vast array of self-help books out there, but there are several aspects of this topic that you will find relevant as you gain experience investing. A little persistence, a little courage, and continued efforts will carry you far.

> *That's why they call it "fishing." If you never failed to catch a fish,*
> *then they would call it "catching." – unknown.*

NEVER GIVE UP

The basics on being persistent:

> *To strive, to seek, to find, and not to yield. – Alfred Lord Tennyson.*

Always remain vigilant in safeguarding your investments.

> *When you are in any contest you should work as if there were—to the*
> *very last minute—a chance to lose it. – Dwight D. Eisenhower.*

Remember that every day in the market is a new day. The market does not remember yesterday. Anything can happen.

> *Let a man who has to make his fortune in life remember this maxim:*
> *Attacking is the only secret. Dare and the world yields, or if it beats*
> *you sometimes, dare it again and you will succeed.*
> *– William Makepeace Thackeray.*

The basics, again:

> *Never, never, never, never give up. – Winston Churchill.*

> *You just can't beat the person who never gives up. – Babe Ruth.*

> *Victory is always possible for the person who refuses to stop fighting.*
> *– Napoleon Hill.*

GET TOUGH AND CONFIDENT

Of course, investing—or most anything else—is not easy at first.

> *All things are difficult before they are easy. – Matthew Henry.*

> *If thou wouldst conquer thy weakness thou must not gratify it.*
> *– William Penn.*

Build up your weaknesses until they become your strong points.
- Knute Rockne.

The way to make it easy is to start doing it. This applies whether you are making your own investments or regularly monitoring a couple of professionals who are doing it for you.

Do the thing we fear, and the death of fear is certain.
- Ralph Waldo Emerson.

The first duty of man is that of subduing fear. We must get rid of fear, we cannot act until then. - Thomas Carlyle.

You gain strength, courage and confidence by every experience in which you really stop to look fear in the face...You must do the thing which you think you cannot do. - Eleanor Roosevelt.

Do one thing every day that scares you. - Eleanor Roosevelt.

When we understand that we cannot be destroyed, we are liberated from fear. - Thich Nhat Hanh.

Keep at it. Keep monitoring your investment situation. Keep talking to knowledgeable investors, and reading good old books on the topic. I beg forgiveness from my publishing-industry readers, but please also avoid at all cost the dozens of trendy "new investing secrets" books that come out every year.

Mental toughness is essential to success. - Vince Lombardi.

Commitment is what transforms a promise into reality.
- Abraham Lincoln.

It's not that I'm so smart, it's just that I stay with problems longer.
- Albert Einstein.

There is no such thing as a great talent without great willpower.
- Honoré de Balzac.

Nothing is so common as unsuccessful men with talent. They lack only determination. - Charles Swindoll.

To whatever degree of involvement you want with your investments, know that you can become competent.

Do, or do not, there is no try. - Yoda character, Star Wars, George Lucas, 1980, film.

Clear your mind of "can't." - Dr. Samuel Johnson.

The word "impossible" is not in my dictionary. - Napoleon Bonaparte.

What appears to us as the impossible may be simply the untried.
– Seyyed Hossein Nasr.

ALWAYS WORK TO MAKE PROGRESS

While some of your friends may sit at home passively watching television, all the while complaining about their limited means, you can open that investment account and start reading a good basic investing book. A much better use of your time.

You can overcome anything if you don't bellyache. – Bernard M. Baruch.

It's wonderful what we can do if we're always doing.
– George Washington.

It has been my observation that most people get ahead during the time that others waste. – Henry Ford.

It had long since come to my attention that people of accomplishment rarely sat back and let things happen to them. They went out and happened to things. – Leonardo da Vinci.

Don't talk about what you have done or what you are going to do.
– Thomas Jefferson.

Just do it. – Nike (athletic gear company) marketing slogan.

Take some simple steps.

You will not become a good investor overnight. It is the repeated small steps that will get you there.

Small attempts repeated will complete any undertaking. – Og Mandino.

No problem can withstand the assault of sustained thinking. – Voltaire.

Winners never quit and quitters never win. – Vince Lombardi.

Il faut d'abord durer. (Above all, endure). – Ernest Hemingway's favorite maxim.

Nothing in the world can take the place of Persistence. Talent will not; nothing is more common than unsuccessful men with talent. Genius will not; unrewarded genius is almost a proverb. Education will not; the world is full of educated derelicts. Persistence and determination alone are omnipotent. The slogan "Press On" has solved and always will solve the problems of the human race. – Calvin Coolidge.

Repeat these basic steps often.

And especially all the little mistakes you make along the way. From these you will gain true experience and wisdom.

> *You can't expect to win unless you know why you lose.*
> *– Benjamin Lipson.*

> *The only real mistake is the one from which we learn nothing.*
> *– John Powell,* The Secret of Staying in Love.

> *Ever tried. Ever failed. No matter. Try again. Fail again. Fail better.*
> *– Samuel Beckett.*

> *I have not failed. I have just found 10,000 new ways that will not work.*
> *– Thomas A. Edison.*

> *Men succeed when they realize that their failures are the preparation for their victories. – Ralph Waldo Emerson.*

> *A failure is not always a mistake, it may be simply the best one can do with the circumstances. The real mistake is to stop. – B. F. Skinner.*

> *The majority of men meet with failure because of their lack of persistence in creating new plans to take the place of those which fail.*
> *– Napoleon Hill.*

> *Move fast and break things. Unless you are breaking stuff, you are not moving fast enough. – Mark Zuckerberg, Facebook corporate motto.*

Keep at it. That is the secret.

> *The three great essentials to achieve anything worthwhile are, first, hard work; second, stick-to-itiveness; third, common sense.*
> *– Thomas A. Edison.*

> *There is genius in persistence. It conquers all opposers. It fires confidence. It annihilates obstacles. Everyone believes in a determined man. People know that when he undertakes a thing, the battle is half won, for his rule is to accomplish whatever he sets out to do. – Orison Swett Marden.*

> *Genius is nothing but a great aptitude for patience.*
> *– George-Louis de Buffon.*

> *Genius is 1% inspiration, and 99% perspiration.*
> *– Thomas A. Edison.*

> *When nothing seems to help, I go look at a stonecutter hammering away at his rock, perhaps a hundred times without as much as a crack showing in it. Yet at the hundred and first blow it will split in two, and I know it was not that blow that did it, but all that had gone before.*
> *– Jacob Riis.*

I work every day—or at least I force myself into my office or room. I may get nothing done, but you don't earn bonuses without putting in time. Nothing may come for three months, but you don't earn the fourth without it. - Mordecai Richler.

If you have ever studied any difficult subject, you know this already. If you have ever written a book or completed any major project of long duration, you know this already. Gaining a basic working knowledge of investing, or becoming a half-competent investor, is no different. You must put in a certain initial quantity of time, learning and effort.

ALWAYS WORK TO CAPTURE OPPORTUNITY

To catch the market when it does something silly and puts something on sale, you have to be there. You have to be watching it. You have to be looking for the discrepancies, and be ready to pounce.

Eighty percent of success is showing up. - Woody Allen.

Being smart, or knowledgeable about investing, is not enough. You have to be out there looking for good investments.

Ability is of little account without opportunity. - Napoleon Bonaparte.

The more you work at finding good investments, the more good investments you will find.

*Do not wait to strike till the iron is hot; but make it hot by striking.
- William Butler Yeats.*

*You can't wait for inspiration. You have to after it with a club.
- Jack London.*

Inspiration does exist, but it must find you working. - Pablo Picasso.

*The wise man will make more opportunities than he finds.
- Roger Bacon.*

I'm a great believer in luck, and I find the harder I work the more I have of it. - Thomas Jefferson.

Everything comes to he who hustles while he waits. - Thomas A. Edison.

Things may come to those who wait, but only the things left by those who hustle. - Abraham Lincoln.

Opportunities multiply as they are seized. - Sun Tzu.

Circumstances? What are circumstances? I make circumstances.
– Napoleon Bonaparte.

True, you may not find any good investment opportunities today. But come back tomorrow, and keep looking.

The wheel of fortune turns round incessantly, and who can say to himself,
I shall today be uppermost. – Confucius.

Unless you are out there looking, you will miss your opportunities.

PART 5

Cycles, Situations & Philosophy

Keep Some Cash Available

It is very wise to always have some cash available. It is also very wise to always sell off some of your winning investments. This creates the aforementioned cash, which you then have available to fund your next investment. Some comments on this virtuous circle follow below.

> *[Warren Buffett] thinks of cash differently than conventional investors...*
> *He thinks of cash as a call option with no expiration date, an option on*
> *every asset class, with no strike price. It is a pretty fundamental insight.*
> *Because once an investor looks at cash as an option—in essence, the*
> *price of being able to scoop up a bargain when it becomes available—it*
> *is less tempting to be bothered by the fact that in the short term, it earns*
> *almost nothing. – Alice Schroeder,* The Snowball: Warren Buffett and the
> Business of Life, *Globe and Mail, September 24th, 2012.*

ALWAYS HAVE CASH—WHY?

You always want to have some cash available.

> *There are three faithful friends—an old wife, an old dog, and ready*
> *money. – Benjamin Franklin.*

> "Ready money'" refers to cash or equivalents, such as money market funds or government bonds such as Treasuries, for which there is a highly liquid market and the ability to convert to cash easily. You might ask, "How much cash?" to which the answers vary a bit more. In terms of your living expenses, anywhere between 6 months' to 3 years' worth is probably sufficient to weather anything but an apocalypse. In terms of assets, it is advisable to have roughly 5 to 25% as cash, and possibly more if you really cannot find any worthy investment ideas or do not like the market. However, realize that having a lot of cash is not a long-term investment strategy, and in periods of high inflation would be counterproductive (more in the forthcoming chapter on inflation).

Because it is always better to have it before you need it.

> *Necessity never made a good bargain. – Benjamin Franklin.*

> You never want to be in a position where you are forced to sell assets. When you are forced to sell assets, it is usually because you got over-extended at the same time that things took a downturn. And if things

took a downturn, you will then be forced to sell at what is probably a short-term dip in the market—not a good trade.

If you already have cash when the market goes down, then you are able to purchase the bargains that only get offered then.

> *A stock market decline is as routine as a January blizzard in Colorado. If you're prepared, it can't hurt you. A decline is a great opportunity to pick up the bargains left behind by investors who are fleeing the storm in panic. - Peter Lynch.*

> *In the middle of every difficulty comes opportunity. - Albert Einstein.*

> *When written in Chinese, the word "crisis" is composed of two characters. One represents danger and the other represents opportunity.*
> *- John F. Kennedy.*

But to have this cash and be ready, you have to have sold before the market went down.

Always Have Cash—How?

Always sell some of a successful investment early in its success, once it starts to look good and has made you some money.

> *One must simply get out while the getting is good. The secret is to hop off the elevator on one of the floors on the way up. In the stock market one good profit in hand is worth two on paper. - William J. O'Neil.*

> *Repeatedly I have sold a stock while it still was rising—and that has been one reason why I have held onto my fortune. Many a time, I might have made a good deal more by holding a stock, but I would also have been caught in the fall when the price of the stock collapsed.*
> *- Bernard Baruch.*

When succeeding, always sell a little bit early on.

You may not be getting out at the top (and timing that is impossible anyway), but you will be ensuring a profit, and ensuring you have your invested capital back as cash, ready for the next opportunity.

> *Nobody ever lost money taking a profit. - Bernard Baruch.*

> *I made all my money by selling too soon. - Bernard Baruch.*

When succeeding, always sell a little bit early on.

Yes, it is psychologically difficult to pick up your winnings and leave the game—

one always hopes for more. This, of course, is why many people stay in Vegas until they have lost everything. But leaving the party early is the only way to keep your money safe so that tomorrow you can come back and play again.

Baseball is like a poker game. Nobody wants to quit when he's losing; nobody wants you to quit when you're ahead. – Jackie Robinson.

When succeeding, always sell a little bit early on.

And if you are employing a money manager, always give them the freedom to decide how much cash they will hold.

Investors who see their fund managers holding a lot of cash tend to think that they are not getting their money's worth, which is wrong. If investors would realize that what they are paying for is someone to have the expertise to know when to buy a call option called cash, and move in and out of that, then perhaps there might be more value placed on that service. – Alice Schroeder, The Snowball: Warren Buffett and the Business of Life, *Globe and Mail, September 24th, 2012.*

Allow your money managers to live by this same rule.

Market Cycles

Individual stocks, sectors of the market, or sometimes the market as a whole, will inevitably go through overvalued bubble periods. When these bubbles inevitably burst, the market then goes through cheap trough periods. This is a natural cycle. It is important to recognize these different stages as they inevitably occur and recur.

Ignoring bubbles is a special case of ignoring risk in general.
– Howard Marks.

There is hardly a more conventional subject in economic literature than financial crises. – Charles Kindleberger, Manias, Panics and Crashes.

Wall Street breeds panics the way Oklahoma breeds twisters. – unknown.

There are only two emotions in Wall Street: fear, and greed.
– William M. Lefevre, Jr.

In Normal Times

There is not that much to say about normal times...

Anyone can hold the helm when the sea is calm. – Publilius Syrus.

...Except that you should always beware. Things will not stay "normal" for long.

Just because the river is quiet does not mean the crocodiles have left.
– Malay proverb.

The Growth of Bubbles

Whether an entire bull market or merely an individual stock, the reason for the initial rise is usually very reasonable.

An invasion of armies can be resisted, but not an idea whose time has come. – Victor Hugo.

When patterns are broken new worlds emerge. – Tuli Kupferberg.

Initial prosperity then feeds on itself, becoming a self-fulfilling feedback loop.

Men's spirits are lifted when the times are prosperous, rich and happy, so that their pride and arrogance grow. – Cato.

Huge markets attract people who measure themselves by money. If someone goes through life and measures themselves solely by how much they have, or how much money they earned last year, sooner or later they're going to end up in trouble. - Warren E. Buffett.

In a buying frenzy, there is, through the effect of contagion, a universal urge to participate in the whirlwind of speculation. - Marc Faber.

When Alan Greenspan spoke about irrational exuberance in 1996 he misrepresented bubbles. When I see a bubble forming I rush in to buy, adding fuel to the fire. - George Soros, Central European University lecture, October 27th, 2009.

At first, as in all these gambling mania, confidence was at its height, and everybody gained. Many individuals grew suddenly rich. A golden bait hung temptingly out before the people, and one after the other, they rushed to the marts, like flies around a honeypot. - Charles Mackay, Extraordinary Popular Delusions and the Madness of Crowds. [Discussing the 17th century Dutch tulip bubble.—Ed.]

Once things really start to rise, "reasonableness" no longer applies.

The four most expensive words in the English language are "this time it's different." - John Templeton.

Every generation laughs at the old fashions but religiously follows the new. - Henry David Thoreau.

Bubble territory is entered when the old rules and limitations are cast aside and ignored. Since everyone wants the rise to continue, excuses are found as to why the old limits should no longer hold.

Instead, peer pressure, wishful thinking, and mob psychology become dominant...

Insanity in individuals is something rare—but in groups, parties, nations and epochs, it is the rule. - Friedrich W. Nietzsche.

I can calculate the motions of heavenly bodies but not the madness of men. - attributed to Isaac Newton, c.1850. [After he lost money in the South Sea Bubble.—Ed.]

Nothing defines humans better than their willingness to do irrational things in the pursuit of phenomenally unlikely payoffs. This is the principle behind lotteries, dating, and religion. - Scott Adams.

The great masses of the people will more easily fall victims to a big lie than to a small one. - Adolf Hitler.

Though this last quotation is most often cited in the political context, it addresses the same psychological failing in people that also contributes to bubbles. "Profits don't matter for Internet stocks!" circa 1999, or "Home prices will always keep going up!" circa 2006.

...with easily-made, newfound money providing the fuel to keep the bubble going...

At particular times a great deal of stupid people have a great deal of stupid money...At intervals...the money of these people—the blind capital, as we call it, of the country—is particularly large and craving; it seeks for someone to devour it and there is a "plethora"; it finds someone, and there is "speculation"; it is devoured, and there is "panic."
- Walter Bagehot.

During every manic phase, cash is always regarded as a totally unattractive investment alternative. - Marc Faber.

Graham's observations that investors pay too much for trendy, fashionable stocks and too little for companies that are out-of-favor, was on the money...why does this profitability discrepancy persist? Because emotion favors the premium-priced stocks. They are fashionable. They are hot. They make great cocktail party chatter. There is an impressive and growing body of evidence demonstrating that investors and speculators don't necessarily learn from experience. Emotion overrides logic time after time. - David Dreman.

...and heavy promotion from whatever segments of the press and financial industry are most involved. People are finally paying attention to them, which directly translates into business for them, and so they are naturally loath to call an end to the party, even if the party is clearly fading.

It is difficult to get a man to understand something when his salary depends on his not understanding it. - Upton Sinclair.

Hysterical "bulls" care nothing whatever about the earnings or dividend returns on a stock. The only note to which they attune their actions is the optimistic slogan, "It's going up!" and the higher it goes, the more they buy, and the more their ranks are swelled by new recruits.
- Henry Howard Harper, The Psychology of Speculation, *1926.*

Stock prices have reached what looks like a permanently high plateau.
- Irving Fisher, Yale University Professor of Economics, 1929.

Of course, two weeks later, the stock market crashed and the Great Depression began.

The above factors cause bull markets to last longer than common sense would expect.

Bull markets last longer than bear markets. – Mark Mobius.

It is also commonplace in human affairs that men continue to labor on major undertakings a long time after the ideas upon which these efforts were based have become obsolete. – Fred Charles Iklé, Every War Must End.

What the wise man does in the beginning, the fool does in the end. – Warren E. Buffett.

> To wit, Joseph Kennedy, Sr.'s apocryphal story about getting out of the 1929 stock market when he started hearing stock tips from shoeshine boys. What was exotic to the early, perceptive player became common market practice for all regular players and finally spread to irresponsible inexperienced players entering the market. Meanwhile, returns went from high to medium to low, with risk doing the reverse.

This is also why experienced players tend to avoid bull markets or, upon recognizing the mounting signs, do not play them for very long and get out early.

For best performance in a bull market, rent a kid. – John T. Bennett, Jr.

Clear? Huh! Why a four-year-old child could understand this report. Run out and find me a four-year-old child. I can't make head or tail out of it. – Groucho Marx, Duck Soup, *Bert Kalmar and Harry Ruby, 1933, film.*

Young men thought they could do anything. – Albert H. Gordon. [Wall Street veteran and Crash of 1929 survivor, reflecting on its cause.—Ed.]

As a bull market reaches its later stages, it is useful to remember that not many of the primary players keep making money for long.

During a gold rush, the people that make the money are those selling picks and shovels. – unknown.

The electric light is very probably a great invention and let us take it for granted that its future development will be vast. But this, unhappily, cannot be urged as a reason why the pioneer companies should be prosperous. – The Economist, *1882.*

Benjamin Franklin may have discovered electricity, but it was the man who invented the meter who made the money. – Earl Wilson.

THE INEVITABLE BUST

Nothing is infinite or capable of unchecked growth forever.

Anyone who believes exponential growth can go on forever in a finite world is either a madman or an economist. - Kenneth Boulding.

The excessive increase of anything causes a reaction in the opposite direction. - Plato.

If something cannot go on forever, it will stop. - Herbert Stein.

The only cause of depression is prosperity. - Clement Juglar.

Everything in the world may be endured, except continual prosperity. - Johann Wolfgang von Goethe.

Bull markets are born on pessimism, grow on skepticism, mature on optimism, and die on euphoria. - John Templeton.

No stock will keep going up forever, and especially not when people think "it's different this time."

Even the masses eventually lose their gullibility (or naïveté, to be gentler).

Fatigue makes cowards of us all. - Vince Lombardi.

During times of universal deceit, telling the truth becomes a revolutionary act. - George Orwell.

There are thousands of ways which lead to deception, and there is only one way which leads to the truth. - Jean Jacques Rousseau.

How many legs does a dog have if you count his tail as a leg? Four. You can call a tail a leg if you want to, but that does not make it a leg. - Abraham Lincoln.

They might take a while, and are often late, but the crowd eventually turns.

The old narrative no longer holds.

An era can be said to end when its basic illusions are exhausted. - Arthur Miller.

Bubbles end when people stop believing the false narrative and start thinking for themselves. - Peter Thiel.

Upon which, they realize expectations might be just a little too good to be true.

And those players or investment opportunities left in at the end are mostly not compelling.

It is easy to look good in a boom. But also, every boom—and I have lived and worked through four or five—puts crooks in at the top.
– Peter F. Drucker.

I have seen wicked men and fools, a great many of both; and I believe they both get paid in the end; but the fools first. – Robert Louis Stevenson.

Having exhausted further support, the end of a bubble usually comes quickly and violently.

I have a general rule: Whenever something becomes worth more than the whole state of California, sell it. – Alan Blinder, discussing the Internet bubble.

It is the nature of a speculative boom that almost anything can collapse it. – John Kenneth Galbraith, The Great Crash.

Markets take the stairs up, but the elevator down. – old Wall Street adage.

After the initial fear and valuation drop, there may be a rebound, but it is unlikely to be long lasting.

It is an interesting but not uncommon phenomenon in economics that the expectation of a devaluation can be highly destabilizing but that the devaluation itself can be beneficial. – Ben Bernanke, November 8, 2002, speech to honor Milton Friedman.

Uncertainty finds expression in volatility. Increased volatility requires a reduction in risk exposure. This leads to what Keynes calls increased liquidity preference. This is an additional factor in the forced liquidation of positions that characterize financial crises. When the crisis abates and the range of uncertainty is reduced, it leads to an almost automatic rebound in the stock market as the liquidity preference stops rising and eventually falls. That is another lesson I have learned recently. – George Soros, lecture at Central European University, October 27, 2009.

In less technical terms, this is called a "dead cat bounce." Even something as fully dead and with no future prospects as the proverbial dead cat will still often see a short and temporary bounce upwards if it hits bottom fast enough.

Once a real bubble breaks, it can get very ugly for a while.

Things are going to get a lot worse before they get worse. – Lily Tomlin.

This is no market for young men. At least us old men remember what

a real bear market is like, and the young men haven't got a clue.
– Jeremy Grantham, Marketwatch *interview September 21, 2011.*

Major manias are usually once-a-generation affairs and lead to some serious economic damage once they come to an end. – Marc Faber.

You may think that since it was all a delusion on the profit side, the loss also must have been imaginary; that if nothing was added to the wealth of the country, neither was anything taken away. But that is not the way of it. First there was the direct loss of diverting that credit from all the possible uses of production to the unproductive use of speculation. Secondly, a great deal of it was consumed by two to three million speculators, large and small, who, with that rich feeling upon them, borrowed money on their paper profits and spent it. In this refinement of procedure what happens is that imaginary wealth is exchanged for real wealth; and real wealth is consumed by those who have produced nothing in place of it. Thirdly—and this was the terrific loss—the shock from the headlong fall of this pyramid caused all the sensitive sources and streams and waters of credit to contract in fear. The more they contracted the more fear there was, the more fear the more contraction, effect acting upon cause. The sequel was abominable pain.
– Garet Garrett, A Bubble that Broke the World, *1932.*

And so it was in the 2000 Internet bubble. And so it was in the 2007 housing bubble. And so it will be in future bubbles.

On to the Next Cycle

Markets are cyclical. Randomly so, but cyclical nonetheless.

Whatever men attempt, they seem driven to overdo. When hopes are soaring, I always repeat to myself that two and two still make four.
– Bernard Baruch.

The markets are not random, because they are based on human behavior, and human behavior, especially mass behavior, is not random. It never has been, and it probably never will be. – Jack D. Schwager.

As long as there is human nature, there will be market cycles.

And after a major cycle, there is usually a long pause before things start up again.

Major decline traumas like 2000-02 and 2007-08 take a long time to overcome. After 1929-32 and 1937-38, the public stayed fearful of stocks at least until the mid-1950s. In Japan, after 22 years of disappointing

*markets, they still have not returned. Maybe every situation is different
but human nature stays the same. After greed, fear rules. – Robert Farrell,
market comment, May 5th, 2012.*

A natural impulse is to expect, or hope, that the prior heroic stocks or sectors
recover their prior heights.

*There is a danger of expecting the results of the future to be predicted from
the past. – John Maynard Keynes.*

*It is dangerous...to apply to the future inductive arguments based on
past experience, unless one can distinguish the broad reasons why past
experience was what it was. – John Maynard Keynes.*

*It used to be a good hotel, but that proves nothing—I used to be a good
boy. – Mark Twain.*

> In this aspect of human nature, people are always looking back to what
> they just had, rather than looking forward to what might come.

But the bubble perpetrators rarely get another upturn right away.

*In every major economic downturn in U.S. history, the villains have been
the heroes during the preceding boom. – Peter F. Drucker.*

Today's hero is often tomorrow's blockhead. – Peter L. Bernstein.

And you should not base your investment hopes on a quick rebound.

*How quickly investors flock to better-performing mutual funds, even
though financial researchers have shown that the "hot" funds in one time
period very often turn out to be the poorest performers in another.
– David Dreman,* The New Contrarian Investment Strategy.

*Past performance is no indication of future returns. – Standard
investment industry disclaimer, some version of which will be included in
most communications with clients.*

You must find the next new thing through your own insight, thinking, and
research.

*Markets change continuously and so must you. What worked last year,
last month, or even last week may very well not work today.
– Dean Lundell.*

*Yes. In the garden, growth has it seasons. First comes spring and summer,
but then we have fall and winter. And then we get spring and summer
again. – Chance the Gardiner (Peter Sellers) character,* Being There,
Kosinski/Jones, 1979, film.

> Find the next thing that will go up—before everyone else does.

CONTRARIAN NOTES REGARDING BUBBLES AND BUSTS

To be fair, much of the time it is hard to tell if something is becoming a bubble or not.

> *More often than not stocks, bonds, gold, pork bellies etc. are neither wildly popular, nor wildly unpopular at any particular moment so it's hard to tell when the crowd gets crowded enough to oppose.*
> *– John Rothchild,* The Bear Book.

The trick is to look for where there seems to be an overly unanimous positive or negative consensus.

> *Skepticism and pessimism are not synonymous. Skepticism calls for pessimism when optimism is excessive. But it also calls for optimism when pessimism is excessive. – Howard Marks.*

> *The prevailing wisdom is that markets are always right. I take the opposite position. I assume that markets are always wrong. Even if my assumption is occasionally wrong, I use it as a working hypothesis.*
> *– George Soros,* Soros on Soros.

> *I would say if Charlie and I have any advantage it's not because we're so smart, it is because we're rational and we very seldom let extraneous factors interfere with our thoughts. We don't let other people's opinion interfere with it. We try to get fearful when others are greedy. We try to get greedy when others are fearful. We try to avoid any kind of imitation of other people's behavior. And those are the factors that cause smart people to get bad results. – Warren E. Buffett.*

It is during these periods of consensus that the crowd is most likely to have things wrong, and to have forgotten all about cycles.

> *Historically, stocks are embraced as investments or dismissed as gambles in routine and circular fashion, and usually at the wrong times. Stocks are most likely to be accepted as prudent at the moment they're not.*
> *– Peter Lynch.*

> *When everyone thinks central bankers, money managers, corporate managers, politicians or any other group are the smartest guys in the room, you are in a bubble. – Doug Kass.*

> *And it never failed that during the dry years the people forgot about the rich years, and during the wet years they lost all memory of the dry years.*
> *– John Steinbeck,* East of Eden.

The public is right during the trends, but wrong at both ends.
– Humphrey Neill.

And it is during these periods that analysts, commentators, the press, and most "professionals" become least useful.

You don't want analysts in a bear market and you don't need them in a bull market. – Gerald M. Loeb.

When even the analysts are bored, it's time to start buying. – Peter Lynch, Beating the Street.

Buy the market when the banks are firing, and sell it when they are hiring. – old Wall Street proverb.

They don't ring a bell at the top or the bottom. – old Wall Street proverb.

It is at times like these that going with the crowd actually presents the most risk.

The central principle of investment is to go contrary to the general opinion, on the grounds that if everyone agreed about its merits, the investment is inevitably too dear and therefore unattractive.
– John Maynard Keynes.

You pay a very high price in the stock market for a cheery consensus. Uncertainty actually is the friend of the buyer of long-term values.
– Warren E. Buffett.

The market usually does whatever will disappoint the greater number of people. – old Wall Street proverb.

Whereas by going against the crowd, you can hope to find the best bargains.

Fear is the foe of the faddist but the friend of the fundamentalist.
– Warren E. Buffett.

We like it when markets are bearish. It's an interesting psychological phenomenon that when markets are bullish, I feel very uncomfortable and not too happy, because it's more difficult for us to find bargains. When markets are down, I'm a much happier person. When we hear about recessions, disasters, revolutions, we know there will be an opportunity. – Mark Mobius.

Most people get interested in stocks when everyone else is. The time to get interested is when no one else is. You can't buy what is popular and do well. – Warren E. Buffett.

People make markets and act more emotionally than rationally. Markets, therefore, tend to go to extremes that take expectations and valuations well beyond what is fundamental and rational. At the tops of booms everyone sees the wisdom of being a long-term investor (thus rationalizing paying high prices for overvalued securities). At the bottoms, long-term investing is decried and trading and limited exposure are accepted as the only way to go. Recognizing extremes and the inevitable counter-moves that follow is important strategic knowledge. – Robert Farrell, market comment, December 18th, 2011.

To buy when others are despondently selling and to sell when others are greedily buying requires the greatest fortitude and pays the greatest reward. – John Templeton.

Be fearful when others are greedy and greedy only when others are fearful. – Warren E. Buffett.

To recapitulate: Look for excessive bad (or good) news.

The worse a situation becomes, the less it takes to turn it around, the bigger the upside. – George Soros.

You can have cheap equity prices or good news, but you can't have both at the same time. – Joe Rosenberg.

Happiness is a rounding bottom. – unknown.

> I am pretty sure this refers to a chart pattern that has stopped going down, gradually found a bottom, and stabilized prior to hopefully going back up—but this could be referring to a completely unrelated topic.

And strive to react contrary to the crowd.

Achetez aux canons, vendez au clairons. (Buy on the cannons, sell on the trumpets). – French proverb.

Buy when everyone is selling. And hold until everyone is buying. – J. Paul Getty.

The time to buy is when there is blood in the streets. – Baron Rothschild.

The time to buy is at the point of maximum pessimism. – John Templeton.

When it's time to buy, you won't want to. – Walter Deemer.

Always buy your straw hats in the winter. – Bernard Baruch.

Berkshire buys when the lemmings are heading the other way. – Warren E. Buffett.

> The best investors invest precisely when feeling most nervous. Conversely, when things are going well and average investors are confident, this is actually a dangerous time to invest.

Happy hunting!

When the brothel burns down, even the pretty girls have to run out.
– Warren E. Buffett.

When it gets dark enough you can see the stars. – Leo Salk.

It is also when you can pick the best stocks.

CLOSING NOTES REGARDING BUBBLES AND BUSTS

No, it is not different, or never-before-seen, or unique, or new, this time around.

There is nothing new under the sun. – Ecclesiastes 1:9.

There is nothing new under the sun but there are lots of old things we don't know. – Ambrose Bierce.

Such pauses and cycles have happened many times in the past and will almost certainly recur in the future.

It is said an eastern monarch once charged his wise men to invent him a sentence, to be ever in view, and which should be true and appropriate in all times and situations. They presented him the words: "And this, too, shall pass away." – Abraham Lincoln, speech, referencing a Persian Sufi proverb.

History doesn't repeat itself, but it does rhyme. – Mark Twain.

Those who do not learn from history are doomed to repeat it.
– George Santayana.

History teaches us the mistakes we are going to make. – Laurence J. Peter.

The only thing new in the world is the history you don't know.
– Harry S. Truman.

That men do not learn very much from the lessons of history is the most important of all the lessons that history has to teach. – Aldous Huxley, Collected Essays, *Case of Voluntary Ignorance.*

We learn from history that we learn nothing from history.
– Georg W. F. Hegel.

The details this time may seem novel and unpredictable.

The Chinese believe in constant change, but with things always moving back to some prior state. They pay attention to a wide range of events; they search for relationships between things; and they think you can't understand the part without understanding the whole. Westerners live in a simple, more deterministic world; they focus on salient objects or people instead of the larger picture; and they think they can control events because they know the rules that govern the behavior of objects. – Richard E. Nesbett, The Geography of Thought: How Asians and Westerners Think Differently.

May you live in interesting times. – Chinese proverb (or curse).

But there are never really any shortcuts, or alternatives to common sense.

During my eighty-seven years I have witnessed a whole succession of technological revolutions. But none of them has done away with the need for character in the individual or the ability to think. – Bernard M. Baruch.

The process and end result will always be the same.

Just because everything is different doesn't mean anything has changed. – Irene Peter.

Technology changes, economic laws do not. – Hal Varian & Carl Shapiro, Information Rules.

And the basic rules of valuation will always reassert themselves.

Then the Gods of the Market tumbled, and their smooth-tongued
*   wizards withdrew*
And the hearts of the meanest were humbled and began to believe
*   it was true*
That All is not Gold that Glitters, and Two and Two make Four
And the Gods of the Copybook Headings limped up to explain it
*   once more.*

As it will be in the future, it was at the birth of Man
There are only four things certain since Social Progress began.
That the Dog returns to his Vomit and the Sow returns to her Mire,
And the burnt Fool's bandaged finger goes wabbling back to the Fire;

And that after this is accomplished, and the brave new world begins
When all men are paid for existing and no man must pay for his sins,
As surely as Water will wet us, as surely as Fire will burn,
The Gods of the Copybook Headings with terror and slaughter return!
– Rudyard Kipling, The Gods of the Copybook Headings.

Being a Generalist and Adapting

There will always be something cheap somewhere. Forget about the stock you missed yesterday. Forget about stocks in your favorite industry. Forget about your favorite geographic region. Explore new places, look everywhere, and eventually you will find something worthy.

> *Life is a banquet, and most poor suckers are starving to death.*
> *– Patrick Dennis,* Auntie Mame.

LEARN TO LOOK EVERYWHERE

But first, you need perspective, so that you do not confuse your apples and oranges.

> *He who thinks everything must be in bloom when the strawberries are in bloom doesn't know anything about apples. – Greek proverb.*

> ...or tulips, as the case may be. The point is, if you know only one industry (or one business, or one geographic area, or other limiting factor), it will give you little useful information into everything else, and could even mislead you. Individual stocks, and individual sectors, often move in different directions—and to understand why, you need to know a little about each of them. This helps you better connect the dots and foresee how these moves might occur.

Therefore, broaden your knowledge...

> *Try to learn something about everything and everything about something. – Thomas Huxley.*

> *The whole secret of life is to be interested in one thing profoundly and in a thousand things well. – Horace Walpole.*

> Endeavor to maintain as wide a range of interests as manageable.

...both in terms of fields of study, in terms of geography, and in all things.

> *I notice that when all a man's information is confined to the field in which he is working, the work is never as good as it ought to be. A man has to get perspective, and he can get it from books or from people —preferably from both. – Harvey Firestone.*

> *We are now one business world, one financial world. You can no longer make a decision about the attractiveness of U.S. chemical stocks without*

knowing what's going on in Europe. – Peter Vermilye.

Your investments can be affected by anything. Keep yourself informed.

As you expand your bounds, do so slowly and never forget what you know you know versus what you know you don't know.

What an investor needs is the ability to correctly evaluate selected businesses. Note that word "selected." You don't have to be an expert on every company, or even many. You only have to be able to evaluate companies within your circle of competence. The size of that circle is not very important; knowing its boundaries, however, is vital.
– Warren E. Buffett.

Know the limits or boundaries of what you know.

Ignore Missed Opportunities

There will always be an endless supply of good investment ideas and opportunities.

You can't kiss all the pretty girls. – unknown.

There are finer fish in the sea than have ever been caught. – Irish proverb.

Against stupidity the gods themselves contend in vain.
– Friedrich von Schiller.

There will always be new mis-priced investment opportunities.

There is no rush, even if media, marketers and overenthusiastic advisers might hint otherwise.

The stock market is a no-called-strike game. You don't have to swing at everything—you can wait for your pitch. The problem when you're a money manager is that your fans keep yelling, "Swing, you bum!"
– Warren E. Buffett.

You do not lose anything by declining to make an investment, even if it does later go up. Again, there will always be some other opportunity—so better to miss a good opportunity through reasonable care than to rush into something and be wrong.

I think and think for months and years. Ninety-nine times, the conclusion is false. The hundredth time I am right. – Albert Einstein.

Very few investment ideas, once examined, are compelling. Wait until you find one that is.

THERE'S ALWAYS SOMETHING CHEAP SOMEWHERE

When your favorite sector is overvalued, uncertain, or not interesting, you want to be able to look elsewhere. Without carrying it to too far an extreme, learn to make money not in just one or two fields, but in whatever area might seem cheap today.

> *Many are stubborn in pursuit of the path they have chosen, few in pursuit of the goal. - Friedrich W. Nietzsche.*

> *To be strong, you have to be like water: if there are no obstacles, it flows; if there is an obstacle, it stops; if a dam is broken, then it flows further; if a vessel is square, then it has a square form; if a vessel is round, then it has a round form. Because it is so soft and flexible, it is the most necessary and the strongest thing. - Lao Tzu.*

> *Soros saw no point in knowing everything about a few stocks in the hope of anticipating small moves; the game was to know a little about a lot of things, so that you could spot the places where the big wave might be coming. - Sebastian Mallaby,* More Money Than God: Hedge Funds and the Making of a New Elite.

> *It is not a stock market, but a market of stocks. - unknown.*

That way, it will not matter where you find opportunity—it will always be a felicitous coincidence.

> *Do not seek to have events happen as you want them to, but instead want them to happen as they do happen, and your life will go well.*
> *- Epictetus.*

> *Welcome anything that comes to you, but do not long for anything else.*
> *- André Gide.*

> *Carpe diem, quam minimum credula postero. (Seize the day, put no trust in tomorrow). - Horace.*

There are always great potential ideas out there.

> *No great man ever complains of want of opportunity.*
> *- Ralph Waldo Emerson.*

> *If you look at 10 companies you'll find one that's interesting. If you look at 20, you'll find two; if you look at 100, you'll find 10. The person that turns over the most rocks wins the game. - Peter Lynch.*

> There are always endless profitable opportunities surrounding you. It merely requires some looking, and sometimes with a fresh eye, to find them. So always keep looking.

Psychology, Philosophy, and Common Sense

Despite all that insightful people might understand about the market, most participants remain members of the ignorant herd. Similarly, while short-term financial (or other) results should not usually much matter, this daily reading of the tea leaves almost predictably stampedes prices first one way, then the other. Next up, some contrarian thoughts on avoiding popular delusions and crowd madness.

To suppose that the value of a common stock is determined purely by a corporation's earnings discounted by the relevant interest rates and adjusted for the marginal tax rate is to forget that people have burned witches, gone to war on a whim, risen to the defense of Joseph Stalin and believed Orson Wells when he told them over the radio that the Martians had landed. – James Grant, Minding Mr. Market.

Behavioral finance is not a branch of standard finance: it is its replacement with a better model of humanity. – Meir Statman.

THE MARKET IS AN IGNORANT HERD

Because people by nature are rarely content to sit still, the herd that makes up the market is also usually running, mostly mindlessly, one way or the other.

The stock market is always going lower (when it is headed down) and always is going higher (when it is headed up). Sounds stupid, doesn't it? But that about expresses the public psychology. The crowd rides the trend and never gets off until they're bumped off. – Humphrey Neill.

I feel very strongly that, in the short run, the market is illogical, capricious, wanton and wild in the way that it prices financial assets. It behaves just as you would expect any mechanism driven by fear and greed to behave. – Robert G. Kirby.

Most of the time common stocks are subject to irrational and excessive price fluctuations in both directions as the consequence of the ingrained tendency of most people to speculate or gamble... to give way to hope, fear and greed. – Benjamin Graham.

Everyone always thinks yesterday's trend will continue into today, and everyone always wants to make just a little more money from that trend for just one more day.

Why are people so quick to copy each other? Probably because our animal genes and subconscious lead us to believe (erroneously) that "safety in numbers" (i.e., doing exactly the same thing as everyone else) applies in the market as well.

When people are free to do as they please, they usually imitate each other.
– Eric Hoffer.

We do not err because truth is difficult to see. It is visible at a glance. We err because this is more comfortable. – Alexandr Solzhenitsyn.

Better mad with the rest of the world than wise alone.
– Baltasar Gracián.

Investors may be quite willing to take the risk of being wrong in the company of others, while being much more reluctant to take the risk of being right alone. – John Maynard Keynes.

I believe that the public wants to be led, to be instructed, to be told what to do. They want reassurance. They will always move en masse, a mob, a herd, a group, because people want the safety of human company. They are afraid to stand alone because they want to be safely included within the herd, not to be the lone calf standing on the desolate, dangerous, wolf-patrolled prairie of contrary opinion. – Jesse Livermore.

> For the readers who would like to go against the herd, but find themselves lacking in fortitude, hire a good contrarian "value" investment manager.

And, ever since markets first evolved, we've repeated this herd behavior.

The evidence reveals repeated patterns of irrationality, inconsistency, and incompetence in the ways human beings arrive at decisions and choices when faced with uncertainty. – Peter L. Bernstein, Against the Gods.

Only two things are infinite: the universe, and human stupidity, and I'm not sure about the former. – Albert Einstein.

Therefore, recognize the dynamics of the prevalent herd mentality.

He who studies books alone will know how things ought to be, and he who studies men will know how they are. – Charles Caleb Colton.

There is one principle which a man must follow if he wishes to succeed, and that is to understand human nature. – Henry Ford.

> The market is never "how it ought to be." The market is always in whatever barely balanced state the herd has left it in.

And, fortunately, for those investors courageous enough to think for themselves, there is money to be made here.

Because people are simple-minded in how they try to understand what goes on in the market, they like to own what is comfortable instead of what's uncomfortable. They make big errors in valuation. Therefore, if you really understand this, you can make money as a value investor.
– Peter L. Bernstein.

Since most investor decisions are based on herd emotions more than anything else, investments often get over-valued or under-valued. For the investor willing to put their emotions aside, ignoring the herd to investigate the contrary opinion often yields ideas.

(ALMOST) ALWAYS BET AGAINST THE HERD

If most investors out there never really think things through, then why in the world would you invest your money alongside them and make the same popular bets on the same popular companies that everyone agrees with?

It is not worth an intelligent man's time to be in the majority. By definition, there are already enough people to do that. – G. H. Hardy.

The stock market is always wrong, so that if you copy everybody else on Wall Street, you're doomed to do poorly. – George Soros.

Indeed, that is how the stage gets set for disappointments (i.e., market downturns and financial losses), by too many people thinking they are right.

Remember, it [the market] is designed to fool most of the people most of the time. – Jesse Livermore.

[An intelligent] investor [gets] satisfaction from the thought that his operations are exactly opposite to those of the crowd.
– Benjamin Graham.

So start by looking at things others are not considering or looking in areas ignored or unpopular.

For an idea ever to be fashionable is ominous, since it must afterwards be always old fashioned. – George Santayana.

As a rule, I always look for what others ignore. – Marshall McLuhan.

To see what is in front of one's nose requires a constant struggle.
– George Orwell.

Find topics that have been ignored recently, or industries and companies that are considered too old and boring. Or, conversely, seek new technologies that the herd considers too speculative or strange or impractical, but which you find reason to believe will succeed.

And rely on your common sense to figure out what investments might really be worth intrinsically.

Common sense is the knack of seeing things as they are, and doing things as they ought to be done. – Josh Billings.

We must always think about things, and we must think about things as they are, not as they are said to be. – George Bernard Shaw.

It is a fine thing to be honest, but it is also very important to be right. – Winston Churchill.

The height of ability consists in a thorough knowledge of the true value of things. – François, duc de La Rochefoucauld.

Consider what the investment will be worth tomorrow, assuming modest success and a modest reception by the market herd.

Nobody is saying this will be easy...

Common sense is not so common. – Voltaire.

One pound of learning requires ten pounds of common sense to apply it. – Persian proverb.

Common sense in an uncommon degree is what the world calls wisdom. – Samuel Taylor Coleridge.

Common sense is genius dressed in its working clothes. – Ralph Waldo Emerson.

Actually, it is not difficult in terms of the effort or quantity of work required. It is difficult in the sense that you must have the courage and conviction to think for yourself.

...or much fun along the way, as you eschew the popular investments.

People who think deeply and seriously are on bad terms with the public. – Johann Wolfgang von Goethe.

We pay a high price for being intelligent. Wisdom hurts. – Euripides.

Of what use is a philosopher who never offends anyone? – Diogenes.

Great spirits have often encountered violent opposition from weak minds. – Albert Einstein.

Our wretched species is so made that those who walk on the well-trodden

path always throw stones at those who are showing a new road.
– Voltaire.

Indeed, the man who has fully educated and developed himself in a
higher sense can always reckon to have the majority against him.
– Johann Wolfgang von Goethe.

> Your goal is to deeply consider and think about your investments, and
> eventually be right. This often means not making the same nifty-popular-
> trendy-fashionable investments that your friends are making or that the
> financial media is fawning over.

In fact, you can sometimes take it as a positive sign when the average person
dismisses your investment ideas.

When a true genius appears in the world, you may know him by
this sign, that the dunces are all in confederacy against him.
– Jonathan Swift.

When everyone is against you, it means that you are absolutely wrong,
or absolutely right. – Albert Guinon.

But beware when even unconventional, non-conformist, independent thinkers
might also disagree with you.

The race is not always to the swift, nor the battle to the strong—but that's
the way to bet. – Damon Runyon.

Just because everyone says it's raining outside is no reason not to take an
umbrella. – François D. Sicart.

I'm an optimist, but I'm an optimist who carries a raincoat.
– Harold Wilson.

> Do be a contrarian, but don't get completely carried away.

MAKE FEWER BETS, SAFER BETS, BIGGER BETS

Be more patient. Wait until you think you have discovered something that others
have not yet noticed.

An investor is better off doing nothing until he sees money over in the
corner just waiting to be picked up. Most investors make the mistake of
believing they always have to be doing something, investing their idle
cash. In fact, the worst thing that happens to many is to make big money
on an investment. They are so flushed, excited, and triumphant that they
say to themselves, "Okay let me find another one!" – Jim Rogers.

Thus it is that in war the victorious strategist only seeks battle after the victory has been won, whereas he who is destined to defeat first fights and afterwards looks for victory. – Sun-Tzu.

Wait for the fat pitch or nearly sure thing.

Being selective is especially important when starting out because you do not have enough capital to waste on mediocre ideas.

I've also felt that a shortage of capital is not necessarily a bad thing. It forces you to make choices as to what businesses you engage in and don't engage in. Any business that has all the capital it could possibly need is in trouble, because nobody is there making choices as to how it uses its capital. – John Whitehead.

And even when you do have a lot of capital, being selective is still the better, more profitable approach.

If you took our top fifteen decisions out, we'd have a pretty average record. It wasn't hyperactivity, but a hell of a lot of patience. You stuck to your principles and when opportunities came along, you pounced on them with vigor. – Charles Munger.

Around here I would say that if our predictions have been a little better than other people's, it's because we've tried to make fewer of them. – Charles Munger.

And when you find a better-than-average opportunity, and fully examine it and it still holds up, then give it a decent-sized allocation.

Most people invest 100% of their capital in hope of a 10% return. I prefer to wait until I can invest 10% of my capital for a 100% return. – Doug Casey.

If you have a highly-diversified portfolio, then you will most likely get a market return, which over long periods of time is thought to be somewhere around 10% (nominal). This is fine for protecting your purchasing power, but not for growing your wealth. To grow your wealth, you must find those truly attractive opportunities, and then make larger bets on them.

Really think it through. Really critique it. Ask your critical friends. Then, if it still looks good, bet enough to matter.

When you're absolutely certain you're right, no trade is too big. And the bigger your gains in a year, the more aggressive you can be. – George Soros.

Concentration is my motto—first honesty, then industry, then concentration. - Andrew Carnegie.

Concentration; put all your eggs in one basket, and watch that basket. - Andrew Carnegie.

Nobody has ever bet enough on the winning horse. - unknown.

Once you've done all the work to finally find something good, you should invest enough to matter. Not so much that, if you lose it, it will kill you, and yet enough so that if you make at least a 50% or 100% return, it will make a meaningful difference to your wealth.

Avoid "rebalancing" as this is mostly a waste of time and potential gains.

To suggest that this investor should sell off portions of his most successful investments simply because they have come to dominate this portfolio is akin to suggesting that the Bulls trade Michael Jordan because he has become so important to the team. - Warren E. Buffett.

Our favorite holding period is forever. We are just the opposite of those who hurry to sell and book profits when companies perform well but who tenaciously hang on to businesses that disappoint. Peter Lynch aptly likens such behavior to cutting the flowers and watering the weeds. - Warren E. Buffett.

If you are going to sell something, it should be because it is nearing a full valuation and you do not see further growth anytime soon. As much as you want to be a pig when it starts to go up, you do not want to miss your window of opportunity to sell once it approaches full value.

If you are right, and if you stick with it, be prepared for the following to regularly occur.

First they ignore you, then they laugh at you, then they fight you, then you win. - Mahatma Gandhi.

All truth passes through three stages. First, it is ridiculed. Second, it is violently opposed. Third, it is accepted as being self-evident. - Arthur Schopenhauer.

Not everyone will immediately recognize the wisdom of your investment. You should be prepared for this and not care what others think.

In summary:

It's not given to human beings to have such talent that they can just know everything about everything all the time. But it is given to human beings

*who work hard at it—who look and sift the world for a mispriced bet—
that they can occasionally find one. And the wise ones bet heavily when
the world offers them that opportunity. They bet big when they have the
odds. And the rest of the time, they don't. It's just that simple.
– Charles Munger, speech at USC Business School, 1994.*

> Patiently keep looking until you think you have found a nearly sure thing,
> then bet a reasonable amount.

UNCERTAINTY IN PROBABILITIES, FORECASTS, HEDGES

It is useful to know what the odds are, but always remember that any one bet can
always go either way.

Probability is the very guide of life. – Cicero.

*I know now that there is no one thing that is true—it is all true.
– Ernest Hemingway.*

Forecasts too are useful, but always remember that they are, ultimately, little
more than just a guess.

Forecasts can be injurious to your wealth. – Dean LeBaron.

*Be sensitive to the subtle differences between intuition and "into-
wishing." – Ed Seykota.*

Even if you are right about the future direction of things, it can always take longer
to get there than you might have originally expected.

*It is often much easier to tell what will happen to the price of a stock than
how much time will elapse before it happens. – Philip A. Fisher.*

*Wall Street's graveyards are filled with men who were right too soon.
– William Hamilton.*

*The market always does what it's supposed to do—but never when.
– unknown.*

And even if your stock idea should have been right or if your investment manager's
picks should have been successful, the rest of the world could have irrationally
gone elsewhere.

*There is nothing so disastrous as a rational investment policy in an
irrational world. – John Maynard Keynes.*

> Always remember that humans are irrational, and they will often make
> lousy long-term choices in order to avoid short-term inconvenience.

If stock values are based on the anticipation of future earnings, then to be a successful investor, beforehand you must have anticipated how others today will anticipate these future earnings.

Successful investing is anticipating the anticipations of others.
– John Maynard Keynes.

You should make educated bets—not a shopping cart full of "maybe one of these will work" hopes.

Diversification is a protection against ignorance. [It] makes very little sense for those who know what they're doing. – Warren E. Buffett.

[Regarding diversification:] One buys two of everything and in the end owns a zoo. – Warren E. Buffett.

Obsession with broad diversification is the sure road to mediocrity. Most people who own more than two mutual funds are over-diversified.
– John Neff.

> Note: Neff was speaking in an age during which most mutual funds had pretty broad mandates and could invest in almost anything. So while this comment remains valid for such a classic fund, it is not meant to include today's sometimes very narrowly-focused funds, which I feel the average investor should mostly avoid.

There is little point in hedging your bets. A perfect hedge is impossible anyway. And if you have done your homework and understand the bet you are making, then why attempt to hedge it? Such investor behavior does not make sense, costs money and effort, does not work in the long run, and contributes to a culture of risk where you erroneously think you are protected.

The only perfect hedge is in a Japanese garden. – Eugene Rotberg.

There is no sure thing, no easy money.

There is only one thing about which I am certain, and that is that there is very little about which one can be certain. – W. Somerset Maugham.

The only certainty is that there is no certainty. – Robert Rubin.

Never does nature say one thing and wisdom another. – Juvenal.

> There is no perpetual-motion machine. A "guaranteed investment" is an oxymoron because if there is no risk then you are not making an investment and surely the return must be very low or negligible. Human nature and motivation do not change.

A Few Notes on Investing Styles

Avoid those who make their decisions based purely on chart patterns (also known as "technicians," "technical analysts," "chartists," etc.).

> *The central proposition of charting is absolutely false, and investors who follow its precepts will accomplish nothing but increasing substantially the brokerage charges they pay. There has been a remarkable uniformity in the conclusions of studies done on all forms of technical analysis. Not one has consistently outperformed the placebo of a buy-and-hold strategy. – Burton Malkiel,* A Random Walk Down Wall Street.

> If technical analysis worked so well, then everyone would be doing it.

Investment managers who look for "growth" companies are acceptable as long as the investment manager is trying to find still-small companies not yet discovered, and she is not paying full price for already-growing companies everyone already knows about.

> *It is anticipation of growth rather than growth itself that makes for lively speculation and big profits in the so-called growth stocks. – Nicolas Darvas.*

> *Buy growth, but don't pay for it. – Martin Whitman.*

> Note: this is usually referred to as GARP investing (i.e., Growth at a Reasonable Price).

Beware picking investment managers (or individual mutual funds) with too narrow a focus. It is unlikely that your picks would ever be much in sync with the market. Instead, find yourself a few good generalist managers, as opposed to a selection of narrow specialists.

> *An investor cannot earn superior profits from stocks simply by committing to a specific category or style. He can earn them only by carefully evaluating facts and continuously exercising discipline. – Warren E. Buffett.*

> *The only big loss for the investment management profession over these years has been the disappearance of the balanced manager. The stylish cafeteria of specialized managers that we see today leads to a mishmash of risks and covariances that most clients fail to understand. – Peter L. Bernstein.*

> A further problem with this approach lies with the structure of many industry segments. Since many are dominated by only a few companies, the narrow fund will most often find itself dominated by these companies.

So the investor will find themselves paying a fund management fee, for results that could be largely achieved by independently buying a few of the larger segment companies.

Look for the investment manager (or mutual fund manager) who likes things that are currently out of favor and unpopular.

What has been in fashion once, will come into fashion again.
– Japanese proverb.

If we assume that it is the habit of the market to overvalue common stocks which have been showing excellent growth or are glamorous for some other reason, it is logical to expect that it will undervalue— relatively, at least—companies that are out of favor because of unsatisfactory developments of a temporary nature. This may be set down as a fundamental law of the stock market, and it suggests an investment approach that should be both conservative and promising.
– Benjamin Graham.

Read investment manager and fund manager letters. Look for those who speak of wanting to be at odds with the herd.

And by all means favor the investment (or fund) manager who practices some form of "value" investing.

All intelligent investing is value investing—acquiring more than you are paying for. – Charles Munger.

I have seen no trend towards value investing in the 35 years I've practiced it. There seems to be some perverse human characteristic that likes to make easy things difficult. – Warren E. Buffett.

Value investors: People who place a very high value on having the last laugh. In exchange for the privilege, they have missed out on a lot of laughs in between. – Michael Lewis, The New New Thing.

We are normally put in the category called "value investors". This has always surprised me a bit, because it seems to imply [the existence] of another category called "non-value investors." – Robert G. Kirby.

The fellow who can only see a week ahead is always the popular fellow, for he is looking with the crowd. But the one who can see years ahead, he has a telescope but he can't make anybody believe he has it.
– Will Rogers.

Value (like beauty) is in the eye of the beholder. – Dean LeBaron.

Again: review the fund manager letters. Anyone discussing value and contrarian concepts is probably taking the right investment approach.

PART 6
Protecting Your Wealth

Always Be Wary of Yourself

Sometimes investors can be their own worst enemy. This is usually due to investors not recognizing or respecting their own weaknesses. This can range from "I know I am a horrible judge of financial matters, and therefore should let a professional invest for me" to "I have a weakness for sexy, trendy stocks, even though I usually get burned." Be aware, then beware, your weaknesses.

> *Keep a watchful eye over yourself as if you were your own enemy; for you cannot learn to govern yourself, unless you first learn to govern your own passions and obey the dictates of your conscience. – Kahlil Gilbran.*

> *To win, you must understand the game, you must understand the players, and above all you must understand yourself. – unknown.*

> *The investor's chief problem—and even his worst enemy—is likely to be himself. – Benjamin Graham.*

Beware Success

Current success does not entitle you to continued success.

> *It is very easy to get comfortable in a position of leadership, to believe that you've got all the answers, especially when you begin to enjoy some success. People start telling you that you're the smartest one around. But if you believe them, you're just the dumbest one around. That's one of the reasons it's extremely difficult to stay at the top—because once you get there, it is so easy to stop listening and learning. – John Wooden.*

Success or fame in other fields does not entitle you to success in investing.

> *With fame I become more and more stupid, which of course is a very common phenomenon. – Albert Einstein.*

> *The trouble with most of us is that we would rather be ruined by praise than saved by criticism. – Norman Vincent Peale.*

> *Fortune does not change men; it unmasks them. – Suzanne Necker.*

> A note for the famous actors, rock stars, sports figures, and other kings and queens of popular culture: stories of such people losing their fortunes are as old as the hills. When surrounded with your entourage telling you how great you are, it becomes hard to remember that when it comes to investing you might not be that great, and you would be better off delegating to a professional.

A good coping tactic is to always retain some humility and doubt.

When many people respect you, you must feel you are the lowest, so you will not develop prejudice or arrogance. – Tibetan proverb.

Great men suffer hours of depression through introspection and self-doubt. That is why they are great. That is why you will find modesty and humility the characteristics of such men. – Bruce Barton.

Both on the way up, and on the way down.

You're never as good as everyone tells you when you win, and you're never as bad as they say when you lose. – Lou Holtz.

Still, once you are no longer a neophyte, you should have a little confidence in yourself.

If I have lost confidence in myself, I have the universe against me. – Ralph Waldo Emerson.

Just never too much confidence.

There's only a razor's edge between self-confidence and hubris. – Jack Welch.

In general, pride is at the bottom of all great mistakes. – John Ruskin, Modern Painters.

The true way to be deceived is to think oneself more clever than others. – François, duc de La Rochefoucauld.

The greatest of all faults, I should say, is to be conscious of none. – Thomas Carlyle.

It is unwise to be too sure of one's own wisdom. – Gandhi.

> Be confident because you did your homework, not because you got the last investment idea right.

Because making that big mistake is always possible.

He is always right who suspects that he makes mistakes. – Spanish proverb.

My biggest error? Something that is to happen yet. – Ayrton Senna. [Famous race car driver; subsequently killed in a crash.—Ed.]

Winning can make folks confident... or it can make them cautious. – Louis L'Amour, The Sky-Liners.

So even when you've almost reached success, almost cashed out that winning investment, remain cautious. Remain vigilant. Do not lose everything because you did not bother to check that one last thing.

> *People in their handlings of affairs often fail when they are about to succeed. If one remains as careful at the end as he was at the beginning, there will be no failure. – Lao Tzu.*

KNOW YOUR WEAKNESSES

Know your own mental quirks, to better avoid them or compensate for them.

> *If you want to avoid irrationality, it helps to understand the quirks in your own mental wiring, and then you can take appropriate precautions. – Charles Munger.*

> *If you want to be strong, know your weaknesses. – German proverb.*

This requires some introspection, though not too much.

> *Know thyself. – inscription at temple of Apollo at Delphi.*

> *Only the shallow know themselves. – Oscar Wilde.*

> *Observe all men, thyself most. – Benjamin Franklin.*

Most importantly, never think of yourself as infallible.

> *To have doubted one's own first principles is the mark of a civilized man. – Oliver Wendell Holmes, Jr.*

> *The wise person questions himself, the fool others. – Henri Arnold.*

> *The cleverest of all, in my opinion, is the man who calls himself a fool at least once a month. – Fyodor M. Dostoyevsky.*

> *A very popular error—having the courage of one's convictions: Rather it is a matter of having the courage for an attack upon one's convictions. – Friedrich W. Nietzsche.*

It is precisely when we think we have a pretty theory, or a theory that suits our aesthetics or worldview, that we are apt to fall in love with the theory and forget to question the theory.

> *Nothing is easier than self-deceit. For what each man wishes, that he also believes to be true. – Demosthenes.*

> *Lying to ourselves is more deeply ingrained than lying to others. – Fyodor M. Dostoyevsky.*

> *Who had deceived thee so often as thyself? – Benjamin Franklin.*

We are never deceived; we deceive ourselves.
– Johann Wolfgang von Goethe.

> The worst thing about being deceived is that it requires some abetting by one's self—whether through laziness to check facts or depending on hope rather than probabilities.

After all, some aspect of your worldview could well be fallacious and thereby taint your investment ideas and judgment. Keep an open point of view.

We cling to our own point of view, as though everything depended on it. Yet our opinions have no permanence; like autumn and winter, they gradually fade away. – Chuang Tzu.

> Don't fall in love with your ideas.

What the human being is best at doing is interpreting all new information so that their prior conclusions remain intact.
– Warren E. Buffett.

> Don't shield your ideas from reality.

Every man takes the limits of his own field of vision for the limits of the world. – Arthur Schopenhauer.

Do not condemn the judgment of another because it differs from your own. You may both be wrong. – Dandemis.

There are three truths: my truth, your truth, and the truth.
– Chinese proverb.

Show me a man who claims he is objective and I'll show you a man with illusions. – Henry R. Luce.

> Everyone has quirks. Know yours and don't let them interfere with your investments.

We all have many erroneous ideas. Over time, make it your goal to slowly correct or minimize these.

I do not believe today everything I believed yesterday; I wonder will I believe tomorrow everything I believed today? – Matthew Arnold.

All men are frauds. The only difference between them is that some admit it. I myself deny it. – H. L. Mencken.

The one important thing I've learned over the years is the difference between taking one's work seriously and one's self seriously. The first is imperative; the second is disastrous. – Margo Fonteyn.

Everyone is a damn fool for at least five minutes every day. Wisdom consists in not exceeding the limit. – Elbert Hubbard.

You will always make mistakes. Just recognize that fact and try to catch the mistakes.

Always Be Wary of Others

If you have money, then you have something to lose. Losses can come from outright theft and fraud or from the well-intentioned bumbler who gets you to invest in some hair-brained scheme doomed to failure. In both cases, the only ways to protect yourself are to always consider why and how you might be at risk, and to exercise some skepticism and critical thinking in all matters.

> *Half the world is composed of idiots, the other half of people clever enough to take indecent advantage of them. – Walter Kerr.*

> *I hate mankind, for I think myself one of the best of them, and I know how bad I am. – Joseph Baretti, quoted by James Boswell, 1766.*

Everyone Is Indeed Out to Scam You

In regard to life in general:

> *A paranoid man is a man who knows a little about what's going on. – William S. Burroughs.*

> *There are a terrible lot of lies going around the world, and the worst of it is half of them are true. – Winston Churchill.*

> *The man who is a pessimist before 48 knows too much; if he is an optimist after it, he knows too little. – Mark Twain.*

> Do not be naïve about life.

As regards investing, Wall Street, and the financial markets:

> *Wall Street never changes. The pockets change, the suckers change, the stocks change, but Wall Street never changes, because human nature never changes. – Jesse Livermore.*

> *The one bit of friendly advice which I didn't hear from my friendly broker was: "Do nothing. Get out of the market." That would be too much to expect. Brokers and their account executives are, like casino operators and croupiers, necessarily in business to make money. And on Wall Street, that means commissions. – Nicolas Darvas.*

> *The figural sculptures on the façade of the New York Stock Exchange are titled "Integrity Protecting the Works of Man." – Charles R. Morris,* The Trillion Dollar Meltdown.

> Do not be naïve about investing.

And especially with regard to anything else involving money:

Where large sums of money are concerned, it is advisable to trust nobody.
– Agatha Christie, Endless Night.

When a fellow says it hain't the money but the principle o' the thing,
it's th' money. – Frank McKinney "Kin" Hubbard, Hoss Sense and
Nonsense.

When it is a question of money, everybody is of the same religion.
– Voltaire.

The buyer needs a hundred eyes, the seller not one. – George Herbert.

Business is a combination of war and sport. – André Maurois.

And do not be naïve about money.

Therefore, to protect your wealth:

Every man should have a built-in automatic crap detector operating
inside him. – Ernest Hemingway.

Do not allow yourselves to be deceived: Great Minds are Skeptical.
– Friedrich W. Nietzsche.

Exercise healthy skepticism.

KNOW THEIR MOTIVES AND STRATEGIES

Always consider the other person's possible motivations and conflicts of interest.

No man does anything from a single motive. – Samuel Taylor Coleridge.

A man always has two reasons for the things he does—a good reason and
the real reason. – J. P. Morgan.

What people say, what people do, and what they say they do are entirely
different things. – Margaret Meade.

Look at the means which a man employs, consider his motives, observe
his pleasures. A man simply cannot conceal himself! – Confucius.

Let it be your constant method to look into the design of people's actions,
and see what they would be at, as often as it is practicable; and to make
this custom the more significant, practice it first upon yourself.
– Marcus Aurelius.

Looking for how the other person might make money or benefit from the
deal is usually a good place to start.

Beware the person who paints too rosy a picture.

The man who promises everything is sure to fulfill nothing, and everyone who promises too much is in danger of using evil means in order to carry out his promises, and is already on the road to perdition. - Carl Jung.

Their words correspond to their actions, and their actions correspond to their words. Are not the best people genuine? - Confucius.

In great affairs men show themselves as they wish to be seen; in small things they show themselves as they are. - Sébastien-Roch Nicolas, aka Chamfort.

I have seldom known anyone who deserted truth in trifles that could be trusted in matters of importance. - William Paley.

> If someone is lying about, or exaggerating, the small inconsequential stuff then there's a good chance they are also lying about, or exaggerating, the bigger important stuff (but have not yet been caught). Do not make an investment for which you cannot rely on the source—this is simply too risky.

For example, company management (or investor-relations people) who tout their efforts and sacrifice for the hallowed shareholder.

Chief executives, who themselves own few shares of their companies, have no more feeling for the average stockholder than they do for baboons in Africa. - T. Boone Pickens.

How do you tell a CEO is lying? Their lips are moving. - variation on an old one-liner.

> Part of the CEO's job is to make investors feel good about the company. To this end, many of them will tell you anything they think you want to hear.

Or the person with nothing at stake, no skin in the game.

Be wary of the man who urges an action in which he himself incurs no risk. - Joaquín Setantí.

> Keep note of this when buying a stock, investing in a mutual fund, or hiring an investment manager. Ideally, you want someone with a material amount of their own personal money invested in the same things.

Or the person facing difficulties.

Never trust the advice of a man in difficulties. - Aesop.

Or the flatterer.

> *Be advised that all flatterers live at the expense of those who listen to them. – Jean de La Fontaine.*

> *Flatterers look like friends, as wolves look like dogs – George Chapman.*

Or the paragon of virtue.

> *Those who are believed to be most abject and humble are usually most ambitious and envious. – Spinoza.*

> *Everyone is a moon, and has a dark side which he never shows to anybody. – Mark Twain.*

> *A man is not honest simply because he never had a chance to steal. – Russian proverb.*

Or the deal presented as completely safe (there is no such thing).

> *There is no such uncertainty as a sure thing. – Robert Burns.*

> *If you want a guarantee, buy a toaster. – Clint Eastwood.*

> *There is no free lunch. – Milton Friedman.*

> *If it sounds too good to be true, it is. – unknown.*

> There are no sure things.

Some Coping Techniques

Always figure out who might benefit from the investment you are being offered.

> *Follow the money. – Deep Throat character,* All The President's Men, *William Goldman, 1976, film.*

> > It is perfectly OK for others to make a little money by providing you with investment ideas and services, but it is equally necessary for you to know where and how their profit is earned. After all, since it is coming out of your pocket, you need to make sure you are getting service, value, and a fair price in return.

Always, always, always read the fine print.

> *The big print giveth, and the fine print taketh away. – F. J. Sheen.*

> > For example, please do start by reading the very important (for me!) legal disclaimers in the back of this very book.

> *Nothing in fine print is ever good news. – Andy Rooney.*

Often the bad news, or the real risk, is buried somewhere and your attention is distracted away.

Language is a tool for concealing the truth. - George Carlin.

A memorandum is written not to inform the reader but to protect the writer. - Dean Acheson.

Worry more about how someone might be wrong than about how they might be right.

To succeed in this world, it is much more necessary to possess the penetration to discern who is a fool than to discover who is a clever man. - Charles Maurice de Talleyrand.

In modern business it is not the crook who is to be feared most, it is the honest man who doesn't know what he is doing. - William Wordsworth.

Just because someone is well-meaning and sincere does not mean they are wise.

Take any official proclamation with a large grain of doubt.

Never believe anything until it has been officially denied. - Claud Cockburn.

Deny it! - sign (purportedly) in the executive washroom of a major oil company.

Documents can lie, and rumors can tell the truth. - Donald Rayfield, Stalin and His Hangmen.

Affairs are rarely straightforward, especially when large sums of money are involved.

Focus on avoiding obvious mistakes and scams, rather than chasing big jackpots.

The first point of wisdom is to discern that which is false; the second to know that which is true. - Lactanius.

It is remarkable how much long-term advantage people like us have gotten by trying to be consistently not-stupid, instead of trying to be very intelligent. There must be some wisdom in the folk saying: "It's the strong swimmers who drown." - Charles Munger.

Performance-wise, avoiding mistakes is more important than finding home runs. Remember Rule #1: Never lose money. Rule #2: See Rule #1.

Nothing is safe that does not show it can bear discussion and publicity. - Lord Acton.

Once someone has been caught in an intentional lie, you can no longer trust them in anything.

There's not much ivory in a rat's mouth. – Chinese Proverb.

A single lie destroys a whole reputation for integrity. – Baltasar Gracián.

There is no such thing as a minor lapse of integrity. – Tom Peters.

Falsum in uno, falsum in omnibus. (False in one thing, false in everything). – source unknown, used in legal doctrine.

Many foxes grow grey, but few grow good. – Benjamin Franklin.

What upsets me is not that you lied to me, but that from now on I can no longer believe you. – Friedrich W. Nietzsche.

> If the person(s) in charge of an investment opportunity are disreputable, have prior issues, or simply do not "smell right," then you should pass. In cases like this, there is a good chance your intuition is right. The world is full of other investment opportunities, and you lose nothing (except the risk of losing everything) by passing on this one.

Once a company or industry or geography has gone bad, stay away.

There's small choice in rotten apples. – William Shakespeare.

One bad apple spoils the bunch. – Proverb.

There is never just one cockroach in the kitchen. – Warren E. Buffett.

> Occasionally, something might start to smell bad. It could be within a single company where cutting corners now seems to be accepted. Or it could occur in a given industry, where perhaps a once-attractive field now has too many late-to-the-party flimflam artists. Or, it could focus on a geographic area, where perhaps one country's politics ensure that its public companies are no longer masters of their own fate. In any case, this means that sometimes it is simply too difficult (and risky) to try to separate the wheat from the chaff, or the one or two good investments from the many bad ones. Move on to another group of investment ideas.

Beware seeming honesty.

If we suspect that a man is lying, we should pretend to believe him; for then he becomes bold and assured, lies more vigorously, and is unmasked. – Arthur Schopenhauer.

I have known a vast quantity of nonsense talked about bad men not looking you in the face. Do not trust that conventional idea. Dishonesty

will stare honesty out of countenance, any day in the week, if there is
anything to be got by it. – Charles Dickens.

Many of the most successful fraudsters were successful for so long precisely because their victims got the impression that they were the very paragons of honesty and virtue. Do not rely only on these impressions.

Beware excessive complexity.

The study of money, above all other fields in economics is one in which
complexity is used to disguise truth or to evade truth, not to reveal it.
– John Kenneth Galbraith.

The longer the explanation, the bigger the lie. – Chinese proverb.

If the latest "investment opportunity" pitched to you sounds a little "off," just keep listening for a little longer. Or if a financial statement seems slightly wrong, be quiet, but check the next one twice as carefully. Eventually, the fraudster will show his hand.

Beware fancy investment vehicles, complicated partnerships, exclusive clubs and the like.

If venture capital involved no risk, it would be called "sure-thing capital."
– unknown.

Hedge funds remind me of the Groucho Marx line about clubs. The ones
that will take your money may not be the ones you want to invest with.
– Shelby White.

Complicated structures only obfuscate the investor (and the tax man). Likewise, exclusivity has been used as a shield to discourage investors from asking questions.

Be aware of psychology, motivations, and why people do things.

It is just as important to have studied men, as to have studied books.
– Baltasar Gracián.

Be aware of simple human nature, motivations, and patterns. Read history, read biography. These things are always true and will always be repeated.

Be aware of who the person in question associates with and where the person has worked in the past.

When the character of a man is not clear to you, look at his friends.
– Japanese proverb.

And always beware appearances.

> *Things are not always what they seem; the first appearance deceives many: the intelligence of a few perceives what has been carefully hidden.*
> *– Phaedrus.*

> *In monetary matters, appearances are deceiving; the important relationships are often precisely the reverse of those that strike the eye.*
> *– Milton Friedman.*

> *At all times, look at the thing itself—the thing behind the appearance.*
> *– Marcus Aurelius.*

> *The wise man never trusts in appearance. – Confucius.*

> *Never assume the obvious is true. – William Safire.*

Look for companies and managers with a history of behaving honorably.

> *It is not the oath that makes us believe the man, but the man the oath.*
> *– Aeschylus.*

> *Honor is a harder master than the law. – Mark Twain.*

>> Because dealing with honorable people will protect you. The law, while it may deter some crooks and perhaps eventually punish others, is powerless to return to you money that your crook has long since spent. (For more on fraud detection, read the next section.)

And stay true to your own moral compass.

> *If you don't stand for something, you will fall for anything. – Malcolm X.*

> *Those who stand for nothing, fall for anything. – Alexander Hamilton.*

>> Have and maintain high standards.

On the Inability to Eradicate Fraud

No amount of prevention or legislation has ever had (or ever will have) a material effect on human gullibility or criminality. Fraud and fraudsters will always be out there—beware!

BECAUSE FOOLS EXIST

There is an endlessly renewing supply of potential victims.

There's a sucker born every minute. – various, including P. T. Barnum.

Think about how stupid the average person is. And then realize that half of them are stupider than that. – George Carlin.

*You can fool too many of the people too much of the time.
– James Thurber.*

And of immoral people willing to take advantage.

Tricks and treachery are the practice of fools, that do not have brains enough to be honest. – Benjamin Franklin.

It is morally wrong to allow a sucker to keep his money. – W. C. Fields.

Thus the two will meet, and fraud will inevitably occur.

*You can fool all the people some of the time, and some of the people all the time, but you cannot fool all the people all the time.
– Abraham Lincoln.*

There must be a vast fund of stupidity in human nature, else men would not be caught as they are, a thousand times over, by the same snare; and while they yet remember their past misfortunes, go on to court and encourage the causes to which they were owing, and which will again produce them. – Cato.

And not only in small matters of investments—also in large matters of national importance, or worse.

The great enemy of the truth is very often not the lie—deliberate, contrived and dishonest—but the myth—persistent, persuasive and unrealistic. – John F. Kennedy, Yale commencement address, 1962.

*The greater the lie, the greater the chance that it will be believed.
– Adolf Hitler.*

As long as people believe in absurdities they will continue to commit atrocities. – Voltaire.

Thus may poor fools believe false teachers. – William Shakespeare.

> People are always looking for someone to tell them that everything will be OK, that the problem will go away, or that there is a simple solution. Unfortunately, the world remains complex.

Do not think you might be immune. Everyone has some element of wishful thinking or is gullible in some regard, and is thus vulnerable to fraudulent schemes arising from those directions.

So careless are most people in the search for truth; they are more inclined to accept the first story that comes to hand. – Thucydides.

Who is ready to believe, is easy to deceive. – German proverb.

All people are most credulous when they are most happy.
– Walter Bagehot.

We are inclined to believe those whom we do not know because they have never deceived us. – Dr. Samuel Johnson.

A man that hath the patience to go by steps may deceive one much wiser than himself. – Marquis of Halifax.

Everything happens to everybody sooner or later if there is time enough.
– George Bernard Shaw.

> Beware your own inevitable moment of weakness.

AND BECAUSE FRAUD IS NOT PREVENTABLE

Creating new laws against new frauds will never deter all fraudsters.

Good people do not need laws to tell them to act responsibly, while bad people will find a way around the laws. – Plato.

> A recent and surely classic example is the Bernard Madoff fund fraud. What he did was clearly illegal; his ability to perpetrate it was not from a lack of laws, but from a failure of enforcement and regulation, exacerbated by the inclination of investors (and even counterparties and regulators) to trust a leading industry figure.

When men are pure, laws are useless; when men are corrupt, laws are broken. – Benjamin Disraeli.

Nothing is illegal if one hundred businessmen decide to do it, and that's true anywhere in the world. - Andrew Young.

Recent examples as of this writing would include the mortgage "robo-signing" frauds and the failure by commodity firms to protect supposedly "safe" customer money (e.g., the MF Global bankruptcy).

The first thing we do, let's kill all the lawyers. - William Shakespeare, Henry VI.

Laws cannot prevent illegal behavior. Contracts cannot prevent your counterparty from acting against you. Eventual legal remedies can cost a lot of money, drag on forever, and perhaps not even be worth pursuing.

Laws and safeguards do not make people any smarter about detecting fraud.

The ultimate result of shielding men from the effect of folly is to fill the world with fools. - Herbert Spencer.

Life is never fair, and perhaps it is a good thing for most of us that it is not. - Oscar Wilde.

Indeed, making people think they are safe only makes them that much more gullible, because they then think something bad cannot happen. Arguably, most of our learning comes from negative experiences—in this context, from losing real money.

The legislators and regulators will always have amongst their number the corruptible or the incompetent placed there for political patronage.

Quis custodiet ipsos Custodes? (Who is to guard the guards themselves?). - Juvenal, The Satires.

And good times often hide a fraud for a long period, during which people fail to question something that nonetheless does not "smell" right (e.g., again, Bernard Madoff's Ponzi scheme fraud).

Every great crisis reveals the excessive speculations of many houses which no one before suspected, and which commonly indeed had not begun or had not carried very far those speculations, till they were tempted by the daily rise of price and the surrounding fever. - Walter Bagehot, Lombard Street.

You only find out who is swimming naked when the tide goes out. - Warren E. Buffett, Berkshire Hathaway 2001 annual report.

Others may well be aware of the fraud or suspect something. But if they are benefiting from it, or if voicing their suspicions would "rock the boat," then people are often silent for a long time.

At the end of the day, as the investor, you are ultimately responsible for the safety of your money.

When they raid the whorehouse, they also seize the piano player.
– various, including Harry S. Truman.

> Do not invest in questionable enterprises, or with questionable people, lest you get caught up in the fallout of the scam once it is inevitably uncovered.

It is impossible for a man to be cheated by anyone but himself.
– Ralph Waldo Emerson.

> Most of the time, you probably could have avoided the fraud. Did you invest in something you didn't really understand? Not check history and references? Get greedy about a story that was truly too good to be true and ignore the warning signs? There will almost always be something you could have picked up on.

But do not completely give up.

You must not lose faith in humanity. Humanity is an ocean; if a few
drops of the ocean are dirty, the ocean does not become dirty.
– Mahatma Gandhi.

Laws control the lesser man. Right conduct controls the greater one.
– Chinese proverb.

> There will always be good and less-good people. It is your job to use your judgment to protect yourself.

A Warning About Debt

I offer a few brief words on debt and why you should only very carefully and hesitantly be a borrower or a lender. Mostly, this can only get you into trouble.

Never a borrower nor a lender be. – William Shakespeare, Hamlet.

…As a Borrower

What will it cost to buy that new house or car?

If you would know the value of money, go and try to borrow some.
– Benjamin Franklin.

The cost of borrowing is always the interest rate demanded, which varies.

Why does the cost of borrowing vary?

A banker is a fellow who lends you his umbrella when the sun is shining, but wants it back the minute it begins to rain. – Mark Twain.

When the well is dry, we learn the worth of water. – Benjamin Franklin.

Creditors have better memories than debtors. – Benjamin Franklin.

In a good economy when everyone has a job, debt is cheap because lenders believe they are more likely to be repaid. In difficult times, it is the reverse, because lenders want to be paid more for the risk they are taking.

Do not borrow for frivolous pleasures.

Debts are nowadays like children, begat in pleasure, but brought forth in pain. – Moliere.

Be not made a beggar by banqueting upon borrowing.
– Ecclesiasticus 18:33.

Better bread with water than cake with trouble. – Russian proverb.

Leasing that sports car when you can barely make the monthly payment is probably not a good idea.

Nor for more than you can safely and easily repay.

It is a fraud to accept what you cannot repay. – Publilius Syrus.

Credit is a system whereby a person who cannot pay gets another person who cannot pay to guarantee that he can pay. – Charles Dickens.

Buying a modest principal residence for your family, where you already have some savings and where your income can easily support the mortgage, is probably OK.

Nor to speculate with.

You can use leverage, and it's the only way a smart guy can go broke. If you do smart things and use leverage and do one wrong thing along the way, it could wipe you out, because anything times zero is zero.
– Warren E. Buffett.

Don't use margin. If you're smart, you don't have to borrow money to make money. If you're dumb, you may go broke. – Albert Hettinger.

A margin call is what alerts you to the fact that your life is going to hell and that you never should have gotten into the market when you did, let alone on margin. – Andrew Tobias.

A reminder that if you get a margin call you do not have the additional funds to cover, you will be unable to prevent your broker selling out your position. And even if the stock goes back up the next day, it's too late— that money is lost.

And preferably not from anyone you know.

Before borrowing money from a friend decide which you need most.
– American proverb.

It is very difficult to escape debt.

The only man who sticks closer to you in adversity than a friend is a creditor. – unknown.

A note on the difficulty of eliminating debt: according to the current (2013) personal bankruptcy code of the United States, credit card and educational loans cannot be eliminated. So even if you declare bankruptcy, you will still end up paying much of what little you still earn toward these debts. See the next point.

And it can end badly.

"Pray, sir," said Arthur, repeating his question, "what is this place?"
"This is the Marshalsea, sir."
"The debtors' prison?"
"Sir, the debtors' prison."
"I beg your pardon, but .. Can any one go in here?"
"Any one can go IN," replied the old man; plainly adding by the significance of his emphasis, "but it is not every one who can go out."
– Charles Dickens, Little Dorrit.

Debt is the slavery of the free. – Publilius Syrus.

...OR AS A LENDER

Beware lending money to people you know. It can create resentment, undesired entanglement, and the loss of friendship and good will.

A small debt produces a debtor; a large one, an enemy. – Publilius Syrus.

A little debt makes a debtor, but a great one an enemy. – Thomas Fuller, Gnomologia.

Great indebtedness does not make men grateful, but vengeful.
– Friedrich W. Nietzsche.

And if you absolutely must help someone out, then do it explicitly as a gift, with no expectation of repayment. See your accountant regarding how to make a "forgiving loan" that will not run afoul of various gift tax issues in various localities.

Beware investing in debt of all forms, especially government debt.

Then there is America's debt. It's like an astronomer's black hole, it is of such a magnitude and so complex. I think we will all go into the black hole—and I am sure that on the other side another light will come—but in the hole you will discover that the laws of physics are different.
– Yves Oltramare.

And this was before 2013 when certain US municipalities started to default on their debt—an action largely unheard of just a few years prior.

Navigating Inflation

Although inflation is not itemized in your monthly investment statement, it is the single most important issue an investor needs to consider and keep track of. Preserving your assets is nice. Getting a positive investment return is nicer. But if this return is outstripped by inflation, then you have just lost some of your purchasing power. And for someone trying to manage their wealth over the long term and preserve it for the next generation, maintaining (or increasing) your purchasing power is all you should ever really care about.

Every time history repeats itself the price goes up. – unknown.

The future, according to some scientists, will be exactly like the past, only far more expensive. – John Sladek.

Only the government can take perfectly good paper, cover it with perfectly good ink, and make the combination worthless.
– Milton Friedman.

A nickel ain't worth a dime anymore. – Yogi Berra.

The way money goes so fast these days, they should paint racing stripes on it. – Mark Russell.

WHAT IS INFLATION?

What is inflation?

Inflation is when you pay fifteen dollars for the ten-dollar haircut you used to get for five dollars when you had hair. – Sam Ewing.

People think of inflation as prices going up. It's not. It's the value of money going down. – Ron Muhlenkamp.

Inflation is the time when those who have saved for a rainy day get soaked. – unknown.

Prices do indeed go up (in nominal terms) but that is because the value of money has gone down. It's similar to when one currency declines in value against another, but here it's the currency declining in value against everything.

Why does inflation keep recurring, throughout history, in every country, to every currency?

The more you owe, the more it becomes attractive to devalue the currency in which the nation's debts are denominated. – Warren E. Buffett.

If there is one fact in finance more firmly fixed than another, it is the certainty that the unrestricted issue of paper currency culminates in disaster. – Charles Gordon.

The fundamental flaw in a fiat money system can be summed up as human nature. When the going gets rough, the rough start printing. – Richard Greene.

> For those new to the topic, "fiat money" means money not backed by, and exchangeable into, a fixed amount of gold (or silver or another hard asset)—like the present (2013) US dollar.

Or, more bluntly, why do governments allow inflation to persist?

By continuing the process of inflation, governments can confiscate, secretly and unobserved, an important part of the wealth of their citizens. – Vladimir I. Lenin.

Let me issue and control a nation's money and I care not who writes the laws. – Mayer Amschel Rothschild.

There is no subtler, no surer means of overturning the existing basis of society than to debauch the currency. The process engages all the hidden forces of economic law on the side of destruction, and does it in a manner which not one man in a million is able to diagnose. – John Maynard Keynes.

In 1976, Nobel laureate economist Friedrich Hayek wrote that with the exception only of the 200-year period of the gold standard (1714 to 1914 in Britain), practically all governments of history have used their exclusive power to issue money in order to defraud and plunder the people. According to Hayek's research, history proved two things: 1) that all representative governments eventually abuse their money-issuing privileges, which results in inflation; and 2) that people with access to various types of money always look for the most stable kind—usually gold or silver. Why should it be different this time around? – David Levenstein.

> For example, if the government owes you a fixed-amount pension and then doubles the money supply, then your fixed pension will have only half the purchasing power it used to have. The trick is that this usually takes place slowly, over a decade or more, so you hardly notice it happening—like the frog in boiling water anecdote.

How bad can it get?

The economics of disaster commence when the holders of money wealth revolt. It is as simple as that. The government has little or nothing to say or do about it...They do not fly flags or demonstrate in the streets to express their revolt; they simply get rid of their money...The duller the holders of money wealth are, the longer the government can go on storing up inflation but, by the same token, the more cataclysmic must the eventual dam burst be. The Germans [of the early 1920s] were among the dullest and most disciplined of all holders of money wealth, and this alone permitted the government to build up so huge a pool of unrealized inflation before the burst. - Jens O. Parsson, Dying of Money.

> This happened in 2012 when massive outflows of money from Mediterranean European states (from countries like Greece, Spain, Italy, Portugal, etc.) signaled investors' unwillingness to accept runaway inflation.

Why isn't this discussed more deeply in the popular press? Why don't people seem to know or care?

The few who understand the system will either be so interested in its profits or be so dependent upon its favors that there will be no opposition from that class, while on the other hand, the great body of people, mentally incapable of comprehending the tremendous advantage that capital derives from the system, will bear its burdens without complaint, and perhaps without even suspecting that the system is inimical to their interests. - The Rothschild brothers of London writing to associates in New York, 1863.

Is there any hope for my particular country?

The lesson of history is emphatically that irredeemable paper money results in monetary manipulation, business distrust, a speculative condition of trade, and all the evils which flow from these conditions. - Irving Fisher, The Purchasing Power of Money.

Irredeemable paper money has almost invariably proved a curse to the country employing it. - Irving Fisher, The Purchasing Power of Money.

Paper money eventually returns to its intrinsic value. - Voltaire.

> In other words, it's nothing but paper.

Don't fight the Fed. - old Wall Street proverb.

> Whatever a central bank chooses to do (usually to devalue the currency), there is little the investing class can do about it. Recognize which way interest rates and inflation are moving, and invest accordingly.

OWN COMMON STOCKS

Stocks, more than anything else and certainly over the long term, are your best bet to mitigate the effects of inflation and maintain your purchasing power.

No other investment alternative rivals common stocks as a way of accumulating wealth. Unless you're flat broke, reading this from your death bed, and have no heirs, there will be a time in your life when it will make sense to hold common stocks. – Michael O'Higgins.

In spite of crashes, depressions, wars, recessions, ten different presidential administrations, and numerous changes in skirt lengths, stocks in general have paid off fifteen times as well as corporate bonds, and well over thirty times better than Treasury bills. – Peter Lynch, One Up On Wall Street.

It is my belief that stocks will always outperform bonds on a long-term basis.

Try to buy good-quality companies.

Stocks are simple. All you do is buy shares in a great business for less than the business is intrinsically worth, with managers of the highest integrity and ability. Then you own those shares forever. – Warren E. Buffett.

It's far better to buy a wonderful company at a fair price than a fair company at a wonderful price, so why not invest your assets in the companies you really like? As Mae West said, "Too much of a good thing can be wonderful." – Warren E. Buffett.

You should forget the short term, and not worry about the economy or the direction of the market. Instead, buy a share of a company the way you buy a house: because you know all about it, and want to own it for a long time at that price. In fact, you should only buy what you would be happy to own in the absence of any market. – John Train.

It's straightforward. A good business is one for which there should be decent demand for the next 10 years, and not too much competition.

Ideally, buy good-quality companies when they are on sale.

Great investment opportunities come around when excellent companies are surrounded by unusual circumstances that cause the stock to be misappraised. – Warren E. Buffett.

I define a company as "on sale" when the company encounters a fixable problem that can be corrected or when the market (or herd) as a whole makes a gross error in judgment regarding the company's future.

When a corporation goes into the marketplace to buy back its own stock, it means management thinks the stock is undervalued. This is a smart time to buy. – Nancy Dunnan.

Not necessarily, and not always, but if you happen to see filings indicating that a few of the top executives at a firm are buying stock in the market, or exercising options and not selling, then yes, perhaps. If nothing else, it is a good indicator to take a closer look at that company's situation and prospects.

Look for those businesses, industries, and products that have a sustainable, long-term advantage, and that should see long-term growth.

The key to investing is not assessing how much an industry is going to affect society, or how much it will grow, but rather determining the competitive advantage of any given company and, above all, the durability of that advantage. – Warren E. Buffett.

Start with a growing market. Swim in a stream that becomes a river and ultimately an ocean. Be a leader in that market, not a follower, and constantly build the best products possible. – Robert Noyce.

You can't economize your way to profits; you've got to sell your way. – unknown.

A company that increases its profits merely by cutting expenses will eventually cut its way to death. Favor investments that increase their profits by increasing their revenues.

Growth stocks are a happy and haphazard category of investments which, curiously enough, have little or nothing to do with growth companies. Indeed, the term "growth stock" is meaningless; a growth stock can only be identified with hindsight—it is simply a stock which went way up. But the concept of "growth company" can be used to identify the most creative, most imaginative management groups; and if, in addition, their stocks are valued at a reasonable ratio to their increase in earnings power over time, the odds are favorable for appreciation in the future. – Peter L. Bernstein.

Don't buy the house; buy the neighborhood. – Russian proverb.

You can have a good, profitable company at a seemingly reasonable price—but if it is in a bad industry or is an incumbent in an industry that will shortly see radical change, then beware.

Or just buy a few good mutual funds.

The mutual fund is a wonderful invention for people who have neither the time nor the inclination to test their wits against the stock market, as well as for people with small amounts of money to invest who seek diversification. – Peter Lynch.

A mutual fund can do for you what you would do for yourself if you had sufficient time, training, and money to diversify, plus the temperament to stand back from your money and make rational decisions. – Venita Van Caspel.

Buying a mutual fund is almost like hiring a money manager—just look for an independent contrarian thinker, whose long-term historic results are good but do not mirror the broader market.

But, avoid index funds because they are probably too broad.

Index funds are an honest expression of incompetence. It's a vote for the inability to choose a good manager, so you put the money in an index fund. It's not saying I don't believe there is such a thing as a good manager. It's not saying I believe in efficient markets. – Barr Rosenberg.

If you want to outperform other people, you have got to hold something different from other people. If you want to outperform the market, the thing you mustn't hold is the market itself. – Anthony Bolton.

To be explicit, if you hold a broad index fund, such as an S&P 500 tracking fund or exchange traded fund (ETF), then your returns will almost certainly mirror the underlying index, or "the market itself," very closely.

Also, avoid hedge funds as these are often nothing special—and those that are good usually have too much fine print in their contracts for all but the most well-informed investors.

It's true that the best minds are drawn to the hedge fund business. But there are not as many great minds out there as there are hedge funds being started. – Antoine Berheim.

Hedge funds are a compensation scheme, not an asset class. – Paul Isaac.

This quotation refers to the still-current (2013) general fee structure of "2 & 20", or annually billing the client 2% of assets under management and paying 20% of any returns. This "compensation structure" is even more egregiously true of the fund-of-funds variety (which take an additional cut); thankfully these are now a bit on the wane.

OTHER ANTI-INFLATIONARY PRACTICES AND ASSETS

Always have an employable skill.

The best way to prepare for inflation is to be the best at what you do, leveraging your earning power. – Charles Munger.

In other words, always be able to get a job. Have a skill (or two) that will always be in demand. Or own a business providing a product or service for which there will always be demand.

Cash is no refuge from inflation, and should not typically constitute the bulk of your holdings. Even in "bubbly" periods you can usually find something, whether by betting against whatever the bubble may be in, or in just holding gold or land. So stay mostly invested.

Bankers know that history is inflationary and that money is the last thing a wise man will hoard. – Will & Ariel Durant.

The value of most currencies, including ours, is going to decline in purchasing power. I still believe, over a 10-year period, I would rather own stocks than cash. – Warren E. Buffett.

But remember, this is Buffett speaking. So when he says "stocks" what he really means are stocks that fit his definition of "value" (i.e., profitable businesses, where there will be long-term demand for the firm's goods or services and where the stock is not grossly overpriced). For a more complete understanding, read some of his excellent writings, and/or hire an investment adviser (or two) who adheres to a "value" investment style.

Land is usually a good long-term store of value.

Buy land. They're not making it anymore. – Will Rogers.

But avoid purchasing at the top of a real estate craze (e.g. Japan circa 1990, or North America and Europe circa 2006). You will recognize a craze if this is the only topic in the newspapers, on television, and at cocktail parties. A number of your acquaintances will also start training to become real estate brokers, or look into "flipping" houses. When this starts to occur, it is probably better to rent until the inevitable crash comes.

In Xanadu did Kubla Khan
A stately pleasure-dome decree:
Where Alph, the sacred river, ran
Through caverns measureless to man
Down to a sunless sea.
– Samuel Taylor Coleridge, Kubla Khan.

Waterfront property, as a specific example, is something they are hardly making any more of—and thus demand should usually be strong. Fifty years ago, cutting a new canal to create water access was allowed, but current environmental regulations no longer permit this. While developers can create any number of new housing developments inland, they cannot create any more nice houses on the nice beach right near the nice town. Therefore, those houses, if not bought at the heights of any period of real estate craziness, should be good long-term investments in terms of preserving value and purchasing power.

Bismarck's appetite for timberland was insatiable. His theory was that the price of land would gradually appreciate in line with population growth, or about two percentage points annually. His studies had convinced him that German forests would grow 2.75% a year, so that his real return for timberland would be around 4.75% per annum, because inflation at the time was virtually zero. If there was inflation, he was sure timberland and log prices would appreciate in line with the inflation. He thought that with very little risk, this was a spectacular compounding of wealth. As it turned out, Bismarck was absolutely right. – Barton Biggs, Hedgehogging.

As long as the sun shines, the trees will grow. – Jeremy Grantham.

Timberland can also be a good specific investment idea as explained above. The benefit is that you can just let it grow in years when prices are down. However, if you are to be an owner of timberland, you really need to be able to invest for the long haul (in decades), you must have enough to diversify (several locations, to avoid losing it all in one fire, for example), and you must arrange for management of the work (pruning, cutting, selling, re-planting, etc.).

Gold is also a good long-term store of value.

Gold and silver are money. Everything else is credit. – J. P. Morgan.

Gold is the money of kings; silver is the money of gentlemen; barter is the money of peasants; but debt is the money of slaves. – Norm Franz, Money and Wealth in the New Millennium.

Gold is not a financial asset to be compared with dot-com stocks or Miami condos and it is not a commodity like pork bellies or crude oil. It is the ultimate currency for the truly sophisticated wealth holder in a time of substantial unreserved credit promotion. – Paul Brodsky.

Gold is precious because it is scarce, compact, and impossible to dilute through the mischief of government. Its monetary qualities are conferred not by government decree but by the acclamation of history. Governments can write gold out of the script as legal tender but they are powerless to remove the metal's monetary qualities. – John C. Hathaway, October 31, 2006 market letter.

The modern mind dislikes gold because it blurts out the unpleasant truth. – Joseph Schumpeter.

Since earliest recorded history, a means of safeguarding some of your wealth involved keeping some of it in gold. Methinks neither the world nor humanity has changed that much.

The great thing to remember about gold is that it's the most valuable and most easily marketable commodity in the world. You can go to any town in the world, almost to any village, and hand over a piece of gold and get goods or services in exchange... And the next thing to remember...is that gold is virtually untraceable. Sovereigns have no serial numbers. If gold bars have Mint marks stamped on them the marks can be shaved off or the bar can be melted down and made into a new bar. That makes it almost impossible to check on the whereabouts of gold, or its origins, or its movements round the world. – Ian Fleming, Goldfinger.

You have the choice between trusting to the natural stability of gold, and the honesty and intelligence of the members of government. And with all due respect for those gentlemen, I advise you, as long as the capitalist system lasts, to vote for gold. – George Bernard Shaw.

[Discussing gold:] There's no sensible reason not to have some. If you're going to own a currency, if you don't—it's not sensible not to own gold. Now it depends on the amount of gold. But if you don't own, I don't know 10%, if you don't have that and then it depends on the world, then there's no sensible reason other than you don't know history and you don't know the economics of it. – Ray Dalio.

Always own some gold (some combination, or all, of jewelry, coins, bullion, mining stocks, gold and precious metal mutual funds). Remember that currencies go through long-term, generational cycles.

When the currency is strong, inflation is low, and no one has any interest in precious metals, buy some more gold. When inflation is high and currencies are devalued, trade some of your now-expensive gold for other real assets (like real estate) or stock in good companies.

Utilities, or companies that have a geographic monopoly on something we will always need, can be reasonable long-term stores of value.

Owning utilities is not a way to get rich; it's a way to stay rich.
– Warren E. Buffett.

Utilities are an old standby because they have a natural monopoly granted by the government, a rate (and built-in profit margin) practically guaranteed by the government, and customers who will consume their water and electricity with little sensitivity to the broader economy.

Beware anything perishable.

Never invest in anything that eats or needs painting. – Billy Rose.

Businesses in which the product needs to be fed (e.g., cattle), or can readily spoil (e.g., milk), or requires very high fixed-cost, constant maintenance regardless of use (e.g., a ski resort during a warm winter), are mostly investments for the professional investor to trade, and not a long-term holding for the novice investor who might not have the resources to keep the investment through a tough period.

Country Risk

Not all countries present the same investment opportunities and risks. When making investments in assets of different countries, you need to be especially concerned with their financial markets, respect for the law, and systems of government. These aspects can and will affect the performance of your investments.

> *Opinions alter, manners change, creeds rise and fall, but the moral laws are written on the table of eternity. – Lord Acton.*

> *Upon the sacredness of property civilization itself depends—the right of the laborer to his hundred dollars in the savings bank, and equally the legal right of the millionaire to his millions. – Andrew Carnegie*, Wealth, *from the* North American Review.

FAVOR FREER, OPEN SOCIETIES

Citizens of free societies will produce more because they are more assured of keeping the fruits of their production. This makes companies doing business in these locales more profitable and thus better holdings for investors.

> *Only those cities and countries that are free can achieve greatness... In free countries we also see wealth increase more rapidly, both that which results from the culture of the soil and that which is produced by industry and art; for everybody gladly multiplies those things, and seeks to acquire those goods the possession of which he can tranquilly enjoy.*
> *– Niccolò Machiavelli.*

And companies in countries with open trade policies tend to be stronger global competitors—and better investments—than companies hiding behind protectionist policies.

> *When every country turned to protect its national private interest, the world public interest went down the drain, and with it the private interests of all. – Charles Kindleberger,* The World in Depression, *1929-1939.*

Whereas societies that strangle productivity through corruption and red tape do not encourage entrepreneurs or beget profitable investment opportunities.

> *The more corrupt the state, the more numerous the laws. – Tacitus.*

> *If you have ten thousand regulations you destroy all respect for the law.*
> *– Winston Churchill.*

The more laws and order are made prominent, the more thieves and robbers there will be. – Lao Tzu.

The more complicated the forms assumed by civilization, the more restricted the freedom of the individual must become. – Benito Mussolini.

Consider the circumstances that fostered historic periods of great wealth creation:

- 1600s, Netherlands, greater legal structure and religious freedom lead to global commerce.
- 1800s, Europe and North America, free-market capitalism speeds the industrial revolution.
- Late 20th century, US West Coast, universities and flexible labor markets attracted technology risk-takers.

The ideal is probably somewhere in the middle, both in terms of regulations...

Without government a nation would instantly collapse. With too much government it takes considerably longer. – Cullen Hightower.

My reading of history convinces me that most bad government results from too much government. – Thomas Jefferson.

...And in terms of the level of freedom enjoyed.

When the people fear their government, there is tyranny; when the government fears the people, there is liberty. – Thomas Jefferson.

Therefore, look for countries that fall somewhere in the middle, both for your residences and your investments.

BEWARE DICTATORSHIPS, LACK OF RULE OF LAW, NO TRANSPARENCY

In arbitrary societies, you can expect your investment profits (and losses) to be arbitrary.

When virtue is lost, benevolence appears; when benevolence is lost, right conduct appears; when right conduct is lost, expedience appears. Expediency is the mere shadow of right and truth; it is the beginning of disorder. – Lao Tzu.

In a disorderly society, your investment profits will not depend on how savvy you are about picking a company to invest in. Rather, these profits will depend on whether the ruling class in that society continues to let your investment company keep those profits. Not a good way to invest for the long term.

You also cannot expect that such societies—however entrenched the rulers may appear—will last forever and thus these are not good places to store wealth.

A kingdom founded on injustice never lasts. - Lucius Annaeus Seneca.

Every observance of history inspires a confidence that we shall not go far wrong; that things will mend. - Ralph Waldo Emerson.

And the end, when it inevitably comes, can come very suddenly.

Civilization and Anarchy are only seven meals apart.
- Old Spanish proverb.

From fanaticism to barbarism is only one step. - Denis Diderot.

> Note two most important things: First, these transitions can be very sudden and unexpected (most recent example, the 2011 "Arab Spring" in Egypt and Libya), so as an investor you cannot plan for them. Second, it does not really matter whether the new regime is better or worse than the old—anything viewed as tainted by the old regime will probably be seized or nationalized or shunned. Either way, as an investor, you can very suddenly and unexpectedly lose a lot of money—so this is not a good way to invest.

A reminder about how these societies work:

It doesn't matter how the people vote; what matters is who counts the votes and how they do it. - Stalin.

Where the law ends, tyranny begins. - William Pitt.

A reminder about the kind of people who are in charge:

Power does not corrupt men; fools, however, if they get into a position of power, corrupt power. - George Bernard Shaw.

When small men begin to cast long shadows, it is a sure sign that the sun is setting. - unknown.

> This sort of regime is interested in two things: remaining in power, and milking the country's assets for the benefit of their entourage. Creating a good environment for investors, or working to grow GDP, or anything else, tend to be far secondary goals.

A reminder about how power is maintained:

Violence is the last refuge of the incompetent. - Isaac Asimov.

> If they were to competently run their country, they would not need to use violence.

Whatever needs to be maintained through force is doomed.
– Henry Miller.

> Although no society lasts forever, those maintained through force usually disappear sooner.

Not believing in force is the same as not believing in gravity.
– Leon Trotsky.

> A country that uses force against its own citizens will have no qualms about how it interacts with foreign investors. To think that you are protected by any supposed "legalities" is naïve.

Again, you cannot reliably make money for very long in a corrupt society.

Power tends to corrupt, and absolute power corrupts absolutely.
– John Acton.

A government of laws, and not of men. – John Adams.

> Where there is "rule of law," you and the companies you invest in can (mostly) reliably defend your assets. Where there is no sufficiently well-established rule of law, you cannot.

Or in a society where the rulers can take what they want from you at will—because eventually, they will.

If you give me six lines written by the hand of the most honest of men, I will find something in them which will hang him. – Cardinal Richelieu.

It is legal because I wish it. – Louis XIV.

Healthy societies usually have a wide range of politics.

No government can be long secure without a formidable opposition.
– Benjamin Disraeli.

Whereas un-healthy societies present many dangers for the investor, especially when these societies inevitably come under attack.

You don't want to be in the same woods as a wounded bear.
– Russian proverb.

You may not be interested in war, but war is interested in you.
– Leon Trotsky.

You cannot make a revolution with silk gloves. – Joseph Stalin.

In war it does not matter who is right, but who is left.
– Winston Churchill.

Turmoil does occur. The outcome for investors in countries experiencing conflict is usually not pretty and is to be avoided.

Beware Unbalanced or Indebted Societies

Nature does not like stability. Things tend to swing one way or the other.

The forces of a capitalist society, if left unchecked, tend to make the rich richer and the poor poorer. – Jawaharlal Nehru.

The world has enough for everyone's needs, but not enough for everyone's greed. – Mahatma Ghandi.

We may have democracy, or we may have wealth concentrated in the hands of a few, but we can't have both. – Louis Brandeis, quoted by Raymond Lonergan in Mr. Justice Brandeis, Great American.

Democracy is the theory that the common people know what they want, and deserve to get it good and hard. – H. L. Mencken, Sententiae.

Historically, this tends to happen regardless of prior "best intentions."

Democracy is a device that ensures we shall be governed no better than we deserve. – George Bernard Shaw.

For the investor (or the wealthy), the danger becomes more acute as the gap between them and the poor widens.

If a free society cannot help the many who are poor, it cannot save the few who are rich. – John F. Kennedy.

This society cannot go forward, the way we have been going forward, where the gap between the rich and the poor keeps growing. It's not politically viable; it's not morally right; it's just not going to happen. – Michael R. Bloomberg.

When people have lost their money, they strike out unthinkingly, like a wounded snake, at whoever is most prominent in their line of vision. – Theodore Roosevelt.

As things become more unbalanced, the greater number of poor people will elect officials who will implement policies unfriendly to business and the wealthy. "Unfriendly" translates to confiscatory tax rates and nationalization of businesses at far below fair value. And, in extreme versions, this degenerates into riots and pogroms.

A slower-moving version of these dangers occurs when societies run up deficits by funding spending they cannot afford.

Christmas is the time when kids tell Santa what they want and adults pay for it. Deficits are when adults tell the government what they want— and their kids pay for it. - Richard Lamm.

It is incumbent on every generation to pay its own debts as it goes. A principle which if acted on would save one-half the wars of the world. - Thomas Jefferson.

A debtor nation does not love its creditor. - John Maynard Keynes.

Large deficits usually lead to hyperinflation or national debt default, or both. In turn, creditor countries usually do not take too kindly to this, often retaliating with punitive trade measures, and escalating up to asset seizures and even war. This cycle does not usually end well for involved investors.

Unfortunately, heading down this path seems to be human nature.

A balanced budget cannot be,
  Amend the process as you will
The dripping snouts within the trough
  Will not forgo the tasty swill.
- Art Buck.

And, unfortunately, it usually ends the same way.

Any government, like any family, can for a year spend a little more than it earns. But you and I know that a continuance of that habit means the poorhouse. - Franklin D. Roosevelt.

Everyone points out Greece's default record, but the history of a lot of sovereign nations is not a good one when it comes to lending them money. - James S. Chanos.

Nations default when they can't pay. This happened in the 1930s and has started happening again today [2012—Ed.]. Default, whether outright (through debt repudiation) or de facto (currency/debt debasement) is rarely orderly (although Greece managed to live in default for over 50 percent of the last two centuries). It tends to happen when all other choices have been exhausted. - Paul Gambles.

Some recent major examples: United States (1930s), England (1950s), Japan (1990s), Italy / Spain / Southern Europe (2010s).

Which is why they say:

Blessed are the young, for they shall inherit the national debt.
- Herbert Hoover.

And which is partly why I dedicated this book to my three children, for their taxes will be paying for my retirement, whether they like it or not.

Governments Do Not Exist to Protect the Investor

Realize that governments have never much improved.

Government is at a stand; little better practiced now than three or four thousand years ago. – John Adams.

A phenomenon noticeable throughout history regardless of place or period is the pursuit by governments of policies contrary to their own interests. – Barbara W. Tuchman, The March of Folly.

The worst evils by which mankind has ever had to endure were inflicted by bad governments. – Ludwig von Mises.

Although the goals have always been clear...

The budget should be balanced, the treasury should be refilled, public debt should be reduced, the arrogance of officialdom should be tempered and controlled, and the assistance to foreign lands should be curtailed lest Rome become bankrupt. People must again learn to work, instead of living on public assistance. – Cicero, 55 BC.

If a state is governed by the principles of reason, poverty and misery are subjects of shame; if a state is not governed by the principles of reason, riches and honors are the subjects of shame. – Confucius.

We all know what to do, but we do not know how to get re-elected once we have done it. – Jean-Claude Juncker, Prime Minister of Luxembourg, The Economist, *March 15, 2007.*

...The incentives very rarely align to the benefit of the governed.

Under capitalism, man exploits man. Under communism, it's just the opposite. – John Kenneth Galbraith.

...everyone but an idiot knows that the lower classes must be kept poor, or they will never be industrious. – Arthur Young, 1771.

The comfort of the rich depends upon an abundant supply of the poor. – Voltaire.

Politics: A strife of interests masquerading as a contest of principles. The conduct of public affairs for private advantage. – Ambrose Bierce.

We have always known that heedless self-interest was bad morals; we know now that it is bad economics. – Franklin D. Roosevelt.

What experience and history teach is this—that people and governments never have learned anything from history, or acted on principles deduced from it. – Georg W. F. Hegel, Lectures on the Philosophy of History.

Thus history repeats itself.

And the governmental gene pool usually remains weak.

Know, my son, with how little wisdom the world is governed.
– Count Axel Oxenstierna, Chancellor of Sweden, early 1600s.

The best minds are not in government. If any were, business would steal them away. – Ronald Reagan.

An important exception may be Singapore, where the government makes a point of paying high salaries to people in high positions, and recruits very competitively versus private enterprise. However, at just over 50 years of age, Singapore is still a very young exception to the rule.

And slow to adapt.

Politics move very slowly in a world where problems move very fast.
– Roland Dohrn.

This is why you should expect little from government.

I don't make jokes. I just watch the government and report the facts.
– Will Rogers.

A good government remains the greatest of human blessings, and no nation has ever enjoyed it. – William Ralph Inge, Outspoken Essays: Second Series; The State, Visible and Invisible.

Men and nations behave wisely once they have exhausted all other alternatives. – Abba Eban.

A COUPLE OF COUNTRY NOTES

By the way, I like Brazil.

They have a joy for life in Brazil unlike any country I've ever seen.
– Morena Baccarin.

Brazil is the country of the future and always will be. – Brazilian joke.

With vast natural resources, huge agricultural capacity, and a civilized government, Brazil has a lot of potential.

And find some nice comments regarding the United States.

You can always count on Americans to do the right thing—after they've tried everything else. – Winston Churchill.

America was not built on fear. America was built on courage, on imagination, and unbeatable determination to do the job at hand. – Harry S. Truman.

American culture encourages the process of failure, unlike the cultures of Europe and Asia where failure is met with stigma and embarrassment. America's specialty is to take these small risks for the rest of the world, which explains this country's disproportionate share in innovations. – Nassim Nicholas Taleb, The Black Swan.

America is great because America is good, and if America ever ceases to be good, America will cease to be great. – Alexis de Tocqueville.

The things that will destroy America are prosperity-at-any-price, safety-first instead of duty-first, the love of soft living, and the get-rich-quick theory of life. – Theodore Roosevelt.

There is nothing wrong with America that cannot be cured by what is right with America. – William J. Clinton.

During my lifetime most of the problems the world has faced have come, in one fashion or the other, from mainland Europe, and the solutions from outside it. – Margaret Thatcher.

Throughout history, the region making the greatest contributions to the advancement of civilization was usually also the best place to invest. Hopefully there will always be such a place, somewhere.

Your Taxation

Everyone must pay taxes. But you are not obliged to domicile yourself in the most expensive zone, nor to remain in a zone that becomes overly expensive. Many wealthy people change domiciles, and even their citizenship, for reasons of taxation. It's not something you should contemplate lightly, but everything has its price. The government services you benefit from, up to and including your passport and citizenship, should be viewed as services you are buying with your taxes. So, like anything else, should the price become excessive, consider shopping elsewhere.

Capital punishment: The income tax. – Jeff Hayes.

SOME TAXATION IS UNAVOIDABLE

The government will always want its share.

*In this world nothing can be said to be certain, except death and taxes.
– Benjamin Franklin.*

The Congress shall have the power to lay and collect taxes on incomes from whatever source derived, without apportionment among the several states, and without regard to any census or enumeration. – 16th Amendment to the U.S. Constitution, 1913.

Taxation is, arguably, the primary function of government.

And, to be fair, government usually provides something in return.

*I like to pay taxes. With them I buy civilization.
– Oliver Wendell Holmes, Jr.*

Taxes, after all, are the dues that we pay for the privilege of membership in an organized society. – Franklin D. Roosevelt.

A real patriot is the fellow who gets a parking ticket and rejoices that the system works. – Bill Vaughan.

*In moderate governments there is an indemnity for the weight of the taxes, which is liberty. In despotic countries there is an equivalent for liberty, which is the lightness of the taxes. – Baron de Montesquieu,
The Spirit of the Laws, 1747.*

But that does not mean tax policy will always be justified or equitable.

*Civilization is the eternal sacrifice of one generation to the next.
– Edward Bulwer-Lytton, Alice.*

There may be liberty and justice for all, but there are tax breaks only for some. – Martin A. Sullivan.

The Rich aren't like us—they pay less taxes. – Peter De Vries.

The income tax has made liars out of more Americans than golf. – Will Rogers.

> Legislators seeking funds for their pet projects pull tax policy one way. Private entities who can afford lobbyists push the opposite way for special tax breaks. Reconciling these two forces requires treating a third party unfairly.

Or simple. Indeed, obfuscation and misdirection are how the State hides its hand.

The hardest thing in the world to understand is the income tax. – Albert Einstein.

Tax reform is when you take the taxes off things that have been taxed in the past and put taxes on things that haven't been taxed before. – Art Buchwald.

The art of taxation consists in so plucking the goose as to obtain the largest amount of feathers with the least possible amount of hissing. – J. B. Colbert.

Give the masses what they want in nominal terms and take it back in real terms. – unknown.

When unavoidable, a sense of gallows humor at the inevitable will always help.

The trick is to stop thinking of it as "your" money. – apocryphal words of a government tax auditor.

What is the difference between a taxidermist and a tax collector? The taxidermist takes only your skin. – Mark Twain.

The only thing that hurts more than paying an income tax is not having to pay an income tax. – Lord Dewar.

Taxation with representation ain't so hot either. – Gerald Barzan.

I love to go to Washington—if only to be near my money. – Bob Hope.

So hire a good accountant, and pay only what you must.

Day in and day out, your tax accountant can make or lose you more money than any single person in your life, with the possible exception of your kids. – Harvey Mackay.

Anyone may so arrange his affairs that his taxes shall be as low as

possible. He is not bound to choose that pattern which best pays the Treasury. Everybody does it, rich and poor alike, and all do right; for nobody owes any public duty to pay more than the law demands.
– Judge Learned Hand.

Note: There is a big difference, and a very clear line, between "avoidance" and "evasion." In the case of the entirely permissible former, you avoid taxes by not incurring them to begin with, whether by moving or transacting elsewhere or by other entirely legal means and choices. The latter, on the other hand, consists of illegally hiding activity or lying in order to evade taxes that your choices or actions, if known, would normally require paying. This is not encouraged.

But Beware Arbitrary or Excessive Taxation

Remember that the State is never your friend in this matter.

Taxes are not levied for the benefit of the taxed. – Robert Heinlein.

In the most sinister version, taxation is a tool to grow and maintain power.

An unlimited power to tax involves, necessarily, the power to destroy.
– Daniel Webster.

The way to crush the bourgeoisie is to grind them between the millstones of taxation and inflation. – Vladimir I. Lenin.

Hopefully, the perceptive investor would have noticed early on where things were heading, and left or removed their money.

And states can also go through misguided periods.

When a new source of taxation is found it never means, in practice, that the old source is abandoned. It merely means that the politicians have two ways of milking the taxpayer where they had one before.
– H. L. Mencken.

Or temporarily veer closer to socialism than most good capitalists would like.

There is nothing in socialism that a little age or a little money will not cure. – Will Durant.

Socialism collapsed because it did not allow prices to tell the economic truth. – Oystein Dahle.

A democratic government is the only one in which those who vote for a tax can escape the obligation to pay it. – Alexis de Tocqueville.

The problem with socialism is that eventually you run out of other people's money. – Margaret Thatcher.

Complete equality cannot be legislated.

The worst form of inequality is to try to make unequal things equal. – Aristotle.

A perfect equality will indeed be produced; that is to say, equal want, equal wretchedness, equal beggary, and on the part of the partitioners, a woeful, helpless, and desperate disappointment. Such is the event of all compulsory equalizations. They pull down what is above. They never raise what is below: and they depress high and low together beneath the level of what was originally the lowest. – Edmund Burke, Thoughts and Details On Scarcity, *1795.*

Equality, Fraternity, Poverty. – unknown. [Satirical spoof of French national motto "Liberty, Equality, Fraternity," and usually dusted off whenever France veers more towards its socialist constituents.—Ed.]

And efforts to do so usually produce negative effects on investments, businesses, and wealth in such targeted areas.

The democracy will cease to exist when you take away from those who are willing to work and give to those who would not. – Thomas Jefferson.

You cannot legislate the poor into freedom by legislating the wealthy out of freedom. What one person receives without working for, another person must work for without receiving. The government cannot give to anybody anything that the government does not first take from somebody else. When half of the people get the idea that they do not have to work because the other half is going to take care of them, and when the other half gets the idea that it does no good to work because somebody else is going to get what they work for, that my dear friend, is about the end of any nation. You cannot multiply wealth by dividing it. – Adrian Rogers.

There will always be those who work harder, make more money, and become wealthy. The challenge for the state is to fund itself mostly from the wealthy, and yet not take so much that the wealthy will be discouraged and move elsewhere.

Your Nationality and Where You Keep Your Assets

Even countries go bad. For the wealthy person looking to preserve assets over a lifetime or for the benefit of the next generation, to ignore this risk is to ignore human history. Therefore, no matter where you currently live (and yes, I explicitly include Americans here), you must always monitor the situation in your current country, and always consider where else you might want to reside—even to the point of keeping investment, real estate and business toeholds in other jurisdictions.

A man's feet should be planted in his country, but his eyes should survey the world. – George Santayana.

CONSIDER WHERE YOU BANK AND INVEST

Always remember that anywhere in the world, and at any point in time, your wealth can simply be taken from you.

All persons are required to deliver on or before May 1, 1933 all gold coin, gold bullion, and gold certificates now owned by them to a Federal Reserve Bank, branch or agency, or to any member bank of the Federal Reserve System. – President Franklin D. Roosevelt, Executive Order 6102, April 5, 1933. [Announcing a prohibition on private citizens owning gold.—Ed.]

Yes, even in the United States. And those who lost their gold then did not expect this either. Technically, the gold was seized in exchange for $20 per ounce; shortly thereafter, the Treasury raised the international rate to $35 per ounce. This dollar devaluation was in effect a 43% one-time tax on all gold in private hands.

A government that is big enough to supply all your needs is big enough to take all you have. – Thomas Jefferson.

Remember that no society lasts forever. Never has, and never will.

If Rome and Sparta could perish, what state could hope to live forever? – Jean-Jacques Rousseau.

A nation may be said to consist of its territory, its people, and its laws. The territory is the only part which is of certain durability. – Abraham Lincoln, message to Congress, December 1, 1862.

Many countries have a revolution, coup or major monetary devaluation every generation or so (if not more frequently). If you live in one of these countries, what is your long-term planning for your family's fortune? For larger developed countries, this might happen less often, but it still does, and a smart family should incorporate this fact into their planning. Even global superpowers eventually see over-extension, contraction, and turmoil (consider Egypt, China, Rome, and England, in roughly that order, as a partial list).

And that no nation is special or somehow exempt from history.

Nature is indifferent to the survival of the human species, including Americans. – Adlai E. Stevenson.

Every nation ridicules other nations, and all are right.
– Arthur Schopenhauer.

Everyone wants to think their country is special and their people and leaders are exempt from making the mistakes of others. This is very wishful thinking.

So constantly observe how conditions evolve in geographies where you have links.

When you see that trading is done, not by consent, but by compulsion— when you see that in order to produce, you need to obtain permission from men who produce nothing—when you see money flowing to those who deal, not in goods, but in favors—when you see that men get richer by graft and pull than by work, and your laws don't protect you against them, but protect them against you—when you see corruption being rewarded and honesty becoming a self-sacrifice—you may know that your society is doomed. – Ayn Rand, Atlas Shrugged.

There is a bit of conspiracy, and of authoritarianism, in every democracy; and a bit of democracy in every dictatorship. – George F. Kennan.

Be aware of which direction the pendulum is swinging, and act accordingly.

Always Watch Elsewhere (Don't Be an Isolationist)

Just because you live in one country and for the moment like it, that does not mean you should ignore more attractive or safer opportunities elsewhere—whether as a matter of diversification or as a measure of "insurance" for some portion of your wealth.

*It was not tax evasion that brought clients to Switzerland; it was
fear of war, revolution, and inflation. A former French minister said:
"Switzerland is a reflection of our mistakes," and another added, "It has
saved the fortunes of the French." We had gotten the money that sought
refuge, not because we were Swiss per se, but because we had escaped
many of the accidents of history. – Yves Oltramare.*

I am not an Athenian or a Greek, but a citizen of the world. – Diogenes.

For people to say just because I'm a resident of the United States [or any
other country—Ed.] *that I'm going to restrict my investments to the
United States is terribly myopic, and numerous studies have shown that
it really curtails investment opportunities. The more one thinks about
global investment opportunities, the greater the chances of success.
– Gary Brinson.*

Your patriotism will not protect your wealth. Do remain patriotic to your country,
but if your country's institutions are failing to act fairly, do not hesitate to protect
your wealth from their grasp.

*Patriotism is often an arbitrary veneration of real estate above principles.
– George Jean Nathan.*

*Patriotism is your conviction that this country is superior to all others
because you were born in it. – George Bernard Shaw.*

> You may love your country, but if you are on the wrong side of the next
> irresponsible or authoritarian regime to come to power, your patriotism
> will not protect your wealth or assets.

Countries mostly stay, but governments come and go. Be prepared to protect
yourself against the more noxious ones.

*Just as nomads, people driven out of their native lands, illegal migrants,
political refugees, and the poorest of the poor have long been doing, one
must be prepared for change in society and be determined to live in any
city in any country, learn any language as necessary, and do any type of
work [in order to adapt and survive]. – Jacques Attali.*

*My kind of loyalty was loyalty to one's country, not to its institutions or
its officeholders. The country is the real thing, the substantial thing, the
eternal thing; it is the thing to watch over, and care for, and be loyal to;
institutions are extraneous, they are its mere clothing, and clothing can
wear out, become ragged, cease to be comfortable, cease to protect the
body from winter, disease, and death. – Mark Twain,* The Innocents
Abroad.

Have some portable skills, assets or businesses, and watch to ensure that your country's institutions continue to do the right thing.

Beware Governments and Politicians

Your government is not your friend or some purely benevolent entity.

Government is that great fiction, through which everybody endeavors to live at the expense of everybody else. – Frederic Bastiat.

It is bad to be oppressed by a minority, but it is worse to be oppressed by a majority. For there is a reserve of latent power in the masses which, if it is called into play, the minority can seldom resist. But from the absolute will of an entire people there is no appeal, no redemption, no refuge but treason. – Lord Acton.

A government which robs Peter to pay Paul can always count on Paul's support. – George Bernard Shaw.

Recognize government as such, and live with it as long as it stays within reason.

Be wary of government that starts to get too big.

Government should do for people only what they cannot do better by themselves, and no more. – Abraham Lincoln.

The nine most terrifying words in the English language are, "I'm from the government and I'm here to help." – Ronald Reagan.

The nearest thing to eternal life we will ever see on this earth is a government program. – Ronald Reagan.

The mystery of government is not how Washington works but how to make it stop. – P. J. O'Rourke.

When was the last time a government voluntarily, absent a crisis, became smaller?

Be wary of government in general.

Politics is the entertainment division of the military industrial complex. – Frank Zappa.

The oppressed are allowed once every few years to decide which particular representatives of the oppressing class are to represent and repress them. – Karl Marx.

Behind every form of government lurks an oligarchy. – unknown.

A foolish faith in authority is the worst enemy of truth. – Albert Einstein.

> Government does not exist to protect you. Government exists to perpetuate its own power—it only protects you as and when this proves beneficial to itself.

Remember that all governments, all ruling orders, carry the seeds of their own downfall.

Civilizations die from suicide, not by murder. – Arnold Toynbee.

A society of sheep must in time beget a government of wolves.
– Bertrand de Jouvenel.

A great civilization is not conquered from without until it has destroyed itself from within. The essential causes of Rome's decline lay in her people, her morals, her class struggle, her failing trade, her bureaucratic despotism, her stifling taxes, her consuming wars. – Will Durant.

Big Brother in the form of an increasingly powerful government and in an increasingly powerful private sector will pile the records high with reasons why privacy should give way to national security, to law and order, to efficiency of operation, to scientific advancement and the like.
– William O. Douglas, US Supreme Court Justice, Points of Rebellion.

The right to do something does not mean that doing it is right.
– William Safire.

The illegal we do immediately; the unconstitutional takes a little longer.
– Henry Kissinger, in meeting with Turkish foreign minister Mehli Esenbel, March 10, 1975, National Security Archive, George Washington University.

> Power eventually corrupts. But this is hardly a novel revelation.

So as for governments:

Governments never learn. Only people learn. – Milton Friedman.

Every nation has the government it deserves. – Joseph de Maistre.

As for politicians, beware especially politicians.

The word "politics" is derived from the word "poly," meaning "many,' and the word "ticks," meaning "blood sucking parasites." – Larry Hardiman.

Politics: The gentle art of getting votes from the poor and campaign funds from the rich by promising to protect each from the other.
– Oscar Ameringer.

If a politician found he had cannibals among his constituents, he would promise them missionaries for dinner. – H. L. Mencken.

We hang the petty thieves and appoint the great ones to public office. – Aesop.

In government, the scum rises to the top. – Friedrich von Hayek.

Politicians are like diapers—they should be changed often, and for the same reason. – Mark Twain.

True terror is to wake up one morning and discover that your high school class is running the country. – Kurt Vonnegut.

That's all politics is. You know what politicians are? When are people going to grow up? Politicians are the same jerks you hated in high school and college that wanted to be class president and head of the student council. The brown-nosers, suck-ups, overly-ambitious, insincere—and now they are telling you what to do and you are paying attention to them and you are bowing down? – Gerald Celente.

Power eventually attracts those who would abuse it.

If you always remember that those in charge are not there primarily to help you, then you will be well served.

Idealism is the noble toga that political gentlemen drape over their will to power. – Aldous Huxley.

Those who take the most from the table, teach contentment. Those for whom the taxes are destined, demand sacrifice. Those who eat their fill, speak to the hungry, of wonderful times to come. Those who lead the country into the abyss, call ruling difficult, for ordinary folk. – Bertolt Brecht.

AT WORST, BE PREPARED TO EMIGRATE

Someday, your opinion of right and wrong may unfortunately differ from that of your government.

We can never forget that everything Adolf Hitler did in Germany was "legal" and everything the Hungarian freedom fighters did in Hungary was "illegal." – Martin Luther King, Jr., Letter from Birmingham Jail, April 16th, 1963.

There is no reason to believe that there is one law for families and another for nations. – Mahatma Gandhi.

Right is right, even if nobody does it. Wrong is wrong, even if everybody is wrong about it. – G. K. Chesterton.

Unfortunately this has happened, with pretty regular recurrence, throughout history.

Law cannot restrain evil; for the freedom of man is such that he can make the keeping of the law the instrument of evil. – Reinhold Niebuhr.

Moral codes adjust themselves to environmental conditions. – William J. Durant.

Any fool can make a rule, and any fool will mind it. – Henry David Thoreau.

And unfortunately, this could put you legally at odds with your government, the day you feel compelled to act otherwise.

The wise don't obey useless laws. – Lao Tzu.

Every actual State is corrupt. Good men must not obey laws too well. – Ralph Waldo Emerson.

Blind respect for authority is the greatest enemy of truth. – Albert Einstein.

Do nothing to make you lose respect for yourself or to cheapen yourself in your own eyes; let your own integrity be the standard of rectitude, and let your own dictates be stricter than the precepts of any law. – Baltasar Gracián.

I am free, no matter what rules surround me. If I find them tolerable, I tolerate them; if I find them too obnoxious, I break them. I am free because I know that I alone am morally responsible for everything I do. – Robert A. Heinlein.

If so, recognize how you might be at risk, how you will act, and how you will protect yourself.

A truth spoken before its time is dangerous. – Greek proverb.

Wise men say nothing in dangerous times. – Aesop.

He that spits against the wind spits in his own face. – Benjamin Franklin.

It is dangerous to be right when the government is wrong. – Voltaire.

If you speak the truth, have a foot in the stirrup. – Turkish proverb.

Beware becoming a martyr. It may earn you a footnote in history, but will rarely help your family or your fortune.

Recognize that safety or stability is not permanent, and change can come suddenly.

> *The marvel of all history is the patience with which men and women submit to burdens unnecessarily laid upon them by their governments.*
> *– William E. Borah.*

> *There is no security on earth, there is only opportunity.*
> *– General Douglas MacArthur.*

> *Civilization is a movement and not a condition, a voyage and not a harbor. – Arnold Toynbee.*

> *Freedom is never more than one generation away from extinction.*
> *– Ronald Reagan.*

> *Revolution is impossible until it becomes inevitable. – Leon Trotsky.*

> *A revolution is not a dinner party. – Mao Zedong.*

> You cannot assume that your country will always be safe or that your government will always be reasonable.

Have contingency plans for moving or otherwise protecting your wealth and your family.

> *Be prepared. – Boy Scout's motto, Robert Baden-Powell.*

> *In fair weather prepare for foul. – Thomas Fuller.*

> *Put your trust in God; but be sure to keep your powder dry.*
> *– Oliver Cromwell.*

> *God helps those who help themselves. – unknown.*

> *Even in the sheath the knife must be sharp. – Finnish proverb.*

> You want to be able to get out before things get too bad.

Because sometimes (though rarely), the worst does happen, and you need to leave.

> *You are permitted in time of great danger to walk with the devil until you have crossed the bridge. – Bulgarian proverb.*

> *In war, boots; in flight, a place in a boat or a seat on a lorry may be the most vital thing in the world, more desirable than untold millions. In hyperinflation, a kilo of potatoes was worth, to some, more than the family silver; a side of pork more than the grand piano. A prostitute in the family was better than an infant corpse; theft was preferable to starvation; warmth was finer than honor, clothing more essential than*

democracy, food more needed than freedom. – Adam Fergusson, When
Money Dies: The Nightmare of the Weimar Collapse.

> And if things really do get that bad, you have to do what you can just to
> survive.

SOME KIND WORDS ABOUT BEING DOMICILED IN THE UNITED STATES

Everything written in this chapter applies to everyone, even Americans. But
America and Americans still remain very fortunate in many ways. I feel that much
of what follows, even though mostly said a good while ago, still remains true to
this day.

> *America has the world's best money. Every U.S. dollar is secured by the
> universal demand for it. – Cullen Hightower.*

> *Of all the countries in the world, America is that in which the spread
> of ideas and of human industry is the most continual and most rapid.
> – Alexis de Tocqueville.*

> *Any man who is a bear on the future of this country will go broke.
> – J. P. Morgan.*

> *It is America, not Moscow, that has shown the worker how he can get
> what he most desires—a steadily rising standard of living. – Philip Kerr.*

> *My message to you is: Be courageous! I have lived a long time. I have seen
> history repeat itself again and again. I have seen many depressions in
> business. Always America has come out stronger and more prosperous.
> Be as brave as your fathers before you. Have faith! Go forward.
> – Thomas A. Edison.*

> Hopefully, America, and investments in American companies, will
> continue to do well. But since hope is not an investment strategy, always
> monitor and always watch elsewhere.

Keeping a Low Profile

Unless you are a celebrity of some sort and hungry for publicity for commercial reasons, there is usually no good reason to attract unnecessary attention to yourself. The more widely it becomes known that you have money, the more attention you will attract from people trying to get some of it, whether by legitimate or other means.

PROMISCUOUS WEALTH ATTRACTS UNWANTED ATTENTION

The more obvious you are about having money, the more others will try to get some of it from you, by any and all means.

> *He that displays too often his wife and his wallet is in danger of having both of them borrowed. - Benjamin Franklin.*

> *A fool and her money are soon courted. - Helen Rowland.*

> *Envy is a much more serious mischief-maker than greed.*
> *- Charles Munger.*

> From gold diggers to scammers, they will come knocking.

Wealth will also attract sycophants and make you a target, but this comes with the territory.

> *You cannot buy a friend with money. - Russian proverb.*

> *If you want a friend, get a dog. - unknown.*

> People will want to be with you because of the largess you can dispense, not because they genuinely like you. Be careful with whom you surround yourself.

Always be on your guard.

> *We're surrounded... That simplifies our problem. - Chesty Puller.*

> Once you start to have some money (and even before that), remember that everyone, almost without exception, is trying to sell you something, get something, or take or scam something.

ATTENTION AVOIDANCE

A little humility never hurts.

A wise and reasonable person is unassuming and hides rather than flaunts his talents and wisdom. – Taisou.

Pride ends in humiliation, while humility brings honor. – Proverbs 29:23.

Pride leads to disgrace, but with humility comes wisdom. – Proverbs 11:2.

Being powerful is like being a lady. If you have to tell people you are, you aren't. – various, including Margaret Thatcher.

For whosoever exalteth himself shall be abased; and he that humbleth himself shall be exalted. – Luke 14:11.

Since ancient times, they all say the same thing. Make too much of a target of yourself and sooner or later someone will take a shot at you.

You are probably not that great anyway.

No man is a hero to his valet. – various.

Allowing people to underestimate you is usually a good policy.

Be wiser than other people if you can; but do not tell them so. – Lord Chesterfield.

It is a profitable thing, if one is wise, to seem foolish. – Aeschylus.

The height of cleverness is to conceal one's cleverness. – François, duc de La Rochefoucauld.

It is also good for your business if everyone else does not fully realize how smart you might actually be.

It is always the secure who are humble. – G. K. Chesterton.

This is arguably a "chicken-and-egg" situation. By hiding behind a front of quiet humility, you minimize the amount of noxious attention you might otherwise attract by being too public. This, in turn, further enhances your security. Also, once it is known that you are powerful, you no longer need to overtly advertise the fact.

Be discreet.

Nobody will keep the thing he hears to himself, and nobody will repeat just what he hears and no more. – Lucius Annaeus Seneca.

There are some occasions when a man must tell half his secret, in order to conceal the rest. – Lord Chesterfield.

Avoid escalating or pursuing fights. Your time and resources are better spent on productive projects.

Revenge is sweet, sweeter than life itself. So say fools. – Juvenal.

And avoid making enemies. You never know who you might need help from in the future.

Friends may come and go, but enemies accumulate. – Thomas Jones.

There is no such thing as an insignificant enemy. – French proverb.

> Having people out to get you is bad for business, and thus bad for your wealth.

Legal-Phobia

Avoid lawsuits whenever possible. A calmly negotiated compromise will usually be preferable.

Discourage litigation. Persuade your neighbors to compromise whenever you can. As a peacemaker the lawyer has superior opportunity of being a good man. – Abraham Lincoln.

Never stir up litigation. A worse man can scarcely be found than one who does this. – Abraham Lincoln.

> Look into arbitration, or be reasonable about proposing or taking a settlement.

Because judges and juries do not always arrive at the correct decision.

A jury consists of twelve persons chosen to decide who has the better lawyer. – Robert Frost.

> Being morally in the right, having a winnable case, and employing the more convincing lawyer, are three very different and not causally-related things.

And even if you win, you can lose.

I was never ruined but twice, once when I lost a lawsuit, and once when I won one. – Voltaire.

A long dispute means that both parties are wrong. – Voltaire.

The trend toward increased recourse to the legal system is unfortunate.

Of course, people are getting smarter; they are letting lawyers instead of their conscience be their guides. – Will Rogers.

Lawyers will always want to sue, as that tends to maximize their billable hours. But that is not necessarily your best course of action.

A final note on lawyers:

The best description of "utter waste" would be a busload of lawyers going over a cliff with three empty seats. – Lamar Hunt.

PROLES, POLITICOS, AND THE RICH

Carefully handle those with no power.

Beware of the person with nothing to lose. – Italian proverb.

Because they no longer have anything to restrain them, responses can be unpredictable and excessive. It is therefore as dangerous to reduce someone to destitution as to be the one taking an already poor person's last piece of money or property.

Carefully handle those with a lot of power, because you cannot completely avoid them.

Renunciation of world politics offers no protection from its consequences. – Oswald Spengler.

Just because you do not take an interest in politics doesn't mean politics won't take an interest in you. – Pericles.

Try not to put yourself in a position where it will benefit a politician (e.g., win them votes or popular appeal) to somehow punish, fine, or tax you. Offend enough of the population and a mob will start calling for your head (or your money). Then, some politician will be happy to oblige the mob if he thinks it will win him a few votes.

Carefully handle those with a lot of money.

When money speaks, the truth keeps silent. – Russian proverb.

It can cost those with a lot of money comparatively little to get what they want. Avoid standing between them and what they want, especially when you have more to lose.

FRIENDSHIP AND MARRIAGE

Pick your friends carefully. Not everyone needs a thirty-person entourage.

The best time to make friends is before you need them. – Ethel Barrymore.

Avoid that friend who is greedy for wealth. – Jagarjuna.

Beware the mixing of friendship and business.

A friendship founded on business is better than a business founded on friendship. – John D. Rockefeller.

Marriage. Be warned on the way in.

Maids want nothing but husbands, and when they have them, they want everything. – William Shakespeare.

Suspicion, Discontent, and Strife / Come in for Dowry with a Wife. – Robert Herrick.

Women shop for a bikini with more care than they do a husband. The rules are the same. Look for something you'll feel comfortable wearing. Allow for room to grow. – Erma Bombeck.

Remember, it's as easy to marry a rich woman as a poor woman. – William Makepeace Thackeray.

The converse, and various other modern permutations, is true as well.

Divorce. Be prepared (and get a pre-nuptial agreement) because it happens much more often than you might think.

Divorce is probably of nearly the same date as marriage. I believe, however, that marriage is some weeks more ancient. – Voltaire.

I am a marvelous housekeeper. Every time I leave a man I keep his house. – Zsa Zsa Gabor.

Instead of getting married again, I'm going to find a woman I don't like and give her a house. – Lewis Grizzard.

I never hated a man enough to give his diamonds back. – Zsa Zsa Gabor.

You never realize how short a month is until you pay alimony. – John Barrymore.

Alimony—the ransom that the happy pay to the devil. – H. L. Mencken, The Devil's Dictionary.

Why are divorces so expensive? Because they're worth it. – Kurt Leuthold.

Since divorce is a real risk, take steps to minimize any eventual expense. You should not forfeit half your wealth or half your business because of poor risk planning. Worse, consider how little you would have left after two or three such unplanned divorces.

CONCLUSION

The world is full of predatory elements (always was and always will be).

> *At the end of the decade, no one will be sure of anything except sex will kill you, politicians lie, rain is poison, and the world is run by whores. These are terrible things to accept, even if you are rich.*
> *– Hunter S. Thompson.*

So play nice and try not to make a target of yourself.

> *The seven principles of conduct with people are forbearance, forgiveness, humility, generosity, compassion, good counsel, justice, and fairness.*
> *– Al-Sadiq.*

> *Be civil to all, sociable to many; familiar with few; friend to one; enemy to none. – Benjamin Franklin.*

And thus sustain your happy existence.

> *I'd like to live like a poor man—only with lots of money. – Pablo Picasso.*

PART 7

Protecting Your Future, Family & Legacy

Ensuring You Remain Wealthy

What follows is not specific investment advice, but big-picture generalities on how to ensure you remain in a position to protect and grow your wealth. Stay curious, keep learning, evolve with the times, have lofty goals, and remain vigilant. Just as your investment opportunities and risks will change over time, you too must evolve in order to properly guide, supervise, and protect your fortune.

> *Success is like anything worthwhile. It has a price. You have to pay the price to win and you have to pay the price to get to the point where success is possible. Most important, you must pay the price to stay there.*
> *– Vince Lombardi.*

> *I hope that while so many people are out smelling the flowers, someone is taking the time to plant some. – Herbert Rappaport.*

REMAIN CURIOUS

Continued intellectual activity will help delay senility and keep you out of the retirement home.

> *Curiosity is one of the permanent and certain characteristics of a vigorous mind. – Samuel Johnson.*

> *Anyone who stops learning is old, whether at twenty or eighty. Anyone who keeps learning stays young. The greatest thing in life is to keep your mind young. – Henry Ford.*

There is always something new worth learning.

> *The wisest mind has something yet to learn. – George Santayana.*

> *Wisdom is not a product of schooling but of the lifelong attempt to acquire it. – Albert Einstein.*

> *I am still learning. – Michelangelo, 1562, at age 87.*

> *We are all born ignorant, but one must work hard to remain stupid.*
> *– Benjamin Franklin.*

> *Intellectual growth should commence at birth and cease only at death.*
> *– Albert Einstein.*

Keep Learning

Strive to master your chosen field.

The prudent man always studies seriously and earnestly to understand whatever he professes to understand, and not merely to persuade other people that he understands it; and though his talents may not always be very brilliant, they are always perfectly genuine. – Adam Smith, Theory of Moral Sentiments.

Study as if you were never to master it; as if in fear of losing it. – Confucius.

I hear and I forget. I see and I remember. I do and I understand. – Confucius.

Broaden your knowledge and abilities.

I do not think much of a man who is not wiser today than he was yesterday. – Abraham Lincoln.

I am always doing that which I cannot in order that I may learn how to do it. – Pablo Picasso.

An investment in knowledge pays the best interest. – Benjamin Franklin.

Wise people learn when they can. Fools learn when they must. – various.

The intellectually curious person is always better prepared when the world inevitably changes. Do not count on current prosperity to maintain things, and train your heirs to do the same.

Occasionally learn something useless, or just because you want to.

It is better, of course, to know useless things than to know nothing. – Lucius Annaeus Seneca.

I have never let my schooling interfere with my education. – Mark Twain.

Favor books and unconventional sources. You want thoughtful knowledge and new takes on things, not what everyone else hears in sound bites or trivia on the evening news.

It is the studying that you do after your school days that really counts. Otherwise, you know only that which everyone else knows. – Henry L. Doherty.

A man's reading program should be as carefully chosen as his daily diet, for it, too, is food without which he cannot grow mentally. – Andrew Carnegie.

To acquire the habit of reading is to construct for yourself a refuge from almost all the miseries of life. – W. Somerset Maugham.

A room without books is like a body without a soul. – Cicero.

I have said that in my whole life, I have known no wise person, over a broad subject matter who didn't read all the time—none, zero. Now I know all kinds of shrewd people who by staying within a narrow area do very well without reading. But investment is a broad area. So if you think you're going to be good at it and not read all the time you have a different idea than I do. – Charles Munger.

Embrace Change in General

Change is inevitable.

There is only one thing in business that is certain and that's change. I don't know what tomorrow is going to be like, but I do know this—it's bound to be different from yesterday and today. – Henry Ford, in The Ultimate Book Of Investment Quotations, *Dean LeBaron et al.*

Change does not necessarily assure progress, but progress implacably requires change. Education is essential to change for education creates both wants and the ability to satisfy them. – Henry Steele Commager.

The world hates change, yet it is the only thing that has brought progress. – Charles Kettering.

Change alone is eternal, perpetual, immortal. – Arthur Schopenhauer.

Change is inevitable in a progressive country. Change is constant. – Benjamin Disraeli.

Change is the investor's only certainty. – T. Rowe Price, Jr.

You cannot fight change, or ignore it, or pretend it is not coming—else you will be left behind.

Only the supremely wise and the abysmally ignorant do not change. – Confucius.

The illiterate of the 21st century will not be those who cannot read and write, but those who cannot learn, unlearn, and relearn. – Alvin Toffler.

Cause change and lead; accept change and survive; resist change and die. – Ray Noorda.

Change is the law of life. And those who look only to the past or present are certain to miss the future. – John F. Kennedy.

He that will not apply new remedies must expect new evils; for time is the greatest innovator. – Francis Bacon.

When you are through changing, you're through. – Alfred P. Sloan, Jr.

If you don't like change, you are going to like irrelevancy even less. – General Eric Shinseki.

Better to embrace change.

Anything that has been done in the same way for the past five years needs an investigation or change. – Percy S. Straus.

If you're doing something the same way you have been doing it for ten years, the chances are you are doing it wrong. – Charles F. Kettering.

The most successful businessman is the man who holds onto the old just as long as it is good and grabs the new just as soon as it is better. – Robert P. Vanderpoel.

Some have an idea that the reason we in this country discard things so readily is because we have so much. The facts are exactly opposite—the reason we have so much is simply because we discard things so readily. We replace the old in return for something that will serve us better. – Alfred P. Sloan.

Prosperity belongs to those who learn new things the fastest. – Paul Zane Pilzer.

And be a proactive participant.

There's a way to do it better... find it. – Thomas A. Edison.

The whole universe is change, and life itself is but what you deem it. – Marcus Aurelius.

If we want things to stay as they are, things will have to change. – Giuseppe di Lampedusa, The Leopard.

Nothing stays the same. A man has to go with the times. No man can put a rope on the past and hope to snub it down. The best thing is to learn to ride the new trails. – Louis L'Amour, Kilkenny.

When great events are moving, one must play a part in them. – Winston Churchill.

Only by actively taking part in change can you ensure your future relevance and usefulness.

Embrace Change in Your Business

If you own a business or if your livelihood or wealth particularly depend on any given industry, you must constantly ensure that it and you do not become irrelevant or obsolete. History is full of businesses (and thereby family fortunes) lost to complacency, or whose industries have been irrevocably changed, or who passed up incredible opportunities by dismissing a new idea or technology. Following, some of the more memorable examples:

They were wrong about railroads.

> *What can be more palpably absurd than the prospect held out of locomotives traveling twice as fast as stagecoaches?* – The Quarterly Review, *March, 1825.*

> *Rail travel at high speeds is not possible because passengers, unable to breathe, would die of asphyxia. – Dionysius Lardner, Professor of Natural Philosophy and Astronomy at University College, London, author of* The Steam Engine Explained and Illustrated, *1830s.*

> *No one will pay good money to get from Berlin to Potsdam in one hour when he can ride his horse there in one day for free. – King William I of Prussia, 1864.* [On hearing of the invention of trains.—Ed.]

> If you own the proverbial buggy-whip factory, beware!

They were wrong about the telephone.

> *Well-informed people know it is impossible to transmit the voice over wires and that were it possible to do so, the thing would be of no practical value.* – Boston Post, *1865.*

> *It's a great invention but who would want to use it anyway?* – Rutherford B. Hayes, U.S. President, 1872. [After a demonstration of Alexander Bell's telephone.—Ed.]

> *This telephone has too many shortcomings to be considered as a means of communication. The device is of inherently no value to us.* – Western Union, internal memo, 1876.

> And thus, Western Union missed owning all of the monopoly pre-breakup AT&T as one of their divisions.

> *The Americans have need of the telephone, but we do not. We have plenty of messenger boys. – William Preece, Chief Engineer, British Post Office, 1878.*

> Beware if you own a messenger-boy company.

They were wrong about the automobile.

The horse is here to stay, the automobile is only a fad.
– unknown President of the Michigan Savings Bank, 1903.

> Advice given to Horace Rackham, Henry Ford's lawyer. Rackham ignored the advice and invested $5,000 in Ford stock, selling it later for $12.5 million. No doubt this conservative bank president invested in safe, established, stable industries like horse stables, stagecoaches, and buggy-whips.

That the automobile has practically reached the limit of its development is suggested by the fact that during the past year no improvements of a radical nature have been introduced. – Scientific American, *January 2, 1909.*

They were wrong about airplanes.

Flight by machines heavier than air is unpractical and insignificant, if not utterly impossible. – Simon Newcomb, Canadian-born American astronomer, 1902.

Airplanes are interesting toys but of no military value.
– Marshal Ferdinand Foch, Professor of Military Strategy,
Ecole Supérieure de Guerre, 1911.

> This WW1 officer preferred to send waves of young men charging into machine-gun fire.

I confess that in 1901 I said to my brother Orville that man would not fly for fifty years. Two years later we ourselves made flights. This demonstration of my impotence as a prophet gave me such a shock that ever since I have distrusted myself and avoided all predictions.
– Wilbur Wright, American aviation pioneer, speech to the Aero Club of France, 1908.

> Here, on the other hand, is someone who rapidly caught on to the idea of constant technological advances. Of course, inventors like Wilbur Wright are usually better at understanding this.

They were wrong about radio.

Radio has no future. – Lord Kelvin, British mathematician and physicist, president of the British Royal Society, 1897.

The wireless music box has no imaginable commercial value. Who would pay for a message sent to nobody in particular? – attribution uncertain, found in papers of David Sarnoff, American radio pioneer, 1920s.

While the context of this quotation remains unclear, it's a known fact that David Sarnoff went on to be the driving force behind the RCA Corporation, first in radio, then in early TV.

The radio craze will die out in time. – Thomas A. Edison, 1922.

They were wrong about television.

While theoretically and technically television may be feasible, commercially and financially I consider it an impossibility, a development of which we need waste little time dreaming.
– Lee DeForest, American radio pioneer and inventor of the vacuum tube, 1926.

Television won't matter in your lifetime or mine. – Rex Lambert, Radio Times editor, 1936.

Hopefully he eventually deigned to write about television.

Television won't last because people will soon get tired of staring at a plywood box every night. – Darryl Zanuck, movie producer, 20th Century Fox, 1946.

Underestimating the apathy of the herd is a classic mistake.

Television won't last. It's a flash in the pan. – Mary Somerville, pioneer of radio educational broadcasts, 1948.

Hopefully she eventually added some TV broadcasts to her repertoire.

They were wrong about photocopying.

The world potential market for copying machines is 5,000 at most.
– IBM, 1959.

Dismissal of the eventual founders of Xerox, implying the photocopier lacked a market large enough to justify production. And thus, IBM missed owning Xerox—which would have helped IBM greatly during a difficult period in the late 1980s and early 1990s.

They were wrong about the telecopy (facsimile, or fax).

Transmission of documents via telephone wires is possible in principle, but the apparatus required is so expensive that it will never become a practical proposition. – Dennis Gabor, British physicist and author of Inventing the Future, *1962.*

They were wrong about computers.

I have traveled the length and breadth of this country and talked with the best people, and I can assure you that data processing is a fad that won't last out the year. - *The editor in charge of business books for Prentice Hall, 1957.*

There is no reason for any individual to have a computer in his home. - *Ken Olson, president, chairman and founder of Digital Equipment Corp. (DEC), maker of business computers, 1977.*

> The powerful editor clearly underestimated this "fad." And while Olson was opining only on computers for home-automation tasks, Olson too, failed to imagine today's newer homes in which Internet-connected computers control heating, cooling, lights, locks, music, etc.

They were wrong about space exploration and commercial opportunities.

A rocket will never be able to leave the earth's atmosphere. - The New York Times, *1936.* [Popular paraphrase.—Ed.]

...too far-fetched to be considered. - *Editor of Scientific American, in a letter to Robert Goddard about Goddard's idea of a rocket-accelerated airplane bomb, 1940.* [German V2 missiles came down on London three years later.—Ed.]

Space travel is utter bilge. - *Dr. Richard van der Reit Wooley, UK space advisor to the government, 1956.* [Russia's Sputnik satellite was launched the following year.—Ed.]

There is practically no chance communications space satellites will be used to provide better telephone, telegraph, television, or radio service inside the United States. - *T. Craven, FCC Commissioner, 1961.* [The first commercial communications satellite went into service in 1965.—Ed.]

> Currently, two private companies are vying for contracts to re-supply the space station. Going forward, a company called Planetary Resources announced it is starting work that will eventually culminate in the mining of asteroids. Pronouncements of impossibility from eminent people are expected imminently.

They were wrong about many social issues.

We don't like their sound, and guitar music is on the way out anyway. - *Decca Records, 1962.* [Rejecting The Beatles after an audition.—Ed.]

If anything remains more or less unchanged, it will be the role of women. - *David Riesman, conservative American social scientist, 1967.*

> As a rule, prior generations are usually not very good at predicting the tastes or morals of the next generation.

Finally, there has always been hostility to progress from certain quarters. Ignore these voices.

> *The view that the sun stands motionless at the center of the universe is foolish, philosophically false, utterly heretical, because it is contrary to Holy Scripture. The view that the earth is not the center of the universe and even has a daily rotation is philosophically false, and at least an erroneous belief. – Holy Office, Roman Catholic Church, edict of March 5, 1616.* [Ridiculing scientific analysis that our planet orbits our sun.—Ed.]

> *I am tired of all this sort of thing called science here... We have spent millions in that sort of thing for the last few years, and it is time it should be stopped. – Simon Cameron, U.S. Senator, 1901.* [Regarding the Smithsonian Institute.—Ed.]

> Absent some future Dark Age, science will continue to advance, and in doing so will continue to challenge (and put to rest) many old ideas and false beliefs. Embrace progress.

Evolve Personally

The world and knowledge evolve. You should as well, if you wish to remain relevant and effective.

> *Growth is the only evidence of life. – John Henry Newman.*

> *All things change and we must change with them. – Matthew E. May.*

> *A man who views the world the same at fifty as he did at twenty has wasted thirty years of his life. – Muhammad Ali.*

Seek to make yourself better.

> *The highest form of maturity is self-inquiry. – Martin Luther King, Jr.*

> *We should every night call ourselves to an account: what infirmity have I mastered today? What passions opposed? What temptations resisted? What virtue acquired? Our vices will abate of themselves if they be brought every day to the shrift. – Lucius Annaeus Seneca.*

> *Only one who continually reexamines himself and corrects his faults will grow. – Yamamoto, The Hagakure.*

Continue striving and experimenting. Keep trying new things.

> *Stay hungry. Stay foolish. – Steve Jobs.*

> *Things do not change; we change. – Charles Kittering.*

To know how to wonder and question is the first step of the mind toward discovery. – Louis Pasteur.

It is right to be contented with what we have, but never with what we are. – James Mackintosh.

ALWAYS AIM HIGH

Because, for anything that matters, there's never any reason to aim low.

Empty pockets never held anyone back. Only empty heads and empty hearts can do that. – Norman Vincent Peale.

Blessed is he who expects nothing, for he shall never be disappointed. – Benjamin Franklin.

The minute you settle for less than you deserve, you get even less than you settled for. – Maureen Dowd.

The greater danger for most men lies, not in setting our aim too high and falling short, but in setting our aim too low and achieving our mark. – Michelangelo.

Far better it is to dare mighty things, to win glorious triumphs even though checkered by failure, than to rank with those poor spirits who neither enjoy nor suffer much because they live in the gray twilight that knows neither victory nor defeat. – Theodore Roosevelt.

So you might as well always aim high.

It's a funny thing about life: if you refuse to accept anything but the very best, you will often get it. – W. Somerset Maugham.

Or at least always target a little more than you think you want, a little more than you feel confident of achieving with ease.

If you would hit the mark, you must aim a little above it. – Henry Wadsworth Longfellow.

In the long run men hit only what they aim at. Therefore, though they should fail immediately [read "initially"—Ed.], *they had better aim at something high. – Henry David Thoreau,* Walden.

Even if you don't fully succeed, aiming high means you often come close.

If you aspire to the highest place, it is no disgrace to stop at the second, or even the third, place. – Cicero.

I may not be a first-rate composer, but I am a first-class second-rate composer. – Richard Strauss.

Aim high, and you won't shoot your foot off. – Phyllis Diller.

And even if you fail, by having aimed high there's usually something interesting to salvage from the attempt.

I like thinking big. If you are going to be thinking anything, you might as well think big. – Donald Trump.

Aim for the moon. If you miss, you may hit a star. – variously W. Clement Stone, Oscar Wilde or Les Brown.

Even if you fail at your ambitious thing, it's very hard to fail completely. – Larry Page.

Exercise Vigilance, Caution, and Planning

Lastly, always be thinking about what might happen to affect your wealth, your business, your possessions, and your family.

If a man is wise, he gets rich an' if he gets rich, he gets foolish, or his wife does. That's what keeps th' money movin' around. – Finley Peter Dunn.

A man's most valuable trait is a judicious sense of what not to believe. – Euripides.

Be vigilant, for nothing one achieves lasts forever. – Tahar Ben Jelloun.

A good hockey player plays where the puck is. A great hockey player plays where the puck is going to be. – Wayne Gretzky.

The more scenarios you will have considered, the fewer unpleasant surprises you will face.

From fortune to misfortune is but a step; from misfortune to fortune is a long way. – Yiddish proverb.

Sudden events cannot be handled by the unprepared mind. – Mo Di.

Caution and planning are underrated, but very necessary. It is much better to have planned for, or at least considered, eventualities that never occur, than to be caught unprepared.

The much-maligned idle rich have received a bad rap: They have maintained their wealth while many of the energetic rich—aggressive real estate operators, corporate acquirers, oil drillers, etc.—have seen their fortunes disappear. – Warren E. Buffett.

He who lives a long life must pass through much evil. – Spanish proverb.

To remain rich means to foresee problems, to consider contingency plans, and to deal with the inevitable unpleasant surprises. To remain rich requires work and forethought.

Preparing the Next Generation

The greatest challenge you have is preparing the next generation to be worthy of wealth. For if they are not worthy, not prepared, not mature, or not possessing the right skills and outlook to preserve and grow the family fortune then they will very quickly lose it.

The mental disease of the present generation is impatience of study, contempt of the great masters of ancient wisdom. – Samuel Johnson.

Teach him what has been said in the past… Speak to him, for there is none born wise. – Ptah-Hotep.

The final test of a leader is that he leaves behind him in other men the conviction and the will to carry on. – Walter Lippmann.

REAL RISK STARTS WITH THE THIRD GENERATION

Those who were not present at the earning of the money are at the greatest risk of eventually losing the money.

Dalle stalle alle stelle alle stalle. (From stalls to stars to stalls).
– Italian proverb.

Shirt sleeves to shirt sleeves in three generations. – American proverb.

Fu bo guo san dai. (Wealth cannot last more than three generations).
– Chinese proverb.

There's nobbut three generations atween a clog and clog.
– Lancashire proverb.

Quien no lo tiene, lo hance; y quien lo tiene, lo deshance. (Who doesn't have it, does it, and who has it, misuses it). – Spanish proverb.

This phenomena, addressed by quotations in many cultures and languages, is for me as a wealth manager the single most important concept in this book—indeed, worthy of a book of its own. If there is only one reason why family fortunes fade with later generations, it is because of this.

The generation that made the money had motivations that the third generation, which grows up privileged and at ease, never feels.

Adversity has the effect of eliciting talents which, in prosperous circumstances, would have lain dormant. – Horace.

You have to do your own growing no matter how tall your grandfather was. – Abraham Lincoln.

> Since they never had to work hard or think hard, they often don't know how to do either.

Those born rich and lacking proper guidance often thus lack the right mindset to remain rich. Having never experienced struggle or failure in making it, they lack the sense of responsibility to preserve it.

Some people are born on third base and go through life thinking they hit a triple. – Barry Switzer.

The character which results from wealth is that of a prosperous fool. – Aristotle.

Money without brains is always dangerous. – Napoleon Hill.

> Because they did not have to earn it themselves, these later generations underestimate the trouble it takes to make money and keep it.

Being rich is thus no entitlement to remaining rich. Beware losing it.

I suppose that one reason why the road to ruin is broad, is to accommodate the great amount of travel in that direction. – Josh Billings.

Wealth changes hands—that is one of its peculiarities. – Elbert Hubbard, Little Journeys to the Homes of Great Businessmen.

EDUCATE AND TRAIN THE NEXT GENERATION

To prepare your heirs, you should progressively shift responsibility to them. Best to start training them early.

If you would trust men, you must train them. – Thomas Jefferson.

The fate of empires depends on the education of youth. – Aristotle.

The foundation of every state is the education of its youth. – Diogenes.

If you plan for one year, plant rice. If you plan for 10 years, plant a tree. If you plan for 100 years, educate a child. – Chinese proverb.

> If you do a good job with your own children, that will leave you time to also work on your grandchildren.

Teaching them will be good for both of you.

To teach is to learn twice. – Joseph Joubert.

A father is a thousand schoolmasters. – Louis Nizer.

Help them to realize how history repeats itself.

Every generation imagines itself to be more intelligent than the one that went before it, and wiser than the one that comes after it.
– George Orwell.

Man is too soon old, and too late smart. – German proverb.

Teach them to think for themselves.

The surest way to corrupt a youth is to instruct him to hold in higher esteem those who think alike than those who think differently.
– Friedrich W. Nietzsche.

[It's] much more important to teach children to question what they read. Children should be taught to question everything. – George Carlin.

Start early.

It is easier to prevent bad habits than to break them.
– Benjamin Franklin.

Start modestly.

The only job where you start at the top is digging a hole. – unknown.

Appealing to the next generation's self-interest is a powerful motivator.

Would you persuade, speak of interest, not of reason.
– Benjamin Franklin.

A man will fight harder for his interests than for his rights.
– Napoleon Bonaparte.

Set a good example for the next generation.

Children have more need of models than of critics. – Joseph Joubert.

Children have never been good at listening to their elders, but they have never failed to imitate them. – James Baldwin.

Example is not the main thing in influencing others. It is the only thing.
– Albert Schweitzer.

Avoid yelling at the next generation. It can be counterproductive.

Harsh counsels have no effect. They are like hammers which are always repulsed by the anvil. – Claude Adrien Helvétius.

Choose carefully what you will focus on, for you cannot dictate to them in everything.

Teach the young people how to think, not what to think.
– Sidney Sugarman.

Don't limit a child to your own learning, for he was born in another time.
– Rabindranath Tagore.

Neighbor in elevator to mother: "Such a handsome boy! Tell me, is he an obedient child?"
Mother: "Yes, but I am very careful what I ask him to do."
– Walter Schloss (famed investor) family story, per Grant's Interest Rate Observer, *issue of February 24, 2012.*

The point of educating your heirs is preparing them to responsibly fend for themselves.

In the final analysis, it is not what you do for your children but what you have taught them to do for themselves that will make them successful human beings. – Ann Landers.

Perhaps the most valuable result of all education is the ability to make yourself do the thing you have to do, when it ought to be done, whether you like it or not. – Walter Bagehot.

Make Your Heirs Truly Independent

You will not be here forever.

The most important thing that parents can teach their children is how to get along without them. – Frank A. Clark.

Simply giving your heirs money will not make them independent.

If money is your only hope for independence, you will never have it.
The only real security that a man can have in this world is a reserve of knowledge, experience and ability. – Henry Ford.

Prosperity is a great teacher; adversity is a greater. Possession pampers the mind; privation trains and strengthens it. – William Hazlitt.

Of course give them some money, but not too much, nor too soon. As one wealthy investor puts it...

...enough money so that they would feel they could do anything, but not so much that they would do nothing. – Warren E. Buffett.

Teach them that they are not entitled to remain wealthy simply because they were born that way.

What you are, you are by accident of birth; what I am, I am by myself.
There are and will be a thousand princes; there is only one Beethoven.
– Ludwig van Beethoven.

Teach them how to work, how to do something productive.

Industry, thrift and self-control are not sought because they create
wealth, but because they create character. – Calvin Coolidge.

A man who gives his children habits of industry provides for them better
than by giving them a fortune. – Richard Whately.

Teach them the true value of money, via the trials and tribulations of earning some.

How sharper than a serpent's tooth it is to have a thankless child.
– William Shakespeare.

Nowadays people know the price of everything and the value of nothing.
– Oscar Wilde, The Picture of Dorian Gray.

To learn the value of money, it is not necessary to know the nice things it
can get for you, you have to have experienced the trouble of getting it.
– Philippe Heriat.

The real price of everything, what everything really costs to the man who
wants to acquire it, is the toil and trouble of acquiring it. – Adam Smith.

> This goes back to why the third generation, with no experience in making
> money, is often the generation to lose the money.

Let them learn to handle their own problems—or at least the manageable ones—
because one day, they will have to handle everything.

Too many parents make life hard for their children by trying, too
zealously, to make it easy for them. – Johann Wolfgang von Goethe.

It is not a parent's job to protect their kids from life, but to prepare them
for it. – Blake Segal.

If I had a formula for bypassing trouble, I would not pass it round.
Trouble creates a capacity to handle it. I don't embrace trouble; that's as
bad as treating it as an enemy. But I do say meet it as a friend, for you'll
see a lot of it and had better to be on speaking terms with it.
– Oliver Wendell Holmes.

> Instead of creating a really complicated trust fund for your children, with
> lots of oversight, conditions, and previsions, spend time teaching them
> to fend for themselves, and then trust them to do so.

Blaming the wolf would not help the sheep much. The sheep must learn not to fall into the clutches of the wolf. - Mahatma Gandhi.

Where parents do too much for their children, the children will not do much for themselves. - Elbert Hubbard.

I'm not concerned that you have fallen, I'm concerned that you arise. - Abraham Lincoln.

Teach the next generation to deal with adversity.

The mother eagle teaches her little ones to fly by making their nest so uncomfortable that they are forced to leave it and commit themselves to the unknown world of air outside. - Hannah Whitall Smith.

We receive three educations, one from our parents, one from our school-masters, and one from the world. The third contradicts all that the first two teach us. - Charles de Secondat, Baron de Montesquieu.

Make sure your children experience a decent dose of education from this third source.

Let them learn independence by experiencing it. Start early, and make the doses incrementally larger.

You cannot build character and courage by taking away a man's initiative and independence. - Abraham Lincoln.

You cannot help men permanently by doing for them what they could and should do for themselves. - Abraham Lincoln.

The worst things you can do for those you love are the things they could and should do for themselves. - Abraham Lincoln.

It is only by facing risk and making decisions that people ever truly become independent and responsible. Minimize the restrictions and guidelines, give them freedom, and most often they will rise to the occasion. And if they are not worthy, then no amount of instructions can save them.

GIVE YOUR HEIRS RESPONSIBILITY

The only way to learn responsibility, is to have it. Get your heirs started early.

The only real training for leadership is leadership. - Anthony Jay.

The gem cannot be polished without friction, nor the man perfected without trials. - Confucius.

To whom nothing is given, of him nothing can be required.
– Henry Fielding.

> Best they start early with measured doses of responsibility while you are still around to monitor and correct, than suddenly, late in life and unprepared, and with everything at stake once you are gone.

Responsibility is empowering.

Few things can help an individual more than to place responsibility on him, and to let him know that you trust him. – Booker T. Washington.

And with money equated to power, best they learn to wield it.

Nearly all men can stand adversity, but if you want to test a man's character, give him power. – Abraham Lincoln.

They will sometimes have wrong ideas. Letting them figure this out for themselves is often best.

Sometimes the best way to convince someone he is wrong is to let him have his way. – Red O'Donnell.

It is one thing to show a man that he is in error, and another to put him in possession of the truth. – John Locke.

We are generally the better persuaded by the reasons we discover ourselves than by those given to us by others. – Blaise Pascal.

And they will surely make mistakes.

No physician is really good before he has killed one or two patients.
– Hindu proverb.

> Making mistakes is part of the learning process. Entrust your heirs with small investment accounts to manage or small segments of your business to run. Give them that small sandbox to make their first mistakes in, before they become responsible for everything.

Do Not Shackle Their Future

Reminder: You will not be around forever.

In the long run we are all dead. – John Maynard Keynes.

We are no more than candles burning in the wind. – Japanese proverb.

Reminder: You are not indispensable. Your heirs will figure out how to carry on without you.

The man who thinks he can find enough in himself to be able to dispense with everybody else makes a great mistake, but the man who thinks he is indispensable to others makes an even greater one.
– François de La Rochefoucauld.

The graveyards are full of indispensable men. – Charles de Gaulle.

There is no indispensable man. – Franklin Delano Roosevelt.

I've reluctantly discarded the notion of my continuing to manage the portfolio after my death—abandoning my hope to give new meaning to the term "thinking outside the box." – Warren E. Buffett.

Do not attempt to plan for every contingency. Besides being an impossible task, you will just create unnecessary difficulties for those who come after.

The circumstances of the world are so variable, that an irrevocable purpose or opinion is almost synonymous with a foolish one.
– W. H. Seward.

Everything which is properly business we must keep carefully separate from life. Business requires earnestness and method; life must have a freer handling. – Johann Wolfgang von Goethe.

A common mistake that people make when trying to design something completely foolproof is to underestimate the ingenuity of complete fools.
– Douglas Adams.

Your advisers may constantly clamor for revisions and additions to your basic plan. You should mostly ignore them.

Estate planning is the orderly and systematic transfer of a client's wealth and assets into fees and commissions. – unknown.

Any fool can make things bigger, more complex, and more violent. It takes a man of genius—and a lot of courage—to move in the opposite direction. – Albert Einstein.

> In the world of trusts and wills, the use of the world "violent" above can be understood to mean "draconian limitations on when and under what circumstances your heirs can enjoy their inheritance."

Do not plan too far ahead. Let your heirs make their own plans.

It is a mistake to look too far ahead. Only one link in the chain of destiny can be handled at a time. – Winston Churchill.

As for the future, your task is not to foresee it, but to enable it.
– Antoine de Saint-Exupéry.

In passing things on, you should not get too complicated. For trusts, limit the restrictions and directions. For bequests, the same applies. Instructions that are simple will be the ones best followed. You cannot provide for every single possible situation, so you will ultimately have to place your trust in those who come afterward. After all, it is no longer your problem, but your heirs' Give them the courtesy of reasonable freedom to act as they see fit.

Above all, do not attempt to "rule from the grave."

Fathers do not embitter your children, or they will become discouraged.
– The Apostle Paul.

He that troubleth his own house shall inherit the wind. – Proverbs 11:29.

One should never forbid what one lacks the power to prevent.
– Napoleon Bonaparte.

Give your heirs the tools, give them the means, and allow them small failures. Trust them and eventually let them be free. Leave the future open to them without attempts to meddle or set constraints, because they will face issues which you cannot foresee.

Using Your Wealth

There is no single "right" answer regarding what you should do with your wealth, but most agree that wealth is not to be hoarded—it should be put to use to serve you. In this spirit, there are a couple of essential points that bear repeating.

One is to make sure you use your money to have a little fun—partly to keep perspective on wherever your specialty or more serious focus might lie, but also because, well, what's the point of living (and of having money!) if you don't have a little fun?

The second oft-repeated tenet is to use your money to do some good. This could mean, in the very narrow sense, helping your family. Or, in the broader sense, this could mean contributing to a charity or cause you deem meaningful. But most importantly, this support should begin while you are still alive, rather than delegating it to heirs or executors who may have other priorities. After all, who knows better than you how to ensure your money is used in the right way? And why wait? Start making a positive impact now.

> *If a man runs after money, he's money-mad; if he keeps it, he's a capitalist; if he spends it, he's a playboy; if he doesn't get it, he's a ne'er-do-well; if he doesn't try to get it, he lacks ambition. If he gets it without working for it, he's a parasite; and if he accumulates it after a lifetime of hard work, people call him a fool who never got anything out of his life. – Vic Oliver.*

> *Question: "What thing about humanity surprises you the most?" Answer: "Man.... Because he sacrifices his health in order to make money. Then he sacrifices money to recuperate his health. And then he is so anxious about the future that he does not enjoy the present; the result being that he does not live in the present or the future; he lives as if he is never going to die, and then dies having never really lived." – the Dalai Lama.*

> *There are four things a man should do before he dies: plant a tree, raise a child, build a house, and write a book. – variously Plato, the Talmud, and Chinese proverb.* [Will this book count as partial credit for #4?—Ed.]

> *My mother taught me that you should divide your life into three segments. In the first third of your life, you should learn. In the second third, you should earn. And in the third, you should serve. – John English.*

First, Have Some Fun

Have some fun.

All animals except man know that the principal business of life is to enjoy it. – Samuel Butler.

The true object of all human life is play. – G. K. Chesterton.

Wealth is not his that has it, but his that enjoys it. – Benjamin Franklin.

Health, money, love, and time to enjoy them. – traditional Spanish toast.

Live all you can: It's a mistake not to. – Henry James, The Ambassadors.

Life is far too important to be taken seriously. – Oscar Wilde.

> If you're not trying to enjoy life, then there's little point in being alive, let alone wealthy.

Regularly take time off to relax, reflect, and recharge.

Beware the barrenness of a busy life. – Socrates.

Work is good provided you do not forget to live. – Bantu proverb.

If you can spend a perfectly useless afternoon in a perfectly useless manner, you have learned how to live. – Lin Yutang.

Be sure to take the occasional well-deserved summer vacation.

Sell in May and go away, stay away till St. Leger Day. – unknown.

> This historical version of the saying refers to the last race of the British horse racing season; however this day is unlikely to be known by the non-British, so it is replaced by Halloween in the North American version. The typically slow summer is historically more pronounced in Europe where people take many holidays during this period, and with little volume transacted in the market, it is difficult to buy or sell anything in large size. But, as with any general rule, there have been exceptional years, like the 2009 economic recovery, or phenomena such as the third year of a U. S. Presidential term, when the incumbent wants to get re-elected and therefore stimulates the economy to make everyone happy.

Sample some of the better things in life.

Life is too short to drink cheap wine. – unknown.

I should have drunk more champagne. – John Maynard Keynes, purported last words.

Beer is proof that God loves us and wants us to be happy. – Benjamin Franklin.

Room service? Send up a larger room. – Groucho Marx.

Do some of the things you could not otherwise afford.

Paris is always a good idea. – Audrey Hepburn.

I regard golf as an expensive way of playing marbles. – G. K. Chesterton.

Skiing consists of wearing $3,000 worth of clothes and equipment and driving 200 miles in the snow in order to stand around at a bar and drink. – P. J. O'Rourke.

A boat is a hole in the water, surrounded by fiberglass, into which you pour money. – unknown.

> I am particularly partial to boats (and fishing), so I highly approve of this approach. And it is still probably cheaper than having a mistress (or pool boy or tennis coach, for my fairer readers).

Focus on high-quality goods and comforts as opposed to flashy quantity.

The gratification of wealth is not found in mere possession or in lavish expenditure, but in its wise application. – Miguel de Cervantes.

Some people think luxury is the opposite of poverty. It is not. It is the opposite of vulgarity. – Coco Chanel.

Luxury must be comfortable, otherwise it is not luxury. – Coco Chanel.

There are people who have money and people who are rich. – Coco Chanel.

Never keep up with the Joneses. Drag them down to your level. It's cheaper. – Quentin Crisp.

Living well is the best revenge. – George Herbert.

> As a side benefit, quality properties, cars, watches and the like, are more apt to retain value over the years. So that Ferrari, if you take good care of it, can also be a hedge against inflation.

Beware your perhaps natural inclination to skimp, save, and only work hard. Just as it is unhealthy to be a spendthrift, so too it is unhealthy to be a miser.

The methods that help a man acquire a fortune are the very ones that keep him from enjoying it. – Antoine de Rivarol, La Seconde Semaine.

Perpetual devotion to what a man calls his business is only to be sustained by perpetual neglect of many other things. And it is not by any means certain that a man's business is the most important thing he has to do. – Robert Louis Stevenson.

Who well lives, long lives; for this age of ours should not be numbered by years, days, and hours. – Guillaume de Salluste Du Bartas.

Who lives without folly is not as wise as he thinks.
– François, duc de La Rochefoucauld.

Remember that you cannot take it with you.

You can't take it with you. – unknown.

It is better to live rich than to die rich. – Samuel Johnson.

The art of living well and the art of dying well are one. – Epictetus.

Everybody who lives dies. But not everybody who dies has lived.
– Dhaggi Ramanashi.

Don't forget to enjoy life.

And have a little more fun.

If women didn't exist, all the money in the world would have no meaning. – Aristotle Onassis, quoted in Aristotle Onassis: A Biography, *Nicholas Fraser.*

But maybe not too much fun.

I spent a lot of money on booze, birds, and fast cars.
The rest I just squandered. – George Best.

I never should have switched from Scotch to Martinis.
– Humphrey Bogart, purported last words.

Because, in moderation, a little of everything is good for you.

Total abstinence is an impossibility, and it will not do to insist on it as a general practice. – Queen Victoria.

All work and no play makes Jack a dull boy,
All play and no work makes Jack a mere toy.
– various.

You only live once, but if you do it right, once is enough. – Mae West.

THEN, ACCOMPLISH SOMETHING WORTHY

You are fortunate as you have the monetary means to accomplish something meaningful.

No man has a right to be respected for any other possessions but those of virtue and talents. Titles are tinsel, power a corrupter, glory a bubble, and excessive wealth a libel on its possessor. – Percy Bysshe Shelley.

Being the richest man in the cemetery doesn't matter to me. Going to bed at night saying we've done something wonderful … that's what matters to me. – Steve Jobs.

The highest use of capital is not to make more money, but to make money do more for the betterment of life. – Henry Ford.

To do for the world more than the world does for you—that is success. – Henry Ford.

How will you have a meaningful effect on the world?

To let your wealth just sit there would be a great lost opportunity.

When money stands still, it is no longer money. – Georg Simmel.

Money is a handmaiden, if thou knowest how to use it; a mistress, if thou knowest not. – Horace.

Few rich men own their property. Their property owns them. – Robert Ingersoll.

Your wealth is a tool waiting to be used. It would be a shame not to use it.

There is no class so pitiably wretched as that which possesses money and nothing else. – Andrew Carnegie.

Money is only a tool. It will take you wherever you wish, but it will not replace you as the driver. – Ayn Rand.

Riches do not consist in the possession of treasures, but in the use made of them. – Napoleon Bonaparte.

Prosperity is only an instrument to be used, not a deity to be worshiped. – Calvin Coolidge.

You can make a powerful difference within your community.

Most people won't have opportunity to do full-time service, but those lucky enough to have monetary wealth or some spare time really can make an enormous difference. As someone who's now in the public sector, and is seeing up-close-and-personal the real impact of what we do and what we give, I can tell you: every dollar and every volunteer help, in more ways than you can count. – Michael R. Bloomberg.

Surplus wealth is a sacred trust which its possessor is bound to administer in his lifetime for the good of the community. – Andrew Carnegie.

> *Service to others is the rent you pay for your room here on earth.*
> *– Muhammad Ali.*

Or simply engage in random acts of kindness.

> *You have not lived a perfect day, even though you have earned your*
> *money, unless you have done something for someone who cannot repay*
> *you. – Ruth Smeltzer.*

> *Do not wait for extraordinary circumstances to do good actions; try to*
> *use ordinary circumstances. – Jean Paul Richter.*

> *The greatest pleasure I have known is to do a good action by stealth, and*
> *to have it found out by accident. – Edmund Spenser.*

For it would be a disappointment to go to your grave without having accomplished anything.

> *It is a wise man who lives with money in the bank; it is a fool who dies*
> *that way. – French proverb.*

> *Every person is guilty of all the good he didn't do. – Voltaire.*

> *The man who dies rich, dies disgraced. – Andrew Carnegie.*

> Sometimes called the "founding philanthropist" of the United States, Andrew Carnegie created approximately 3,000 public libraries, funded many schools, and built the eponymous concert hall in New York City. Most of these still stand.

Making a meaningful gift to a charity would be a good step.

> *The man who leaves money to charity in his will is only giving away*
> *what no longer belongs to him. – Voltaire.*

> *It's so much easier to do good than to be good. – B. C. Forbes.*

But of course, only to legitimate, well-run charities.

> *Beware the prophet seeking profit. – Dennis Miller.*

> *With one hand he put a penny in the urn of poverty, and with the other*
> *took a shilling out. – Robert Pollok.*

> I have a personal bugaboo regarding certain charities: there are many out there whose main raison d'être is really to provide a lavish lifestyle to the charity's management team. So before selecting a charity, make sure its expense ratios are low. There are now several good services that monitor and grade charities. Then, donate directly to the charity, not via some aggregator that will be taking a cut.

And ideally, toward causes that will improve and advance humanity.

> *For every effect there is a root cause. Find and address the root cause rather than try to fix the effect, as there is no end to the latter.*
> *– Celestine Chua.*

> On this topic (and as an example), I would rather make a donation to fund medical research to advance the cure for cancer by a year (and thus save millions of lives) than a donation to feed, house, clothe, comfort, or counsel all existing cancer patients for a year. Cure cancer (fix the root cause), and there will no longer be any afflicted to comfort.

Because, in the end, you can't take it with you.

> *Three immutable facts: You own stuff. You will die. Someone will get that stuff. – Jane Bryant Quinn.*

> *The dead take to the grave, clutched in their hands, only what they have given away. – DeWitt Wallace.*

> *Nothing that you have not given away will ever be really yours.*
> *– C. S. Lewis.*

> *He is no fool who gives what he cannot keep to gain what he cannot lose.*
> *– Jim Elliot.*

> *What I spent, is gone; what I kept, I lost; but what I gave away will be mine forever. – Ethel Percy Andrus.*

> *Every man serves a useful purpose: A miser, for example, makes a wonderful ancestor. – Laurence Peter.*

> Your heirs will undoubtedly thank you. But why should they have all the fun?

AFTERWORD
& END NOTES

Closing Thoughts

I would like to end this book with a few short recapitulative comments on the message of this book and a few separate comments on the book itself.

On the Message

I cannot tell you exactly which stocks you should buy or sell, nor when, nor how.

> *I'd only give you advice if I didn't care what happens to you.*
> *– Gregory David Roberts*, Shantaram.

> *Give a man a fish and you feed him for a day. Teach a man to fish and*
> *you feed him for a lifetime. – Chinese proverb.*

No more than I can provide an easy formula or shortcut for doing so (and there are no shortcuts).

> *Knowledge can be communicated, but not wisdom. One can find it, live*
> *it, be fortified by it, do wonders through it, but one cannot communicate*
> *and teach it. – Herman Hesse.*

> *I have found you an argument; I am not obliged to find you an*
> *understanding. – Dr. Samuel Johnson.*

> *You cannot teach a man anything; you can only help him find it within*
> *himself. – Galileo Galilei.*

But, hopefully, I have provided some structure and guidance on how to wisely think about wealth and investing.

> *I never teach my pupils; I only attempt to provide the conditions in which*
> *they can learn. – Albert Einstein.*

> *All we can do is show the way to the traveler; we cannot walk it for him.*
> *We can write the prescription, but we cannot drink the medicine for him.*
> *– Lao Tzu.*

> This book contains both knowledge and wisdom. It is up to the reader to digest this knowledge and wisdom, make it his own, learn how to apply it, and go forth.

So, start by addressing your own financial situation.

> *Never stand begging for something that you have the power to earn.*
> *– Miguel de Cervantes.*

Patience is a minor form of despair disguised as a virtue.
– Ambrose Bierce, The Devil's Dictionary.

Nothing is so fatiguing as the eternal hanging on of an uncompleted task.
– William James.

Continue to think about the precepts in this book and start applying them to how you invest.

Self-suggestion makes you master of yourself. – W. Clement Stone.

Repeat anything often enough and it will start to become you.
– Tom Hopkins.

I hear and I forget. I see and I remember. I do and I understand.
– Confucius.

> Repeat to yourself, once a day for the next year, "I will no longer make any investment without really thinking it through."

And finally, whether you are down in the details of picking stocks or up at the more abstract level of finding a money manager or two to work with, please do take a proactive, involved approach to your finances.

A fool tells what he will do; a boaster tells what he has done; a wise man does it and says nothing. – unknown.

Actions speak louder than words. – Theodore Roosevelt.

Well done is better than well said. – Benjamin Franklin.

Speak little, do much. – Benjamin Franklin.

> Now that you have read all of these (hopefully) useful words of advice, it is time for you to put them to action.

ON THE BOOK

I've been an investor for long enough, and I have seen enough, to share some of what I have learned along the way.

The great thing is to last and get your work done and see and hear and learn and understand; and write when there is something that you know; and not before; and not too damned much after. – Ernest Hemingway.

The time to begin writing an article is when you have finished it to your satisfaction. By that time you begin to clearly and logically perceive what it is you really want to say. – Mark Twain.

To write it, it took three months; to conceive it three minutes; to collect the data in it, all my life. – F. Scott Fitzgerald.

I also like quotations because they help the reader to better remember the message.

Have you ever observed that we pay much more attention to a wise passage when it is quoted than when we read it in the original author? – Philip Hamerton.

Compiling quotations made the creation of this book a bit easier for someone who, at heart, is much more a reader and a thinker than a writer.

There is nothing to writing. All you do is sit down at a typewriter and bleed. – Ernest Hemingway.

So I thank everyone whose kind help and generosity made possible the creation of this book.

The middle of every successful project looks like a disaster. – Rosabeth Moss Kanter.

No author is a man of genius to his publisher. – Henrich Heine.

Your manuscript is both good and original; but the part that is good is not original, and the part that is original is not good. – Samuel Johnson.

In this book, so very, very true.

And I thank every reader who has made it through this far, or even just randomly opened to this page.

From the moment I picked your book up until I laid it down I was convulsed with laughter. Some day I intend on reading it. – Groucho Marx.

The covers of this book are too far apart. – Ambrose Bierce.

Thank you for looking at my book.

The Fine Print

As specified elsewhere in this book, "Always read the fine print." This is that part—where I tell you that this book will not magically change your life (you are responsible for that), and that neither I, nor my editor, nor my employer, nor my wife's second cousin's friend, is responsible for any use to which you put this book.

Working for and as an investment adviser, I am aware of the regulatory expectations and requirements of disclosure. Thus you need to know that this book reflects the views of the author as of the date or dates cited (or publication) and may change at any time. In addition, the opinions expressed in this book are solely those of the author. No representation is made concerning the accuracy of cited data, nor is there any guarantee that any projection, forecast or opinion will be realized. Furthermore, this book should not be construed as investment advice. References to stocks, securities or investments should not be considered recommendations to buy or sell. Past performance is not a guide to future performance. Securities that are referenced may be held in my personal portfolio or portfolios managed by my employer, its principals, employees or associates, and such references should not be deemed as an understanding of any future position, buying or selling, that may be taken.

COMMON-SENSE DISCLAIMER:

It's the stock market. Stocks go up and down, often randomly. You can lose some or all of your money. You and you alone are ultimately responsible for your investment decisions or delegations. If it sounds too good to be true it probably is, despite whatever someone might suggest or promise or lead you to believe. So take some personal responsibility for your investment actions, be cautious and use common sense, and do not go crying and looking to blame someone else when one of your investments loses money—because eventually, and most probably, you will have one that does. And I say "most probably" only because we are prohibited from guaranteeing anything in this business.

BELIEF SYSTEM DISCLAIMER:

This book incorporates quotations from the Bible, the Koran, other ancient, mystical or religious texts; right-wingers and left-wingers; Chairman Mao and Chairman Greenspan; both Karl and Groucho Marx; and even Homer Simpson. However, the use of these quotations is in no way an endorsement of any particular flavor or brand of religion or politics. This oeuvre is a non-partisan, non-sectarian, non-denominational attempt to gather wisdom wherever it may be found. Just as every belief system contains flaws too numerous to point out, every system also contains many isolated grains of wisdom worth preserving and sharing.

ATTRIBUTION DISCLAIMER (AND SOLICITATION FOR HELP):

This book is primarily about investment wisdom and is not a definitive reference book of investment quotations. The overriding goal throughout is to harness memorable quotations to the task of explaining sensible investment concepts. As a result, unfortunately, there will inevitably have been some omissions of perfectly suited quotations, and worse, some misattribution of those included. Though accepting sole responsibility, this author would like to beg forgiveness on the grounds of the richness of the Internet. When you look up a quotation only to find thirteen different attributions, sometimes (for non-literary non-scholars such as myself), one has to make a best guess, or even fall back on the dreaded duo of "various" and "unknown." That said, it is my sincere hope to correct these failures in a future edition, so I invite any reader kind enough to offer corrections, to email me through my website.

Recommended Reading

Bernstein, Peter L. *Against the Gods: The Remarkable Story of Risk*. New York: John Wiley & Sons, 1996.

Brooks, John. *The Go-go Years: The Drama and Crashing Finale of Wall Street's Bullish 60s*. New York: John Wiley, 1999.

Brooks, John. *Once in Golconda: A True Drama of Wall Street, 1920-1938*. New York: John Wiley, 1999.

Browne, Christopher H. *The Little Book of Value Investing*. Hoboken, NJ: Wiley, 2007.

Bruck, Connie. *The Predators' Ball: The Junk-bond Raiders and the Man Who Staked Them*. New York: Penguin Books, 1989.

Burrough, Bryan, and John Helyar. *Barbarians at the Gate: The Fall of RJR Nabisco*. New York: Harper & Row, 1990.

Carret, Philip L. *The Art of Speculation*. New York: Wiley, 1997.

Carter, Graydon. *The Great Hangover: 21 Tales of the New Recession*. New York: Harper Perennial, 2010.

Chancellor, Edward. *Devil Take the Hindmost: A History of Financial Speculation*. New York: Farrar, Straus, Giroux, 1999.

Dreman, David N. *Contrarian Investment Strategy: The Psychology of Stock Market Success*. New York: Random House, 1979.

Einhorn, David. *Fooling Some of the People All of the Time: A Long Short (and Now Complete) Story*. Hoboken, NJ: J. Wiley & Sons, 2011.

Ellis, Charles D., and James R. Vertin. *Classics: An Investor's Anthology*. Homewood, IL: Dow Jones-Irwin, 1989.

Fisher, Philip A. *Common Stocks and Uncommon Profits and Other Writings by Philip A. Fisher*. New York: Wiley, 1996.

Frankfurt, Harry G. *On Bullshit*. Princeton: Princeton UP, 2005.

Fridson, Martin S. *Investment Illusions: A Savvy Wall Street Pro Explodes Popular Misconceptions about the Markets*. New York: Wiley, 1993.

Galbraith, John Kenneth. *The Great Crash, 1929*. Boston: Houghton Mifflin, 1997.

Gessen, Keith. *Diary of a Very Bad Year: Confessions of an Anonymous Hedge Fund Manager with N 1*. New York: Harper Perennial, 2010.

Graham, Benjamin, and Spencer B. Meredith. *The Interpretation of Financial Statements: The Classic 1937 Edition*. New York: HarperBusiness, 1998.

Grant, James. *Bernard M. Baruch: The Adventures of a Wall Street Legend*. New York: Simon and Schuster, 1983.

Grant, James. *Minding Mr. Market: Ten Years on Wall Street With Grant's Interest Rate Observer*. New York: Farrar Straus & Giroux, 1993.

Kessler, Andy. *How We Got Here: A Slightly Irreverent History of Technology and Markets*. New York: Collins, 2005.

Kessler, Andy. *Running Money: Hedge Fund Honchos, Monster Markets, and My Hunt for the Big Score*. New York: HarperBusiness, 2004.

Kindleberger, Charles P. *Manias, Panics, and Crashes: A History of Financial Crises*. New York: Wiley, 2000.

Lefevre, Edwin. *Reminiscences of a Stock Operator*. New York: J. Wiley, 1994.

Lewis, Michael. *The Big Short*. London: Allen Lane, 2009.

Lewis, Michael. *Liar's Poker: Rising through the Wreckage on Wall Street*. New York: Norton, 1989.

Lowenstein, Roger. *When Genius Failed: The Rise and Fall of Long-Term Capital Management*. New York: Random House, 2000.

Lynch, Peter, and John Rothchild. *Beating the Street*. New York: Simon and Schuster, 1993.

Lynch, Peter, and John Rothchild. *One up on Wall Street: How to Use What You Already Know to Make Money in the Market*. New York: Simon and Schuster, 1989.

Mackay, Charles, Martin S. Fridson, and Joseph De La. Vega. *Extraordinary Popular Delusions and the Madness of Crowds / [Charles Mackay]. Confusión De Confusiones / [Joseph De La Vega]*. New York etc.: John Wiley & Sons, 1996.

Markopolos, Harry, and Frank Casey. *No One Would Listen: A True Financial Thriller*. Hoboken, NJ: Wiley, 2010.

Mayo, Mike. *Exile on Wall Street: One Analyst's Fight to save the Big Banks from Themselves*. Hoboken, NJ: John Wiley & Sons, 2012.

Munk, Nina. *Fools Rush In: Steve Case, Jerry Levin, and the Unmaking of AOL Time Warner*. New York: HarperBusiness, 2004.

Niederhoffer, Victor. *The Education of a Speculator*. New York: John Wiley & Sons, 1997.

Reinhart, Carmen M., and Kenneth S. Rogoff. *This Time Is Different: Eight Centuries of Financial Folly*. Princeton: Princeton UP, 2009.

Schwager, Jack D. *Market Wizards: Interviews with Top Traders*. New York, NY: New York Institute of Finance, 1989.

Schwed, Fred. *Where Are the Customers' Yachts?, Or, A Good Hard Look at Wall Street*. New York: Wiley, 1995.

Siegel, Jeremy J. *Stocks for the Long Run: A Guide to Selecting Markets for Long-term Growth*. Burr Ridge, IL: Irwin, 1994.

Stewart, James B. *Den of Thieves*. New York: Simon & Schuster, 1991.

Taleb, Nassim Nicholas. *The Black Swan: The Impact of the Highly Improbable*. New York: Random House, 2007.

Taleb, Nassim Nicholas. *Fooled by Randomness: The Hidden Role of Chance in Life and in the Markets*. New York: Texere, 2001.

Acknowledgements

Thanks are in order. Firstly, of course, to my wife Heidi W. Moore, who graciously supported this extra-curricular book writing project and skillfully helped at many stages.

In my professional world: François D. Sicart, for hiring me into this wonderful career a long time ago, and then more recently for encouraging me to write. Robert W. Kleinschmidt, for creating the collegial atmosphere where I learnt (almost) everything in this book. And a selection of colleagues and friends, for generously taking the time to look at the manuscript and provide valuable feedback at various stages of development, including but not limited to: John C. Hathaway, Heather Perlmutter, Robert Pegg, Elizabeth Bosco, Tom Pandick, Serge Vinograd, Druce Vertes, Luyen Chou, Chris Fusco, and Tom McCloskey.

In the world of books, all my old and new friends for help, advice, recommendations, opinions, and commiserations while completing this project: Elisha Cooper, Elliot Nesterman, Katherine Armstrong, Marianne Wallace, Julia Roederer, Tim Steele, Fabrice Frere, Sylvie Le Floc'h, Amy Toth, Alexis Shapiro, Nick Richman, Rosalie Maggio, Rachel Chou, and Gustavo Cardona.

And, lastly and especially, James Grant, for very generously contributing such a gracious foreword. This early imprimatur of approval helped this author's confidence no end toward finishing the project.

A book like this owes much to the words of others, so I humbly thank all whom I have quoted. If you find yourself particularly liking any of the snippets herein please support that author by buying one of their books, or reading their magazine or newspaper column or even, for my investment industry competitors whom I quote, consider hiring them to manage some of your money.

About the Author

George B. McAuliffe, III, CFA, is a Portfolio Manager at Tocqueville Asset Management L.P. Mr. McAuliffe joined Tocqueville in 1998 and manages discretionary portfolios for individual and family clients, as well as for trusts. He also manages the firm's Intern Program. Mr. McAuliffe a appris le français au Lycée Français de New York, earned a B.A. from Columbia University, and an M.B.A. from the London Business School. Mr. McAuliffe lives in New York City with his wife and children, and occasionally goes fishing on nearby waters.

Made in the USA
Middletown, DE
29 February 2020